The Death of British Agriculture

The Death of British Agriculture

*The Wanton Destruction of a
Key Industry*

Richard A.E. North

Foreword by Christopher Booker

Duckworth

First published in 2001 by
Gerald Duckworth & Co. Ltd.
61 Frith Street, London W1D 3JL
Tel: 020 7434 4242
Fax: 020 7434 4420
Email: inquiries@duckworth-publishers.co.uk
www.ducknet.co.uk

A catalogue record for this book is available
from the British Library

ISBN 0 7156 3144 6

Typeset by Derek Doyle & Associates, Liverpool
Printed in Great Britain by
Biddles Ltd, *www.biddles.co.uk*

Contents

*non-discretionary and discretionary payments – subsidy disparities –
Irish competition – agrimoney and rural development funds – the roots
of parsimony – rebate calculations – the Fontainebleau accord – national
support – the single market – a cause of death*

Contents

of the supermarkets – popular scapegoat – government more to blame – consumer response to price – support and abuses – 'greedy farmers' paying out of their own pockets

16. Quo Vadis? 202

Farmers sinned against – the NFU – 'useful fools' – addressing the central issues – membership of the EU – halfway house – multiple problems – the insoluble dilemma – benefits of membership – the 'elephant in the room' – the EU dimension – 'group bondage' – abolition of MAFF – red tape and regulation – scares – whither salvation? – the conditions for change – vision

17. Joined-up Government 212

Flaws of a common policy – agricultural policies – the need for rural policies – objectives – CAP objectives – the national rural and countryside policy – lack of understanding – decentralisation – the broader policy infrastructure – interplay between different policies – rural policing – public transport – the role of local authorities

18. Subsidise or Die 225

Financial support – removing subsidies – the New Zealand experience – a North American view – the other side of the coin – the subsidy chain – the case for state support – support essential – crisis measures – source of finance

19. Agricultural Support 237

Payment for 'intangibles' – differential payments – political justification – implementation – the 'one-stop shop' – management of the scheme – lands tribunals – the scheme in practice – self-help – global trading

20. Better Regulation 248

Complexity of the subject – a different approach needed – the 'third' way – veterinary medicines – a guarantee of safety? – nothing can go wrong – post-licensing surveillance – the VMD/VCP – judges and juries in their own cause – regulatory capture – excluding the competition – an alternative model – the 'insurance' model – Genetically Modified Organisms – freedom for all – planning and other problems

21. Dealing with Scares 263

The nature of the scare – the 'nyktomorph' – scare elements: universality, novelty, plausibility, uncertainty – scares as an artifact – structure of a

Foreword

Christopher Booker

Most people in Britain, even now, have no real idea of the scale of
the disaster which spread across a vast area of our countryside in
the spring and early summer of the year 2001. For many of those
directly affected it was to become the most harrowing experience
of their lives. Thousands of farmers and their families saw their
livelihoods vanishing before their eyes. Million of animals were
slaughtered, often in brutal and inhumane circumstances. Tens
of thousands of rural businesses were brought to the edge of
bankruptcy or beyond. Estimates of the damage inflicted on
Britain's overall economy soon ranged up to £20 billion.

Yet what turned Britain's 2001 foot-and-mouth epidemic from
a mere practical problem into an unprecedented catastrophe was
the truly grotesque way in which it was mishandled by the government. It seemed every one of the lessons learned the last time
Britain had an epidemic in the 1960s had been wilfully set aside.
Almost every aspect of the response by politicians and officials
seemed calculated to make the disaster worse. When an array of
the world's leading veterinary experts stated that the only practical, scientific answer to an emergency on this scale was a
strategy of mass vaccination, which could have brought the disease to a halt within weeks, their advice was contemptuously
waved aside: not just by the government itself but by the
National Farmers Union, the bureaucratic organisation which so
bizarrely claimed to speak for the interests of farmers.

The foot-and-mouth disaster soon turned into the most glaring
instance of maladministration by a British government in modern
times. And not the least eerie aspect of this calamity was the way
it seemed to bring to a head that sense of some gathering apo-
calypse which, even before the virus entered the nation's sheep
flock in the months before February 2001, had already plunged

British agriculture into the worst crisis it had ever known. In the preceding few years one disaster after another had fallen on Britain's farmers, like a succession of biblical plagues: a string of food scares, from salmonella in eggs to BSE; an explosion of regulation; collapsing prices; plummeting farm incomes; even an epidemic of chemical poisoning among sheep farmers. Even before foot and mouth, plenty of people were asking 'can British agriculture survive?', and offering answers which seemed based on little more than wishful thinking.

What made this particularly inexplicable was that, to an extent which few outside the farming community realised, Britain's farming industry by the late 1990s was in many ways as efficient, both in terms of productivity and quality, as any in the world. On a level playing field it should have been able to compete successfully with any farming industry in Europe. Yet we now face the real possibility that much of that industry may be about to disappear, with social and economic consequences beyond imagining.

Such is the riddle which Richard North addresses in this book. Firstly, why should such an extraordinary disaster have come about? Secondly, is there any way forward, which might offer genuine hope for the future? Or must we just accept that over the next few years we shall see large parts of Britain's countryside falling derelict, as much of what remains of the rural economy collapses, while we become ever more dependent for our survival on food imported from overseas and in particular from our partners in the European Union?

Many explanations have already been offered in recent years as to why British agriculture has ended up in such a lamentable mess. There has been no shortage of candidates for blame, from intensive farming to the power of the supermarkets. Perhaps the most popular explanation is that the fault must lie with the bureaucratic idiocies of the European Union's Common Agricultural Policy, which is the universal umbrella under which all farming in the EU supposedly operates. But this begs an enormous question. Why then do the farming industries of other countries fare so much better under the CAP than Britain's? Why, if we are all meant to be on the same level playing field, should British agriculture be so conspicuously in a far worse plight than any other in Europe?

There is in fact a simple reason why none of these explanations has been remotely adequate to explain the peculiar crisis afflicting British agriculture. This is that none of the politicians, journalists, economists and supposed farming experts putting them forward have anything like the range of knowledge and technical expertise necessary to give proper understanding of an infinitely complex problem.

Certainly at the heart of the problem is the fact that farming, to a far greater extent than any other industry except fishing, is controlled by and at the mercy of a framework set up and imposed by government. More than anything else, the crisis afflicting Britain's agriculture, as the foot-and-mouth disaster has demonstrated, is a crisis created by government. And to this, it is true, the contribution made by the EU's Common Agricultural Policy is enormous. But what has made the plight of Britain's agriculture unique, as this book shows, is how successive British governments have chosen to implement the CAP in a way which is uniquely damaging to their own farming industry.

The first prerequisite for a proper analysis of the ills besetting British farming therefore is a real understanding of the complexities of the CAP, how it is implemented by different countries, and how the UK government manages to operate its rules and funding arrangements in a way which puts British farming at such a huge disadvantage against its competitors. One cannot understand many of the problems affecting Britain's farmers and food producers in recent years without first hand knowledge of the peculiar psychology of what until June 2001 was known as the Ministry of Agriculture, Fisheries and Food, now renamed in a kind of bureaucratic reverse takeover as the Department of the Environment, Food and Rural Affairs.

In addition, however, it is also impossible to understand some of the most destructive pressures on British farming in recent years without real expertise in the science of food hygiene and the dynamics of food scares. These have given rise to so many of the regulations which have undermined the economic viability of British agriculture, in everything from the mass-closure of rural slaughterhouses to the bureaucratic harassment of specialist cheesemakers. Unless it is grasped just how much of this excessive and nit-picking regulation is scientifically unjustified, one cannot appreciate how unnecessarily this too has contributed to the mountain of government-created problems which affect every sector of food production.

It is precisely in his combination of all these qualifications, coupled with an extensive first-hand knowledge of farming and food production, that Dr Richard North is uniquely qualified to analyse just where British farming, or rather its political control, has gone so dramatically off the rails; and why his proposals as to how British agriculture might be rescued from this plight deserve to be at the centre of that debate on the future of our farming and countryside which, in the shadow of the foot-and-mouth catastrophe, is about to enter a new and even more urgent phase.

*

In recent years, as the mood of crisis has darkened over Britain's agriculture, Richard North has played an unusual background role in the story, partly as a technical and scientific expert, partly as maverick campaigner, partly as journalist, analyst and commentator. I first came across him nearly ten years ago. Through a deluge of letters I was receiving in response to my weekly column in *The Sunday Telegraph*, I had begun to take a serious interest in the extraordinary explosion of regulatory pressures which around that time, it seemed, was suddenly affecting people running businesses of almost every kind. Inevitably an industry to which my attention was particularly drawn, since it was one of the most heavily regulated of all was farming.

When I was first contacted by Dr North, I soon realised he had a wealth of experience and knowledge which would be invaluable in trying to unravel the infinite complexities of this bureaucratic labyrinth into which I had stumbled. To begin with, as a former environmental health officer, he had experience as a regulator himself. He was one of the greatest practical experts in the country on every aspect of food safety (as was later recognised when he not only played a key part as an expert witness in a succession of high-profile hygiene court cases but was invited to write the official manual on food inspection for the Chartered Institute of Environmental Health Officers).

One of the formative experiences of his life, however, had been the part he played at the centre of what, up to that time, had been the most damaging food-scare Britain had ever experienced: the hysteria set off in December 1988 by Edwina Currie with her ill-advised comment about salmonella in eggs. The inside story Richard had to tell of that crisis, which brought the egg industry to its knees, was shattering. Not only had the scare over salmonella in eggs been based on wholly bogus science, as an official government report eventually grudgingly accepted. It had originally been deliberately blown up out of nothing to justify the survival of a particular group of official government scientists at the Public Health Laboratory Service, threatened with cutbacks in funding; and who had used an unwitting junior minister, Mrs Currie, to promote the scare. Even more terrifying was the conduct of the MAFF officials, who had set about slaughtering millions of chickens, for what turned out to be no reason at all. They had stopped at nothing, including falsification of scientific evidence, to pursue their policy of mass-destruction, with the result that more than 5000 egg producers had been driven out of business. It was an eye-opening introduction to the kind of ruthless mindset prevailing in MAFF which we were to see at work many times in subsequent years, culminating of course in the foot-and-mouth débâcle of 2001.

Richard and I soon formed a working partnership, investigating every kind of regulatory disaster and absurdity, which we reported through the *Sunday Telegraph*, through columns in the *Daily Telegraph* and the *Daily Mail* and in our first book *The Mad Officials*. But what above all we were concerned with was to build up a wider understanding of why all these things were happening. Why had British life been suddenly hit by this explosion of bureaucracy? What we soon discovered was that, largely unnoticed by either the media or by most politicians, our British system of government was going through one of the most far-reaching revolutions in its history, inspired to a great extent but by no means solely by its ever greater involvement in the highly-bureaucratic new system of government centred on Brussels.

Inevitably, many of the areas we covered related to agriculture and food production. Richard, for instance, played a central part in the forlorn battle to save Britain's smaller slaughterhouses from destruction when in 1993 MAFF introduced a mass of crippling new rules to comply with the EC's new single-market meat hygiene directives. Because these were drawn up to suit the quite different systems of meat inspection traditional on the continent, the new laws were infinitely more damaging to the British meat industry than any other. But this did not prevent MAFF applying them with its usual ruthlessness, with the result that hundreds of sound, efficient businesses were forced into extinction, to no benefit whatever in terms of improved food safety.

We uncovered the horrifying unfolding tragedy of the thousands of sheep farmers and often their wives and children whose health had been irreparably damaged by organo-phosphorus sheep dips, use of which MAFF had made compulsory. Richard himself continued to act as an expert adviser in a succession of landmark battles for the survival of businesses threatened by out-of-control bureaucracy, from abattoirs to specialist cheese-makers. All this time we were building up an ever more comprehensive picture of how our new system of government, so often driven by bogus science, was withdrawing ever further from reality. More and more it was making its laws and enforcing its whims, not through Acts of Parliament, but simply through bureaucratic diktats, 'statutory instruments', issued by officials; with the role of the politicians reduced to little more than signing pieces of paper and then mindlessly defending the worst of their officials' blunders if and when these came to light.

Then, in the years after the great BSE hysteria of 1996, we found ourselves having to report month by month on by far the greatest single catastrophe this new system of government going off the rails had yet led to, the immense crisis now gathering round the future of Britain's agriculture. Through our endless late-night discussions, I could see Richard consistently puzzling away at all the complexities of this growing disaster, trying to work out why, of all the farming industries of Europe, it was Britain's which was faced by such a unique combination of problems. By the year 2000 he had taken up a new job in Brussels and Strasbourg, as research director to the Europe of Diversities and Democracies group in the European Parliament. And it was here that Richard came across the missing pieces of the jigsaw which enabled him at last to see where the heart of the disaster now threatening the future survival of British agriculture lay.

The real problem, buried away in various dense European Commission and Parliamentary reports, was the extent to which all other governments in the European Union had exploited the labyrinthine rules of the Common Agricultural Policy, and their own taxation systems, to give their farmers the maximum possible support; whereas the UK government had consistently done the very opposite. Not only had MAFF laid far more onerous regulatory burdens on Britain's farmers and food producers than those prevailing elsewhere; but it came to light just how damagingly the British Treasury had denied UK producers the financial help available to their competitors. Since we were now in a 'single market', where the only way to survive was to be able to compete on price, the inevitable result was that Britain's farmers had for years been put at a massive disadvantage. To a far greater extent than was generally realised, the playing field had been savagely tilted against them, not by Brussels but by their own government.

When Dr North concluded the researches in February 2001 which led to the commissioning of this book, the very next week British agriculture was plunged into that cataclysm which was to provide such a chilling demonstration of everything we had learned about the true causes of its problems, and everything that this book is about. Inevitably, the foot-and-mouth catastrophe will change the face of Britain's farming forever. But if there is any way our agriculture can be rebuilt to meet all the exacting needs of the twenty-first century, a vital first step will be to understand, appreciate and meditate on the lessons spelled out in the following pages.

Preface

It used to be the case that any book on agricultural problems would deal with the weather, harvests, livestock and all the other matters, arcane and otherwise, which used to dominate the lives of those who till the soil and raise animals for a living. But, as I have observed in my own profession, it used to be the case that the occupation was 90 per cent application and 10 per cent politics. Now it is 90 per cent politics and 10 per cent application.

Decisions made in Whitehall Brussels and even Washington have far more influence on the prosperity – or lack of it – of agriculture than any of the forces of nature. 'Good' farmers these days are judged not by the mud on their boots nor the health of their stock but by the neatness and accuracy of their paperwork, their skill in making the right applications for the right subsidies, and their record-keeping. Even nature has been forced to bow its head to the overweening power of the bureaucrat.

Thus it is that this book about farming is a book about power, about politics and about bureaucracies, about all those parasites that feed off the body of agriculture and are in the process of destroying it. It is an attempt to understand those forces, more powerful than nature but wholly negative. For, while nature creates, builds, grows and sustains life, the forces identified in this book can only destroy. They contribute nothing but misery and, as we see in the Prologue, death and destruction.

It is appropriate, therefore, that this book should be written by a former bureaucrat, a man with an unlikely pedigree as an agricultural writer. What makes me even more unlikely for my present role is that I was born and bred in North London. In the drab postwar years, when money was tight, travel into the country was a rare luxury. Thus, I do not recall seeing a cow, 'in the flesh', until I was thirteen.

But it was as an environmental health officer in a rural district that I first came face to face with that unique animal, the British farmer. From a succession of other professional encounters, not least when I worked for egg producers in the aftermath of the 'salmonella-in-eggs' crisis, I came to develop a profound admiration and respect for the breed.

In that much of the damage visited on the countryside now comes from my urban contemporaries, this is the contribution of a 'city boy' to the protection and perhaps the restoration of something which is both unique and wonderful, an industry which does not deserve the fate dealt to it. I may lack a deep understanding of country ways, a detailed technical knowledge of agriculture and the art of dealing with animals, but I do understand bureaucracies and politics. And it is in these arenas that the Battle for British Agriculture is being fought – arenas where a 'city boy' can operate. I trust I have managed to do justice to the issues and, by this means, repay some of the debt we all owe our 'country cousins'.

Having completed the work, I must thank Jeffrey Titford and Nigel Farage, the only two MEPs in the European Parliament who are dedicated to informing their constituents and the nation of the vacuity of the organisation to which they were sent. Without their tolerance, this book could never have been written. My thanks also to the 'agriculture committee' of the UK Independence Party, John and Julia Longhurst, Stuart Agnew, John Tarrant and Chris Kingsley, working under the capable chairmanship of David Rowlands, all of whom guided my thinking as to what needed to be done.

I must also thank my publisher, Stephen Hill, without whose enthusiasm and persistence this work would never even have been started, Dr Helen Szamuely, who offered much of her penetrating insight into the political processes which so informs this work, and the Countess Mar, whose passionate concern for farming is a shining beacon in the shell of what is left of the House of Lords.

There are too many others to mention, those friends and colleagues who have helped, directly and indirectly, with this book. I hope that this work will justify the trust and assistance they have given me. But I must thank Christopher Booker, whose friendship, wisdom, insight and knowledge have helped shape my thinking during our partnership of nearly ten years, a period when we have done our best to shed light on the destructive forces which are tearing our world apart.

Finally, I must acknowledge, with deep gratitude, the support and patience of my family and my wife, Mary, who freely admits that, if she did not love me so much, she 'would be doing time'.

Bradford, West Yorkshire   R.A.E.N.
2001

Prologue: Death and Destruction

When, on Monday, 19 February 2001, reports came through of a suspect foot and mouth case in an abattoir in Essex, few could have realised that this was the start of a crisis which would grip the nation, rock the government and foment near-riot in the countryside – much less lead to the needless slaughter of several million animals. Nor could anyone even have guessed at what would come to light as the crisis progressed

Initially, commentators were quick to pick up on the link between the Essex slaughterhouse and Burnside pig farm in Heddon-on-the-Wall, Northumberland, owned by brothers Bobby and Ronnie Waugh, which had supplied it with sows. The obvious inferences were drawn. Here, exposed for all to see, was the effect of the Ministry of Agriculture's policy of closing down hundreds of small slaughterhouses, necessitating the transport of animals hundreds of miles, taking infection with them and spreading it through the countryside.

But no sooner had the spotlight settled on Essex and the cluster of cases around the abattoir, than the focus shifted to Hexham, Carlisle and Longtown markets, and then Welshpool, where new cases had been reported. Responding to the scale of the outbreaks, on 21 February the EU Commission announced an immediate export ban. But animals which had mixed freely at the docks were returned to their farms, helping spread the disease. It then took two days for the government to impose a total freeze on animal movements. With that, the countryside was closed for the duration. France ordered the slaughter of 20,000 sheep imported from Britain since 1 February; the Netherlands destroyed over 4,000, plus deer and other livestock. Once again, the UK became the 'leper of Europe'.

Meat prices soared as slaughterhouses were closed down, only some of which were reopened under licence to allow a trickle of animals to be killed. Producer prices crashed while retail prices soared. Prime Minister Blair blamed the supermarkets for having an 'armlock' on the farmers, while the pundits blamed intensive farming and 'cheap food' for the crisis.

Politically, the Labour government secretly welcomed the epidemic. On 27 February, the Countryside Alliance had been forced to call off its 'Liberty and Livelihoods' march, scheduled for 18 March, when more than 500,000 countryfolk had been expected to parade through the centre of London to protest about the proposed hunting ban. Now confined to quarters, they were safely neutralised, leaving the way clear for an early general election on 3 May, a date then about as secret as the fact that Friday followed Thursday. And, with a mere thirty outbreaks reported by 1 March, Agriculture Minister Nick Brown was confidently claiming that the outbreak was under control.

Meantime, the government had launched a policy of 'slash and burn', putting flocks and herds in quarantine and moving in with death squads, supposedly a well-tested policy based on the experience of the last great epidemic of 1967, although it soon transpired that it was anything but 'tried and tested'. In fact, the bureaucrats had been at work, in the form of EU Commission officials, codifying procedures in Council Directives 85/511/EEC and 90/423/EEC. Together with the little-known 'groundwater directive', which effectively prohibited the burial of diseased carcases, these set the scene for chaos.

Firstly, there were only 217 vets in the field – trying to track down over 43,000 sheep from just one market. There was the rigidity of MAFF's rules, which required their officials to be present at each of three crucial stages: the testing of the animals, their slaughter, and their disposal. Then, under the influence of the groundwater directive, the government's Environment Agency ignored the experience of 1967, where quick burial was the preferred option, and plumped for open-air burning. Soon television screens were filled with the awesome spectacle of funeral pyres, with thousands of animals being incinerated in a ghastly, EU-inspired ritual. But just as quickly came reports of many more thousands of massacred animals left in fields to rot. Vets who had been to infected sites had to be stood down for five days before going onto a 'clean' site, and the process started to grind to a halt. The Ministry had simply run out of staff.

On Sunday, 4 March, the outbreaks had risen to sixty-nine and gruesome stories started emerging of bungled kills. Amateur slaughterers had run amok, blasting pigs with shotguns after they had been stampeded by cattle being killed in their presence; one was filmed taking pot shots at sheep in an open field while others gunned down cows from the back of a fast-moving pick-up truck. Despite this, the services of experienced hunt slaughtermen were initially refused for fear their use might bolster the pro-hunt lobby at the time the Bill to ban hunting was going through Parliament. There was also a suggestion of using shooters but, having banned the use of handguns, the government was not too happy to call on this particular well-trained group.

By 8 March, there had been 106 outbreaks. Farmers were being told that they faced weeks more misery as the government's chief vet, Jim Scudamore, warned that the crisis would last a 'long time'. March 12 then saw an outbreak of the disease in France – blamed on the import of live sheep from England. Ireland and then the Netherlands reported outbreaks. Numbers continued to rise in the UK, spreading into Scotland, Wales and most areas of England. Things were looking distinctly bleak.

Losses were multiplying; tourism was badly affected. The situation had got so bad that, on 15 March, MAFF announced plans for a 'pre-emptive strike', the killing of all animals in the three-kilometre zones around infected farms. What seemed then the fantastic figure of a million sheep were earmarked to die and, although cattle were originally included, Nick Brown had to issue a hasty retraction, adding to the sense of crisis and confusion.

By 18 March, outbreaks had topped three hundred. The butcher's bill was estimated at £9 billion, with no end in sight. The government was increasingly being accused of incompetence so, on 19 March, Scudamore was co-opted to visit farmers in Cumbria to justify its actions. Access was carefully controlled. According to David Handley, chairman of the pressure group Farmers for Action:

> The farmers ... who were opposed to the cull were totally barred from attending. We asked if we could sit quietly at the back and at least hear what was being discussed. After all, this is our livelihood being discussed here. We were refused entry on all counts. The only people allowed in were NFU officials, selected vets and the mainstream press. It

was a totally one-sided affair. We then asked Scudamore for
a private meeting. We were informed that in order for that
to happen, we would have to make a request in writing.[1]

For public consumption, Scudamore complained that the
Ministry was having difficulty tracing many of the sheep suspected of carrying the disease, attributing the problem to 'the
lack of movement documentation for many animals'.

Part of the reason why so many sheep had gone missing was
the EU's sheep subsidy system which had encouraged a few
'rogue' dealers to shift ewes around the country to gather more
subsidies than the qualifying sheep they actually owned. A new
meaning to the term 'bed and breakfasting' broke into the public
consciousness. It was learned that sheep had been trucked into
fields overnight, ready for visiting inspectors to count, only to be
moved on the next day to be counted again in a different field –
a black market in 'black' sheep.

As Prime Minister Blair jetted off to an EU summit in
Stockholm, dropping in to see selected farmers in Cumbria –
another carefully stage-managed visit – his election plans were
beginning to look as shaky as a cow with advanced BSE. In
Stockholm, he was overheard confiding to Commission president
Romano Prodi that he had eleven days to decide whether to go
ahead. Back home, Blair made yet another stage-managed visit
to the countryside, taking care, as always, only to meet farmers
selected by the NFU. Thus informed, he decided to take charge,
to be rewarded with a tally of 587 cases.

Needless to say, the rumour mill was running in overdrive – as
it always does in crisis situations. All sorts of theories were being
advanced as to the cause of the epidemic. These ranged from the
intervention of Saddam Hussein to animal rights terrorists deliberately releasing a virus stolen from the government's biological
warfare laboratory at Porton Down. One commentator even
blamed the Mir space station.

These may have been dismissed as 'urban myths' but there
were nevertheless persistent reports that the government had
had prior knowledge of the epidemic – and had even warned
other countries. A party of British campers in New Zealand, in
December, claimed to have been raided by police who wanted to
disinfect their belongings because of foot and mouth in the UK.

Irish farmers had been warned to improve their 'biosecurity' and, on 18 January, the EU Commission had voted to spend £270,000 on testing the potency of emergency vaccine stocks.

There were confirmed reports that MAFF had contacted timber merchants, weeks before the first reported outbreak, to check the availability of railway sleepers to fuel funeral pyres. One merchant claimed to have last heard from the Ministry in 1967. Then there was an intriguing report that MAFF had ordered 'infected area' road signs from an Irish manufacturer, six weeks before the outbreak, while a MAFF official was overheard on a train predicting 'uproar' when it was discovered that 'Tony' had known about foot and mouth being in the country 'for months'. The satirical magazine *Private Eye* put the date more precisely – 4 December.

Then a French stock dealer operating out of the UK, Mr Hugues Inizan, claimed he had sent sheep to France on 31 January, which were tested some weeks later in France and reported to be infected with foot and mouth disease. Although the sheep had later been slaughtered, rather conveniently for MAFF, French sources dismissed the results as 'false positives'.

Despite lofty denials from government, the 'no smoke without fire' brigade was reinforced in its belief of an earlier outbreak by the sheer scale of the epidemic, which even the government's chief scientist was claiming to be 'out of control'. Nick Brown reacted by extending the killing zones to two miles around each farm, while Tony Blair mobilised the Military Police to help co-ordinate the slaughter and the Catering Corps to kill more animals faster. By then, funeral pyres had become politically unacceptable and the Environment Agency had thrown the EU rules out of the window. A fleet of bulldozers moved in to dig massive pits in a disused airfield in Great Orton, Cumbria, capable of burying 500,000 carcases, the first of many sites, one of which, Tow Law in Northumberland, was to be dubbed 'animal Auschwitz'.

Serious alarm was building up in the farming community. The disease had broken out into the Cumbria Fells, and the National Park was facing an 'absolute Doomsday scenario' with the threatened extinction of the unique breed of Herdwick sheep. The body count now exceeded the record set in 1967. Millions more animals were at risk, with estimates of thirty million having to be killed. Farmers and others were seriously questioning the validity of the 'contain and destroy' policy, and the possibility of mass vaccination was being seriously discussed.

In fact, it was being more than discussed. The Soil Association's Patrick Holden was calling for it, and millionaire publisher and pioneering organic farmer Peter Kindersley was planning to take the government to court to challenge the slaughter and force through a vaccination policy. Meanwhile, MAFF's spin machine had been working overtime, blaming the spread of foot and mouth on illegal sheep movements. The source was a 'dirty' pig farmer who had failed to boil swill from a Chinese restaurant which, in turn, had imported meat illegally from the Far East. After demonstrations by Chinese communities in Newcastle, Manchester and London, the latter claim was withdrawn and Blair had to grovel to Chinese community leaders in order to make peace. Nevertheless, Nick Brown still went to the Commons to announce that pig swill would be banned, even though his own vets had reported seeing old lesions in sheep which predated the cases at Heddon-on-the-Wall, demonstrating that the epidemic cannot have started at that pig farm.

Separately, his ministry went into 'anti-vaccine' mode, dredging up every reason it could find as to why vaccination would not work: vaccinated animals became 'infective'; the vaccine took too long to begin working and did not work very well anyway; and – the 'killer' fact – EU rules required all vaccinated animals to be slaughtered. On 27 March, with over 100,000 rotting carcases still lying in the fields and 634 outbreaks declared, Ben Gill, President of the NFU, took a hand. He went on television denouncing vaccination, saying that 'his members' wanted the killing speeded up. Vaccinated animals were the 'walking dead'.

But the tide seemed to be turning. Blair was already seriously considering the vaccination option, two Conservative MPs were openly advocating it, and Paul Tyler for the Liberal Democrats was calling for a change in policy. Professor Fred Brown, a British scientist now working for the US Plum Island Animal Disease Centre, was scathing. A world-renowned scientist and leading expert on foot and mouth, his view was that it was 'crazy' not to vaccinate. He suggested that Scudamore should look for another job – like gardening. His wrath was also directed at

MAFF for turning down a new American diagnostic field test which could detect foot and mouth in forty minutes, cutting days from the process of disposing of infected animals.

Sense was not to prevail. As outbreaks climbed through the thousand mark, the NFU continued its extraordinary campaign against vaccination. Privately, it was believed, Blair actually supported vaccination but – contrary to his publicly professed claim of being able to make 'hard choices' – was torn by indecision. Instead of vaccination, there was only vacillation, immortalised by *Private Eye* as Blair's 'Emergency vacillation policy'.

Along the way, Blair had postponed his election – officially the local elections – to 7 June 2001. With the economic situation deteriorating, dogged by trouble in the NHS, mutinous GPs and teachers and a breakdown in law and order, Blair knew that any further delay could prejudice re-election for a second term. The word went out – cases must decline. And decline they did. By the end of April, with the help of MAFF massaging the figures so outrageously that even the BBC's *Today* programme began to notice, outbreak numbers miraculously began to drop. The downturn, real only to those in air-conditioned offices in Canary Wharf and Millbank, gave Nick Brown his opportunity. He announced to incredulous MPs attending the Commons Agriculture Committee on 23 April that, because the number of outbreaks was coming down, vaccination was no longer necessary.

If anything had been learned by MAFF from the BSE inquiry, which had reported a mere six months previously, it was 'don't put your chief vet on the stage', after the disastrous performance of Keith Meldrum during the BSE crisis. Sure enough, the present incumbent, Jim Scudamore, disappeared from the front line. His place was taken by a 'media friendly' spokesman. This was professional chemist and government chief scientific adviser Professor David King, who presented MPs with a series of graphs, based on computer projections prepared by statisticians from Imperial College, London. By complete coincidence, one of the graphs showed the epidemic skidding to a halt on exactly 7 June.

That still left the cattle, which, in the main, had been housed over winter and thus protected from the legions of infected sheep. Now due to be turned out onto spring grassland, they were poised to add new fuel to the epidemic, cohorts of fresh victims ready for the burning. Although, as early as 30 March, the British government had successfully applied for and had been granted permission by the EU Commission to vaccinate the cattle in Cumbria and Devon, for the very purpose of protecting them from the sheep, Brown had now ruled out this strategy.

Thus deprived of the only sensible control option, MAFF launched a new wave of slaughter, extending the 'cull' to eliminate every sheep in Dumfries and Galloway, Cumbria, Northumbria, the Forest of Dean and Devon. With the aid of a Charollais-cross calf renamed Phoenix, which somewhat implausibly survived five days in a heap of dead cattle, the intensified killing was heavily disguised as a 'relaxation' of the cull. The cattle were to be spared – only the sheep were to die.

And die they did. With two thousand troops mobilised, the body count shot past the two million mark and continued to rise. As it did, tales of utter barbarity began to filter out. This is part of a letter posted on a website and attributed to a soldier serving with the Green Howards in the Worcester area:

... We were briefed that we'd be 'clearing up' – burning and/or burying carcases of animals humanely destroyed by trained vets and slaughtermen. But that's all turned out to be more spin and propaganda. What we're actually doing is 'mopping up' – killing animals they've left behind or can't be bothered to finish off.

My regiment has got all sorts of battle honours for fighting Britain's enemies all over the world, but we're now engaged in heroic hand-to-hand combat with lambs. Their mothers have been shot but some were so frightened by the noise that they'd escaped all over the place.

As we don't have any humane killers, the cleanest way of killing them is just to throw them in the river. We might be trained to kill enemy soldiers, but slitting the throat of a spring lamb, or beating its brains out with a blunt instrument, is just too much for some of the lads, so they'd rather drown them, even if it's not really as quick.

One of my mates was detailed to stand by a pig which was giving birth. As each piglet was born and crawled away he had to smash it with the back of a shovel. Once they'd all been born the pig was shot with all the others. Worst of all are the cows that have been shot but not finished off by the slaughtermen. Some are still crawling around, others are clearly still alive but unable to move. We have to beat them to death with lorry spanners or other heavy lumps of iron. If people really knew that was going on I think there'd be a revolution.

But the people did not know what was going on. There was no revolution. And so utterly set on their task had the state officials become that they even found time to dispose of a pet goat, Misty, slaughtered while the owner's mother was distracted by police in her own home.

Among the hundreds of thousands to follow were six Dutch Zwartbles sheep owned by Dumfriesshire widow Carolyne Hoffe, who had barricaded them into her home in Glasserton, near Whithorn, in order to protect them. Despite a spirited High Court appeal, the authorities prevailed. A vet, backed by police and the Gurkhas, broke into Carolyne's home to execute the government's policy.

Never mind: Blair had got his way. On 8 May, against a backdrop of children in a South London school, he announced his general election. To no one's surprise, it was to be on 7 June. With 'a hymn and a touch of humility',[2] he then pleaded for the voters' 'hearts and minds' in what was later described as a 'toe-curlingly embarrassing' presentation.[3] By then over 1,600 outbreaks had been declared and the corpses of millions of animals were rotting in the ground, their stench pervading the countryside. But the 'phoney war' was over. The political race was on.

By general consensus among what are still described as 'Fleet Street' hacks, foot and mouth was over. They were bored with burning carcases and snivelling farmers and wanted to get on with the 'real life' issues, such as the general election. But, of course, it was not over. Despite the most determined attempts of the Blair government to massage the statistics and dampen down publicity, the disease grumbled on.

Not least of the events that followed was the determined stand by Juanita Wilson, owner of the Mossburn Animal Sanctuary in Hightae, near Lockerbie. She had been told by the Scottish Executive Rural Affairs Department (SERAD) – the local equiv-

alent of MAFF – that her fourteen goats and three sheep must
die. Yet it had been seven weeks since the neighbouring farm had
been 'killed-out' for foot and mouth, well beyond the incubation
period of the disease, and no sign of it had appeared on the sanctuary. Nor did SERAD want to kill the cattle and pigs – magically,
these could not spread the disease. Only the goats and sheep had
to die, although Henry the goose was also due to be put down.
This bird had spent so much time with the sheep that it thought
it was a sheep. Juanita could not bear for it to be left on its own.
She blockaded her sanctuary to prevent the death squads from
carrying out their work.

Fighting to save her animals, she then took her case to the
High Court in Edinburgh, only to have it rejected. It looked all
over by 11 May when the butchers arrived, accompanied by fifty
policemen, at five to six in the morning – despite having agreed
to allow Juanita's vet to kill them at ten. The police closed the
main road past the sanctuary and rerouted traffic through the
tiny village of Hightae with its primary school, all 'in the interests of road safety' – but actually to prevent reinforcements and
journalists from reaching the sanctuary.

That weekend, the *Sunday Times*[4] was dominated by the
headline 'We can't stop crime, say police'. The Police Federation
was to stage its annual conference and was complaining that
forces were so short of officers that they could do little more than
respond to crimes after the event. 'In essence, we arrive when
the wheels fall off,' chairman Fred Broughton said.

But the wheels had not fallen off at Mossburn. Overnight,
Juanita had sacked her legal team, appointed another and lodged
yet another appeal. The judge gave her a stay of execution until
Tuesday. Come the day, Rural Affairs Minister Ross Finnie
announced that the automatic 'cull' would be discontinued and
each farm could be assessed on a 'case-by-case' basis. It was
agreed that the Mossburn animals should be blood tested and the
court case was adjourned. For once, there was to be no slaughter.

Despite this last-minute reprieve, even by the obscene logic of
the day there seemed something very odd going on in the area.
SERAD seemed determined to wipe out every sheep and every
goat in southern Scotland, including the rare breeds which had
been exempted in England.

The explanation seemed to be a deal between the Scottish

Executive and the European Commission, whereby Scotland, as a region of the EU, could apply for 'disease-free' export status ahead of the rest of the United Kingdom, on condition that all sheep and goats along the English border had been eliminated. Yet, if that was the intent, there was no power for the Executive to slaughter merely for this reason. The Animal Health Act 1981 permitted slaughter for disease control purposes only, so the action appeared to be illegal.

Apart from tiny animal sanctuaries such as Mossburn, however, the only protests seemed to be coming from owners of the rare Cheviot sheep on the sixty-five holdings comprising the Duke of Buccleuch's estates in Dumfriesshire. The Earl of Dalkeith, writing to the *Daily Telegraph*,[5] reported that, after 50,000 cattle and sheep on the estates had been slaughtered, the consensus among farmers was breaking down. The Scottish Executive was using 'tactics that come close to moral blackmail and menace', creating a climate of fear and doubt. He was saddened that the prosecution of a policy that so many had initially supported had become so 'robotic'.

One reason for the lack of more general opposition was that many lowland farmers were happy to accept the scorched-earth policy in exchange for generous compensation – sometimes above the normal market value of their animals – and the prospect of ploughing up pastures to receive additional subsidies for growing barley (thus putting more pressure on the arable sector, as the subsidies are drawn from a fixed pool). Those who regarded their animals as more than items in a profit-and-loss account were at odds with the broader farming community. Thus, not only was the government response to foot and mouth destroying animals and farms, it was setting farmer against farmer, neighbour against neighbour, destroying communities as well.

Nevertheless, the spin machine was still working overtime and, on Thursday, 17 May – almost three months to the day since the epidemic had started – the magic day arrived. There were no new cases of foot and mouth. The following day, however, a resident in one of the new 'kill zones' circulated the following e-mail:

We were told on the propaganda-news yesterday that there had been no cases of foot and mouth in 24 hours. However I have heard of three new cases in the area around Settle, where I have a house. The atmosphere in this part of Yorkshire resembles an armed camp at the moment.

In what Christopher Booker called in his *Sunday Telegraph* column that week 'the greatest conjuring trick of this election campaign', the government was concealing the fact that it was killing more animals than at the height of the foot and mouth crisis. In the ten days preceding the 'zero cases' report, MAFF and its army death-squads had killed more than a quarter of a million animals on more than one thousand farms. Between 4 and 12 May alone, the Ministry had 'killed out' 889 farms, an average of 125 a day. The daily average of animals slaughtered in that week had been 32,000, nearly three times the figure for the previous week. And the total number of animals killed, including those under the so-called 'welfare scheme', was set to top six million, or one in ten of all Britain's livestock.

To conceal the scale of the killing, the big, prepared disposal sites had been abandoned and a new law had been passed, the Waste (Foot and Mouth Disease) (England) Regulations 2001, which forced tip operators under threat of criminal prosecution to bury dead animals in ordinary landfill sites, driving a horse and cart through environmental law. The new strategy was to 'blitz' an area with special 'task forces' of vets and soldiers to kill everything in sight. The carcases were transported overnight to keep them out of public sight. 'Rural cleansing' was under way.

Such was the success of the Millbank machine that foot and mouth disease was well on its way to becoming a 'secret epidemic'. The complaints, on the other hand, were not secret. Two of the Ministry's most senior scientists working on foot and mouth published a 'damning indictment' of the contiguous cull in the *Veterinary Record*, arguing that much of the killing had been unnecessary. Commenting on the article, Anthony Gibson, the NFU's South West Director, damned the 'cull' as 'one of the most bloody, tragic and disgraceful misjudgements ever committed in the name of science'. 'Cull' it was not. That term implied selectivity. It had been pointless, indiscriminate slaughter.

And for all the efforts put into controlling the flow of information, the secret was too big to be completely suppressed. By 19 May, MAFF was being forced to declare four more 'new' outbreaks, bringing the total to a staggering 1,611. But the worrying development was the outbreaks in North Yorkshire. Days later, another MAFF task force comprising more than two hundred officials had been drafted into Settle, an 'army of occupation'. The Ministry admitted to seventeen 'cases' (although farmers counted forty-one) and around 69,000 animals had been or were in the process of being slaughtered. By 24 May, Scottish farmers were also on alert after a second outbreak in two days had been confirmed in Eastriggs, near Annan, the first in Dumfries and Galloway for ten days. Ministry vets were trying to hold the line, carefully describing the incidents as 'sparks round the edge of infected farms'.

That day, Nick Brown was preparing to rush off to Settle to talk, as usual, with the carefully selected group of farmers. But not everything went as planned. When he arrived, he was heckled by a small crowd. 'Where were you when we needed you?' shouted one man. The 'cluster' of outbreaks had by then been reported at eighteen and rising. A MAFF spokesman described the situation as 'very worrying'. Indeed it was. The picturesque Yorkshire Dales were the heart of Herriot country and Settle had become a ghost town. Blair had to take time off from his presidential campaign to urge people 'not to relax in the battle to stop the virus spreading'. And there were rumblings of discontent, even from the NFU. Tim Palmer, the Skipton group secretary, complained, 'Our members feel that they have been ignored and that this is not just a blip at the end of the foot-and-mouth crisis. This is a major extension to the epidemic.'

But if there was a 'blip' it was in the publicity. Swamped by the general election news, foot and mouth disease struggled to compete – and lost. Nick Brown huffed and puffed about accusations that his ministry had massaged the figures to give his party a clear run at the election, 'refuting' everything – even when an analysis in the *Daily Telegraph* indicated that the total outbreaks were double those declared by the government, at over 3,000. And no sooner had Blair announced that we were 'on the home straight' than outbreaks were reported in Clitheroe, Lancashire, and Knutsford in Cheshire. Undeterred, he dismissed these as 'sporadic outbursts ... precisely what the experts had expected'.

Day 100 of the epidemic came and went. MAFF blamed the farmers for spreading the disease and put up Professor David

King to explain that, had the government not killed so many animals, a lot of animals would have had to have been killed. As far as the course of the epidemic had gone, the government had not moved its position one iota. As faithfully recorded by the BBC, the epidemic had started at Heddon-on-the-Wall, MAFF had behaved wonderfully, etc., etc.

The only snag was that the epidemic was now on its way to becoming the largest ever in the world, and even Professor King was saying that it was not going to end until August. The prediction of 7 June was but a distant memory. Another 300 tipper lorries were hired, ready to move into Exmoor after the election, while hit teams stood by in Lincolnshire, Swaledale, South Cumbria and the Brecon Beacons. Oh, and Northumberland county trading standards officers announced they were to prosecute Bobby Waugh and his brother Ronnie for starting the epidemic. MAFF had its scapegoat.

By election day, the disease had spread back into Whitby and the Peak District, and was rampant in cattle in Devon and Somerset. Meanwhile, MAFF was planning an extensive blood-testing exercise in undisclosed areas, to root out hitherto undetected infection. Positive animals were to be slaughtered. With rumours of a new 'blitz' after the election, the media pricked up its ears. But Scudamore denied there was to be any intensification of the 'cull' and the media went back to sleep.

The propaganda war had well and truly been won. In the early hours of 8 June, it was clear that Blair had romped home to victory. But six million animals had been slaughtered, and millions more were yet to die. Joining the casualties was Nick Brown, replaced by Margaret Beckett. With Beckett came the Department of Environment, Food and Rural Affairs (DEFRA). MAFF had been culled – or had it?

1. Introduction

Much has been said and written about the 'death' of British agriculture – the end of traditional farming as we know it, or would wish it to be. And, if it is not actually dead, agriculture is certainly on its deathbed. Whatever survives the current crisis will be very different from what we have become used to. When death does intervene, it will not have come naturally, in the manner of a grand old dowager, her life-force spent from the follies of youth and the travails of a lifetime of service. Agriculture is not ready for a dignified and timely death. It has many, many years of good and faithful service left in it. It will not just die. It will have been destroyed by incompetence, neglect, stupidity and error, compounded by a measure of conspiracy, corruption and political opportunism.

Foot and mouth disease was, of course, the last straw. But it was not the disease that did the damage. It was not the disease which, by the end of May 2001, had killed an estimated six million animals. The real destruction was caused by that excuse for an organisation, the Ministry of Agriculture, Fisheries and Food (MAFF). Even after faithfully recording its behaviour for several decades, I have difficulty in comprehending the ease with which it has presided over the destruction of an entire industry. However, even before MAFF had began its deadly work, British agriculture had been terribly damaged.

That its suffering had been long and lingering is evident from the clinical records of its chief tormentor, the annual reports of the Ministry of Agriculture. Here, year after year, can be found chronicles that mark the life-force of the industry ebbing away.

Not least of the harbingers of death were the analyses of farming incomes, the life blood of the industry. Over the last decade, they had fallen by a staggering 70 per cent, with the current average income dropping to below £7,500. Such had been the devastation that the total value of farming produce had fallen from £6 billion in 1995 to an incredible £1.8 billion in the year 2000. And within these global figures were concealed even greater disasters. Lowland sheep and cattle farmers' incomes had declined to 10 per cent of their 1989/90 values. Pig prices were so low that producers were losing money on every animal sold and their incomes had dropped to a catastrophic *minus* 10 per cent. They were paying their consumers for the privilege of supplying them with food. Highly efficient dairy farmers were in the same position, producing milk at 18-20p/litre, yet being paid as little as 16p, compared with 19.3p/litre in 1991. Cull cows were attracting an average of £250 each – compared with an average of £585 five years previously – and calves, which used to be sold at £180, were being shot on the farm because prices had fallen to just £4 a beast.

Not even the 'barley barons' were making money. The farm-gate wheat price, which in 1991 was a comfortable £116/tonne, had plummeted to £64 in 2000; barley had fallen from £110 to £68; oilseed rape from £242 to £120 and peas from £193 to £79 per tonne.

The scale of the price collapse was even more staggering when it was contrasted with overall agricultural productivity, which had improved every year in the previous decade. In 1999, it leapt 2.6 per cent over the previous year. Labour productivity increased by 8.2 per cent, won by shedding still more paid workers, but not without a human cost. One farmer wrote, 'Here on the farm, I have adjusted to the reductions in income by reducing my farm staff from five full-time to one, who does everything from stockman to maintenance of buildings ...'.[1]

In any other industry, such improvements in efficiency would have been applauded and rewarded with increased profits. But the economics of the market no longer applied to farmers. They worked harder and longer, producing more (an increase of 14 per cent since 1995) to earn less. Small wonder that, in the year 2000, over 22,800 farmers and farm workers left the land, while suicides (at 77 for the year) were running at well over one a week. And the Green Party airily dismissed agriculture as 'an arena for profit'.[2]

Thus, even before the foot and mouth epidemic hit in February 2001, the industry was dying on its feet. In a gruesome sense, the death-blow dealt by MAFF through its response to the epidemic did agriculture a favour, putting it out of its misery.

Many farmers had been trapped on unprofitable farms, unable to liquidate their assets because prices had been so low. Then along came MAFF waving substantial compensation cheques, in some cases valuing animals well above the market rate. This was a way out, a way to bring to an end the long, slow, lingering death to which they had been consigned. Consumed in the funeral pyres or buried in stinking pits, the personal nightmares of thousands of livestock farmers were over. They took their 'pension cheques' and ran.

But what we have witnessed is more than a wanton destruction. Wiping out what remained of our small livestock sector has not only radically altered the familiar appearance of our countryside, but torn the heart out of the industry. Without intervention, the remnants will look very different from the one we have today, as will much of what is left of our traditional rural landscape. Unless its corpse can be resurrected, food production will be concentrated far more obviously than ever before in the hands of the big operators. We will see a further giant leap towards the industrialisation of farming, reinforcing all those tendencies in modern agriculture which in recent years have attracted such growing alarm, from the cramming of animals into factory-scale production units to chemically intensive crop-growing on hedgeless prairie fields.

In many places, such as the hillier parts of Wales, Scotland and the south-west and north of England, the land had already become too marginal to justify traditional farming. We will now discover just how much the familiar appearance of our countryside depended on small-scale agricultural production to retain hedges, trees and patchwork fields. Vast tracts of land presently kept under control by sheep and cattle are already beginning to lie derelict, as stone walls tumble and fields and hillsides disappear under a mass of weeds, scrub and sterile bracken. Furthermore, the disappearance of our remaining small farms will knock a gaping hole in our rural economy, as smaller abattoirs, butchers and a host of other businesses likewise vanish, and with them much of that distinctive character which pertains to country life.

Thus, while politicians continue to prate about 'sustainable farming' and 'the Guardian tendency' drivels on about the evils of 'intensive farming', much of British agriculture, as we know it, has become economically unsustainable. In its present form, it is all but at an end. We are indeed witnessing a key industry in its death throes.

Such an outrageous event requires a serious investigation, if not to bring the perpetrators to account, then at least to expose them in the hope that the court of public opinion can deliver a verdict on their deeds. Thus, if you like, this is a 'murder mystery' book, a detective story. But that is only the first part. Agriculture, for all its ills, is not yet a corpse. There is hope of a resurrection. Thus, the second part of the book is devoted to an exploration of strategies needed to bring agriculture back from the edge and, after a period of intensive care, to create the conditions under which it may survive and perhaps prosper.

When it comes to 'fingering' the culprits, the name of the first and most dangerous has, figuratively at least, already been posted on the wanted lists. Unfortunately, the villain has yet to be apprehended. That culprit is, of course, MAFF, and in the next chapter of this book an indictment is prepared, based in part on the account, recorded in the Prologue, of its disastrous handling of the foot and mouth epidemic. But high on the list of suspects, last seen holding the smoking gun of the Common Agricultural Policy (CAP), is the European Union. A simple catalogue of the failings of the CAP would be more than enough to indict the EU as a co-conspirator but, in the work that led up to the preparation of the charge sheet, I have found several sets of fingerprints on the murder weapon.

The line-up of suspects features prominently those who see reform of the CAP as the answer to agriculture's ills: those who, for want of action, would prefer to wait for the 'perfect' policy that only harmonious co-existence under the wing of 'Mother Europe' can bring; those who would prefer to rely on dysfunctional officials snarling their way through eternal negotiations in the Tower of Babel which squats at the heart of modern Brussels; those who are content to see agriculture die rather than admit the fatuity of their own fantasies.

Also in the line-up is our own British government – not just its junior department of state, MAFF – for its shadowy and malign role in starving agriculture of funds, a devastating indictment which brings it to the top of the list of suspects. But then what is startling is the sheer length of the list brought into the light, the variety and identity of the suspects, some of whom are, on the face of it, unlikely culprits. Their true identities and motives have been cloaked in whirling smokescreens of their own making.

Others are more obvious, among whom are the 'greedy' intensive farmers and the supermarkets. The retail giants, in particular, have been cast in the role of villains, especially when the industry leader, Tesco, declared its first £1 billion annual profit in 2001. But no good detective story is complete without its sprinkling of 'red herrings'. Is intensive farming, as such, really a culprit? Are supermarkets really villains, or are they simply the carrion crows, picking over the flesh of an already inert body, long after the real villains have departed the scene? Their role in the carnage is subjected to careful scrutiny.

With the suspects in the frame, so to speak, and their culpabilities examined, the book then moves on to the much more positive but difficult task of identifying a way to resurrect agriculture, one which can perhaps satisfy its urban critics yet provide a sustainable and rewarding living for those who choose to till the soil and tend stock. Here I find that, despite the many criticisms laid at the door of the CAP and the subsidy system embodied within that policy, there is an essential role for public money in the support of agriculture. So firm is this conclusion that one is drawn to the view that, if the CAP – as a vehicle for dispensing subsidies – did not exist, another system would have to be invented to do the same job.

An examination of alternatives thus forms an important element of the second part of this book. Here I have relied heavily on a series of structured discussions with working farmers and other interested parties, an informed cross-section of opinion, articulated by people who have an intimate knowledge of the industry.

But, whether wittingly or not, I find that I have also been heavily influenced by Sir Richard Body, MP, in that, when I revisited his book *Our Food, Our Land* in the course of writing this book, many of the ideas I thought I was developing for myself had already been suggested by him. However, I believe I have taken many of those ideas and developed them further, offering tangible, practical ways by which they could be implemented.

In his own analysis, Sir Richard came to the conclusion that, in order for UK agriculture (and the countryside) to survive, the CAP must be 'repatriated' (code for abolished, with policy reverting to member states). In promoting this course of action, he also concluded that if this meant we would have to leave the EU, so be it. I concur with his analysis, an analysis borne out by time. Plainly, the policy was not repatriated. Agriculture is on its deathbed.

2. Danger – Maffia Killing Fields

As stories of the arrogance of MAFF's killer squads flooded in at the height of the foot and mouth epidemic, many farmers in the egg industry began to experience an uncanny sense of déjà vu. Starting in early 1989, in the wake of the salmonella-in-eggs scare, through to 1993, they had experienced their own version of a MAFF slaughter campaign, during which over three and a half million laying hens had been compulsorily slaughtered, numerous businesses had been wrecked and farmers driven to the point of suicide.

Working for the egg industry, it was then that I first learnt of the draconian powers of the Ministry and their Animal Health Act 1981, the very same legislation used in the foot and mouth epidemic. For instance, in 1990, when I found that a particular Ministry laboratory was so contaminated that virtually every sample going into it came out positive for salmonella, it made no difference at all to a flock which had been declared infected on the basis of its tests. Even when eleven different samples from the same flock, all sent to different laboratories – including another ministry laboratory – turned out to be negative, it made not one whit of difference. The flock was positive because a Ministry vet had signed a notice saying it was, and that was the end of it. It had to be slaughtered.

That was the power of 'Form A', the Infected Place Notice, served then on egg producers and, during the foot and mouth epidemic, on flock and herd owners. The notice is the death warrant, signed by a veterinary officer and, as I learned to my own personal cost,[1] it is 'proof unto itself'. No evidence is required to declare a farm an 'infected place'. The notice signed by a vet is itself the proof of infection.

My colleagues and I knew then that, if egg producers broke the welfare rules, they stood at risk of being prosecuted. But time and again we saw Ministry officials ride roughshod over welfare codes. We saw vets turn up without the faintest idea of how to handle poultry – or even how to open a battery cage. They had no idea what constituted a random sample or how to go about taking one, nor even of the basic hygiene procedures required to prevent cross-contamination between samples.

Worst of all, they were imbued with self-righteousness, convinced they were saving the nation from evil egg producers intent on poisoning babies and grannies. They were locked into the myth that salmonella infection had come down from breeding flocks and infected feed. To sustain their beliefs, they produced 'Janet and John' epidemiology forms, which they solemnly filled in, ticking off loaded questions and ignoring observations which did not fit their preconceptions. Where the facts conflicted, it was not beyond them to alter documents. When they were challenged in the courts, the simple but effective technique of lying usually sufficed to win them their cases. To prevent farmers arguing, they refused to supply documents. Even the laboratory reports which supposedly confirmed infection had to be prised out of MAFF with the help of a High Court judge.

Time after time, when flocks had been slaughtered, the houses cleaned and disinfected, new 'infection-free' feed supplied, with birds restocked from Ministry-approved sources, we found salmonella infection recurring. One farm succumbed three times, despite all Ministry precautions having been adopted. In the face of Ministry indifference, we sought permission to do our own scientific tests, desperate as we were to discover the sources of infection in order to head off yet more state-sanctioned slaughter. When permission was refused and we told the Ministry that the tests would go ahead anyway, officials resorted to a barrage of High Court injunctions and to intimidating registered laboratories. They were told they would lose their licences if they accepted our samples.

When, despite these blocking tactics, we discovered that the infection came from a variety of sources, including airborne drift from infected broiler litter spread on fields adjoining hen-houses, the ministry was not interested. The officials knew the answer already – it was 'feed and infected breeder flocks'. They were not going to let little things like facts get in the way.

The *pièce de résistance* was even more astounding. Throughout the slaughter campaign, senior MAFF officials systematically cheated producers out of their rightful compensation

when flocks were slaughtered. From the start, they had deliberately set out to underpay and then, by refusing to give farmers
details of their calculations, sought to conceal what they knew to
be illegal. Farmers were told that, if they invoked their rights of
appeal to arbitrators, payments would be delayed, effectively
blackmailing them into accepting their offers. According to a subsequent Select Committee report:[2]

> ... MAFF effectively and deliberately rendered them in-
> capable of reaching an informed decision on whether to
> challenge the amount ... Such postponement of compensa-
> tion to poultry owners facing severe losses should never
> have been countenanced in the first place. That it was coun-
> tenanced in the knowledge that owners were being deprived
> of information vital to their case deserves the most serious
> criticism.

In delivering its report the committee was

> ... astonished that MAFF should have treated so unfairly
> men and women already vulnerable and under extreme
> pressure ... Such maladministration as is found in this case
> must never be repeated.

Few egg producers were astonished. MAFF's behaviour was precisely what they had come to expect. But no one in MAFF was
disciplined – no one lost his job. The Ministry paid £600,000 of
other people's money in compensation and life went on. There
was no public inquiry and many of the officials involved have
since been promoted, some to the upper echelons of MAFF and
others to the Food Standards Agency. Those of us directly
involved in the campaign were left with a lasting legacy of bitterness and, above all, a profound contempt for MAFF officials
and their works.
   Even then MAFF was already involved in another controversy,
the compulsory use of highly toxic organo-phosphorous sheep
dips which had caused serious ill health in a large number of
farmers. The Ministry's responses were true to form: denial,
mendacity and prevarication. Again there was no public inquiry
and victims, many suffering debilitating illnesses, were left to

struggle for justice, expending their time, funds and energies seeking redress through an unyielding legal system.

Bovine Spongiform Encephalopathy (BSE) had also emerged as a high-profile issue. As it had with salmonella in laying hens, MAFF locked itself into the legend that 'infected feed' was the cause. So predictable was this finding that we could have written the script. MAFF *always* blames feed when a new disease emerges – be it swine fever, swine vesicular disease, blue-ear disease, fowl-pest or even humble salmonella in laying hens – and was to do so again in the foot and mouth epidemic. This is the same MAFF, incidentally, which could not see a link between the use of organo-phosphorus sheep dips – potent neurotoxins – and the emergence of neurological illnesses in its users.

When the childishly inadequate BSE feed thesis was challenged by Somerset organic farmer Mark Purdey, who offered well-founded and closely argued theories about the role of organo-phosphates compulsorily applied to cattle, he was met with an impenetrable wall of indifference. When that failed, owing to Purdey's dogged persistence, officials mounted a sustained campaign of disinformation and obstruction. We learned the simple truth as it applied to MAFF. Everything the officials said or did was right. They had 'evidence', we had 'anecdotes'. If we disagreed with MAFF officials, there was only one possible explanation: since they were always right, we had to be wrong. The more we argued, the more it proved we were wrong.

When, in February 2001, MAFF was confronted with a major epidemic of foot and mouth disease, it came as absolutely no surprise that its response was to slaughter. Apart from blaming feed, it kills animals. And should that fail, as proved to be the case, it was inevitable that it would then kill even more animals, faster – egged on in this case by Tim Yeo, Conservative Party spokesman on agriculture, who wanted the killing done even more quickly.

But no dispassionate observer could even begin to describe the handling of the epidemic as anything other than an unmitigated disaster. Renowned international experts on foot and mouth, such as Professor Fred Brown, formerly a MAFF scientist and then at the US Institute of Animal Health, condemned the ministry response. But even Brown had not factored in the mindset: MAFF is right and therefore – by definition – everybody else is wrong.

Yet it was MAFF that was wrong, not least because, at the heart of the machine, there was a fatal policy flaw. Britain, historically, had opted for disease-free status, an entirely realistic objective given its island status and its ability to exclude potentially infected material. But, in 1993, with the advent of the EU's 'single market' – which politicians of all three major parties heartily endorsed – the UK dismantled its border controls and opened up its markets to virtually unrestricted imports, legal and illegal. At a stroke, trade policy was 'out of synch' with the disease control needs. The only logical move then was to embark on routine vaccination, to protect against one of the most infectious diseases in the world.

Amazingly, however, in 1990, when harmonisation of foot and mouth controls came on the agenda in the rush to 'complete' the single market, MAFF had convinced the EU that the way forward was to adopt disease-free status, without vaccination. A new directive, 90/423/EC, was framed which forced continental member states – some against their better judgement – to abandon routine vaccination and adopt what was essentially a British policy designed for a 'fortress' island. The scene was set for a disaster of epic proportions.

But what really set the seal on the disaster-to-come was a change in the way livestock was reared and marketed. Hill farmers traditionally acted as 'nurseries' for breeding ewes, and shipped their progeny off the hills to be fattened on lowland grazing. But as margins had been squeezed, they had been unable to live off the income from traditional stocking levels. Bolstered by a growing export trade with France, they had increased ewe numbers. Local markets and local abattoirs – driven by regulatory pressure – had declined in numbers and the mass movement of animals had been accommodated by larger, more distant markets. This accounted for the huge movements of sheep, estimated at 1.35 million in the weeks preceding the epidemic, which were to hasten the spread of the disease.

But not only was the Ministry unable to factor these changes into its control plan, it was not even able to change the plan. That was set in stone, dictated by EU directives and lodged with the Commission in 1993. That plan – derived largely from experience of the 1967 outbreak – was based on dealing with what might be called a 'phase one' outbreak. It relied on early detection of the disease; identification of the affected animals; isolation; and slaughter. There was no 'Plan B'. However, even before the outbreak had been detected by MAFF, it had broken out of 'phase one' into a 'secondary' phase and become an epidemic. Massive secondary infections had already occurred – many of them in locations unknown to MAFF – and the outbreak was already out of control. The policy adopted was wholly inappropriate right from the very start.

In this 'secondary phase', the priority should have been to prevent development to a third and considerably more damaging phase. In this case, phase three is where the disease breaks out and becomes completely uncontained, affecting all species: pigs, cattle and sheep. By the end of March 2001, the disease was largely (but not entirely) confined to sheep but disaster was imminent. Winter-housed cattle, largely protected from disease spread, were to be progressively turned out to grass, when they would become exposed to the disease. There was the terrifying prospect of spread to these animals, leading to an explosive, tertiary epidemic, larger than had so far been experienced. To prevent that, the only credible option was emergency vaccination of all vulnerable stock.

Fortunately for MAFF, owing to a cold, wet spring which delayed grass growth and left pastures too soft, cattle were not turned out on schedule. The explosive 'third phase' did not occur early enough to affect the timing of the general election which was so desired by the Labour administration. But when evidence of increasing spread became apparent, MAFF resorted to time-honoured tactics – it massaged the figures. In any event, MAFF could only conceive of one response: to widen the control areas and slaughter more and more animals. In anticipation of a wider spread into cattle, whole tranches of England's 'green and pleasant land', the Welsh Brecon Beacons and the border areas of Scotland, were turned into killing fields.

The vaccination débâcle

While vaccination was and remained the only effective response to the growing epidemic, the issue became bogged down in claim and counter-claim as to the effect it might have on restoring Britain's export status, a status which, in any case, had been

lost on 21 February when the EU Commission had formally
banned the export of livestock and most animal products from
the UK.[3]

Those resisting vaccination argued that it would delay
resumption for at least two years while advocates held that it
would make no difference. This terrible confusion arose not least
because of the complexity of the rules but mainly because MAFF
failed to clarify the situation. And there was no doubt that the
rules were complex. Firstly, there was an international code set
out by the Paris-based Office International des Epizooties (OIE),
but then there were the internal rules set by the EU – something
which MAFF seemed loath to acknowledge.

The OIE code[4] conditions specified that, where *routine* vaccination was not practised, export trade could be resumed three
months after the last case had been notified, as long as a
slaughter programme was in place and blood testing had been
carried out. Where *emergency* vaccination had been used, the
period was three months after the slaughter of the last vaccinated animal. It was this which led to the NFU-perpetrated
myth, not countered by MAFF, that vaccinated animals had to be
slaughtered. But the OIE code offered options. Where vaccinated
animals were not slaughtered, the clearance period was extended
to a year, or two years after vaccination when infected animals
were not slaughtered.

But what was not recognised by the farming community, nor
clarified by MAFF, was that the OIE rules were not binding on
the EU, which regarded them as a minimum standard.
Therefore, resumption of trade was not to be determined by the
OIE but by the EU. The problem here was that the EU has not
actually made any formal rules for permitting resumption of
exports. Each incident was to be assessed on its merits and,
because of the scale and duration of the UK epidemic, it was confronting a wholly unprecedented situation. The only certainty
was that, if the UK resorted to vaccination, it would be a year
after the campaign had ended before export clearance would be
given.

On the other hand, it was clear that, if animals were not vaccinated, the EU would only permit resumption of trade at some
(unspecified) time after the epidemic had been brought under
control and all traces of the disease had been eliminated. And

there lay the crux of the matter. Some experts argued that vaccination would bring the epidemic to an end earlier while, without vaccination, the epidemic would linger on and on. Thus, the choice was between a year's wait after vaccination had been completed before exports could be resumed, or an unspecified period, the time taken for MAFF to eliminate the disease by its 'slash and burn' policy – plus however long it took for the EU to decide on giving formal clearance. On this, MAFF was silent, exuding confidence that the trauma would soon be over. By not coming clean on the options, the Ministry consigned farmers and their leaders to a fog of confusion, rendering them unable to make informed decisions.

And no hint was given either of the labyrinthine nature of the decision-making process, nor the hurdles the UK would have to surmount before it was in the clear. The first hurdle was a shadowy organisation known as the Standing Veterinary Committee (SVC), one of the EU's nine regulatory committees set up in 1968. Made up of senior veterinary officers from each of the member states, its role would be to consider representations from the British government and decide on the technical criteria for relaxing the export ban. The committee occupied a key position because, while the Commission nominally made the decisions, it could only do so on the basis of a favourable opinion from the SVC. Without this opinion the Commission was powerless. In other words, the SVC actually ran the show.[5]

Furthermore, the SVC – despite being, ostensibly, a technical committee – has been intensely politicised. Representatives take instructions from their governments and vote on crucial issues according to their respective national interests. As in other EU organisations, they vote by qualified majority. A total of eighty-seven votes can be cast, with Germany, France, Italy and the UK each casting ten votes. Spain has eight votes, Belgium, Greece, Netherlands and Portugal each carry five, while Austria and Sweden have four each. Denmark, Ireland and Finland have three votes each and Luxembourg casts two. For a favourable opinion, sixty-two votes must be cast in favour; for there to be 'no opinion' there must be fewer than sixty-two in favour and fewer than sixty-two against; and, for an 'unfavourable opinion', there must be sixty-two or more votes cast against. Nine countries can overrule or block a UK initiative.

Thus, in negotiating export clearance, Britain was in the invidious position of having to negotiate with a group of political veterinarians appointed by foreign nations who also happened to be our major trading competitors, nine of which could completely sabotage our hopes for an early resumption of exports.

However, while the vaccination debate raged on, nothing publicly was forthcoming from either the SVC or MAFF. Only guarded comments from Commission officials indicated that there might be problems. The crucial test of 'absence of disease' had to be proved by the UK government blood-testing a large number of animals. Those found positive would have to be slaughtered, even if they were perfectly healthy.

But, as is so often the case with the EU, that was not to be the end of it. Precisely how many animals had to be tested was never openly declared, either by the SVC or MAFF. MAFF did not enter into the public arena to discuss what was being considered. It was only through being confronted by a series of baffling 'risk assessment' forms that farmers began to find out what was being proposed. Secrecy had become the watchword. At a time when farmers needed information to make up their own minds as to whether vaccination was a viable proposition or not, all they got from MAFF was silence.

Nor, indeed, could MAFF have been much help. Although, in theory, the SVC could make a decision, in practice the issue had become too much of a political hot potato. It was unlikely that the representatives would commit themselves to giving the UK a clean bill of health. For all anyone could guess, the SVC would pass the issue to the Agriculture Council, which would then have three months to make a decision.

Given the political implications, the next best guess was that the Council would oppose any proposal for immediate clearance. Once again, we would be faced with that twilight world which arises from our membership of the EU, where the matter would be passed up to an EU summit. This is what happened in Florence in June 1996, when – as a result of BSE – the then Prime Minister John Major had to negotiate the terms for the lifting of the export ban on British beef. He found himself in uncharted waters. The ban was eventually lifted three years later, on the basis of political as much as technical issues, none of which could have been predicted when the negotiations started.

Thus, throughout the debate on vaccination, there was absolutely no means of knowing when, and under what conditions, the export ban would actually be lifted, and what relative effect vaccination might have on the timescale.

What was stunning about this situation was the façade maintained first by MAFF, and then by Tony Blair, that they remained in control. Farmers were not only being kept uninformed but also being asked to support an increasingly draconian slaughter policy, directed ostensibly at restoring Britain's export status, without being told whether that policy would or could achieve its stated aim. Instead of leadership, honesty and clarity, they were offered drift, obfuscation and confusion.

The roots of madness

Quite why MAFF displays such an uncanny ability to get things wrong, and then to continue reinforcing failure, lies within the realms of psychology. In a study of military incompetence, seeking to understand the reasons why there have been so many spectacular disasters, Norman Dixon, an eminent psychologist, explored the phenomenon of 'cognitive dissonance'.[6] The term describes a mental state that arises when a person possesses knowledge or beliefs which conflict with a decision he has made. In the context of MAFF and the management of the response to foot and mouth disease, senior officials in the organisation were confronted with the inherent conflict brought about by knowledge that the adopted strategy could not work, and was not working, and their decision to persist with that strategy.

Research indicates that cognitive dissonance has a particularly powerful effect on behaviour when there are strong pressures to justify initial decisions. The less justified those decisions, the greater will be the dissonance. Furthermore, the inability to admit error increases with the degree of seriousness of the error made: the more serious the error, the more bizarre will be attempts to justify the unjustifiable. Thus, given the overweening confidence of MAFF that it is always right, it was inevitable that, when its initial slaughter policy showed signs of catastrophic failure, it would resort to further slaughter.

That its actions were destroying the very fabric of the rural economy was of little importance compared with its overpowering need to prove itself right. While a rapid, early vaccination programme could have ended the misery within thirty days of the first reported outbreak, not only could MAFF''s corporate brain not cope with such a drastic shift in policy, but a change of tack would have amounted to an admission of error. This was not an option. Thus, the killing intensified and the 'cure' became worse than the disease.

Lessons learned?

In response to the 1993 select committee report on its cheating of egg producers, MAFF issued a statement accepting the criticisms, stating that 'valuable lessons' had been learned. In fact, nothing had been learned. Throughout the foot and mouth crisis, Ministry personnel ran roughshod over the welfare codes, just as they had done in the poultry slaughter campaign. There are strong indications that the 'contiguous cull' policy of slaughtering healthy animals was illegal, yet – to pursue its policy – MAFF officials bullied, bludgeoned and intimidated farmers, abusing their power and authority by recruiting the police and army to back up their demands.

In the line-up of culprits, therefore, Maffia – as it has been dubbed by *Private Eye* – is rightfully indicted as a destroyer of British agriculture. In Carlisle, where its lethal activities have been most pronounced, cars sport stickers denouncing MAFF as the 'Ministry of Arseholes F***ing Farming'. What a contrast this is to earlier claims by food safety campaigners that MAFF was the 'farmers' friend'. The car stickers had it right. MAFF was a deadly enemy of agriculture. Now it is dead and buried, replaced by the Department of Environment, Food and Rural Affairs (DEFRA), but is this just MAFF by any other name?

3. Enter the Reformers

If one was to line up all the culprits and invite opinions as to who really caused the near-death of British agriculture, many people would point the finger at the European Union for its use of that blunt and unpleasant weapon, the Common Agricultural Policy (CAP). Even the Euro-enthusiast Prime Minister Tony Blair, when he was not blaming supermarkets, was keen to join the band of accusers, declaring in a speech to the World Wildlife Fund that the policy was 'bad for consumers, bad for the environment and ultimately bad for farmers'.[1] Blair, however, could not begin to improve on the last government's view of the policy, expressed in a memorandum by MAFF to the House of Lords European Communities Committee in 1995. It said:

> The huge cost of the policy to taxpayers and consumers far outweighs any benefit to them ... such large transfers into agriculture represent a major misallocation of resources and thus damage the economy as a whole ... the policy is extremely complex in detail, hence difficult and costly to administer and giving scope for fraud.

In our book *The Castle of Lies*, Christopher Booker and I wrote that the CAP is one of the most bizarre creations ever devised by the human mind.

> We are entering here that mysterious, semi-mythical realm of beef mountains and wine lakes, where not only cattle but even plants must be issued with 'passports', where the Sicilian Mafia makes a fortune out of 'paper olives' (olive groves which exist only on paper), yet where British dairy farmers must pay fortunes to each other for official permits to allow their cows to continue producing milk at all.
>   Simply in terms of the mountains of taxpayers' money it disposes of, the CAP puts all the EC's other activities into

the shade. In 1973 when Britain joined the Common Market, the CAP accounted for no less than 91 percent of all Brussels' annual spending, at a cost of just over £3 billion. By 1995 the CAP's share of the EC budget had dropped to only 55 percent, but this was only because other areas of spending had risen much faster. In money terms spending on the CAP had soared to £29.3 billion.

We then referred to our earlier book, *The Mad Officials*, in which we had written about

... the calculation of a Blackburn carpet firm that it would cost less than this sum to cover every square inch of the EC's land area with top-quality carpet. But these direct payments are of course only part of the benefits the CAP bestows on EC farmers. Thanks to tariff barriers designed to keep out cheaper food from the rest of the world, EC citizens must subsidise the farmers twice over, firstly through their taxes, then by having to pay more for food in the shops. In 1993 this gave rise to probably the best-known single statistic about the EC, when the OECD estimated that, in one way or another, the CAP was adding £1,000 a year, or £20 a week, to the food bill of the average UK family.

Even though this figure was disputed, and anyway had fallen considerably as a result of international agreements and changing patterns of world prices, we argued that the CAP nevertheless maintained agriculture in a position of quite extraordinary privilege. We continued:

It soaks up more public subsidies than all other sectors of the EC economy put together. And inevitably, with the dishing out of such astronomic sums of taxpayers' money, by far the greater part serves no useful or productive purpose at all. Billions of pounds go to rich farmers who do not need the financial help anyway. Billions more are siphoned off in wholesale cheating and fraud. Billions more go to paying for produce which is not needed and has to be destroyed or dumped in the poorer countries of the third world. And yet further billions are swallowed up in paying the armies of officials required just to administer such an unbelievably complex system.

Despite further reforms in 1999, spending on the CAP continued on its upward spiral. Nothing we wrote in 1996, or anyone else has written subsequently, has changed the fundamentally corrupt nature of the policy. But since we wrote our book, British agriculture has declined further and is now at the point of death.

Apart from *The Castle of Lies*, the task of evaluating the CAP has been undertaken not least by Richard Cottrell, Conservative MEP for the South-West,[2] by Graham Harvey[3] and in a series of books by Sir Richard Body, MP, culminating in his superb *Our food, Our land*.[4] For a clinical analysis of failures, it would be impossible to find a more compelling source. At the core of that analysis is a damning condemnation of a key facet of postwar agricultural policy – subsidy payments. For Body, and many other critics, that is what destroyed British agriculture – the corrosive effect of public money which has eroded the capability of farmers to service their markets, distanced them their consumers, increased land prices, and driven intensification with the concomitant use of artificial fertilisers, herbicides, pesticides and the rest.

However, it is perhaps possible that the EU – in this very specific context – is not a destroyer. It has a good alibi. The system of production support embodied in the Treaties of the European Union, which is the subject of the indictment, is not unique. The United States and most of the developed world have supported agriculture in this way. Even the UK, before joining the (then) Common Market, supported production with what were known as deficiency payments. Minimum prices were set for certain agricultural commodities and farmers were compensated when their products, sold on the free market, failed to attract those prices. By this means, they were guaranteed minimum incomes, irrespective of the state of the market.

Furthermore, there is another problem in lining up the CAP – or, at least its authors, the EU – as one of British agriculture's destroyers. That problem is simply that the CAP is a *common* agricultural policy, applicable to all fifteen member states.

Should the CAP be a primary cause of decline, every agricultural industry in the EU would be in its death throes. Yet, according to the EU's statistical service, Eurostat (May 2001), agricultural income in the EU increased by 1.9 per cent in the year 2000 (compared with 1999). And while Finland and Denmark achieved 24.8 and 23.8 per cent increases, Britain's income declined 8 per cent. Using 1995 as a base, the overall index of EU agricultural incomes stood at 103.5 while the UK managed only a lamentable 58.9 – the lowest performer in the whole of the EU by a very large margin. The next lowest was Ireland at 87.8, while the index for both Spain and Belgium increased to 117. Clearly the EU, in this context, may be an accomplice but is hardly an assassin.

What Britain needs

Before eliminating the EU from our enquiries, there is room for more subtle probing on the role of the CAP. Here, it is instructive to note that most of the pundits who have involved themselves in the debate about farming, occasioned by the onset of foot and mouth disease, seem to agree on one thing: if there is a silver lining to the débâcle, it is that agriculture – and rural policy – have been put firmly on the political agenda. Media attention has also been focused on the CAP at a level of intensity rarely experienced.

As an example of that media attention, *The Times* published an editorial the morning of the day Blair announced his election date.[5] Its writer opined:

Britain's rural landscape is an asset whose value has been both distorted and reduced by mountains of subsidy designed in and for another age ... The subsidies of the iniquitous common agricultural policy have been cut back in the past decade, but only to be replaced by compensation payments to farmers which, again, are heavily biased in favour of those with huge and highly productive holdings who need no handouts. The European Union's pet monster is still untamed.

'What Britain needs', *The Times* continued,

is a wholly new concept, one that ceases to treat agriculture in isolation from rural strategy. It must begin by asking the question: what kind of countryside do we want, and what are we prepared to pay?

There, in the search for culprits, lies a clue – as clear as a patterned footprint in the mud outside the forced window of a burgled house: *what Britain needs* ... Perhaps it is not the CAP per se that is wrong. It is more likely that the CAP delivered something of a boost to British agriculture (and protected it from domestic frugality). That it contributed to the rationalisation of the industry cannot be laid exclusively at its door. This was happening anyway, both here and globally. But it has outlived its usefulness. Once prosperous farmers are no longer thriving. Insofar as it ever did, the CAP no longer meets the needs of the UK and is in need of reform. Maybe it is that *lack* of reform which was, at least in part, responsible for killing British agriculture.

Agreement on reform

All the traditional political parties agree that CAP reform is necessary. For instance, the Conservative Party in its 2001 manifesto stated:

> The Common Agricultural Policy has damaged consumers, farmers, the taxpayer and the environment. It must be reformed to cut the bill for taxpayers and consumers, provide sustainable long term support for farming, and protect the environment and the countryside. We will renegotiate the CAP so that many decisions currently taken at EU level would be taken by the governments of individual member states.

The Labour manifesto offered something essentially the same:

> ... British agriculture will only thrive in the longer term through a further, radical reorientation of the Common Agricultural Policy (CAP), away from distorting Europe-wide production subsidies towards more national

responsibility for domestic farming, environmental and rural development priorities. CAP reform is now more possible; Labour's engagement with the EU gives us the best chance of making it happen.

Then there was the Lib-Dem offering:

Reform is long overdue. We will promote the sustainability of agriculture and redirect support so that small and family farms are more effectively supported. We will seek to refocus payments on achieving public, environmental and social goals rather than encouraging unnecessary production, while maintaining the current overall level of support for farmers and rural areas.

And there we have it. Reform (or renegotiation, which amounts to the same thing) is the centrepiece of all three main political parties' agriculture manifestos.

An international view

Agreement on the need for reform is not exclusively British. From being one of the main obstacles, the Germans suddenly came 'on-side' in early 2001 after embarrassing revelations that BSE had been present in Germany long before it had been officially admitted. The result was the appointment of a new German agriculture and consumer protection minister, Renata Künast, leader of the Green Party. At last Germany had a minister dedicated to the 'greening' of agriculture and she lost no time in declaring 'The BSE scandal marks the end of agricultural policy of the old style'. Her prescription was that the EU member states should progress to organic farming and other 'environmentally friendly' systems, moving away from production support to environmental subsidies.

Künast's appointment was hailed as shifting the balance of power in the EU, to the extent that the bipartisan alliance of Germany and France, which had scuppered the UK's ambitions for CAP reform, no longer existed. France, it was felt, could no longer rely on Germany's help to block reforms. And even the French agriculture minister, Jean Glavany, seemed to be bending. At the agriculture council held at Östersund in Sweden in April 2001, he spoke of the CAP being 'outdated' and in need of 'reorientation'. Attention was focused on an expected 'mid-term review' planned for 2002 and, speaking to Socialist deputies at his own national assembly, Glavany even dared to criticise President Jacques Chirac for refusing to contemplate reform of the CAP until 2006, when the existing financial agreements were due to be renegotiated.

Chancellor Gerhart Schröder then added his voice in late May, publishing a motion for his SDP Federal Party conference in Nuremberg, due to be held between 19 and 23 November 2001. His party was in favour of a new agricultural policy ' ... which concedes the highest priority to consumer protection and the quality of our food ...' and therefore argued for 'a new definition for the objectives for CAP'.

Empty posturing

Like the UK political parties, and their manifestos, Schröder et al. were indulging in empty posturing. At a breakfast meeting with the European Policy Centre in Brussels in early May, Dr Franz Fischler, EU agriculture commissioner, had already reminded member states of the terms of the Berlin agreement. The mid-term review was intended for procedural adjustments. It could not be hijacked. It would provide only an 'opportunity to re-examine the workings of a number of market regimes such as beef, dairy and arable crops' and to examine how best to use the CAP budget 'while staying within the imposed limits'. Nailing down the lid on the coffin of early reform, he added, 'It is impor-tant to understand that we are not changing the objectives of the CAP as re-formulated in Agenda 2000 and agreed in Berlin.' And no, he did not favour a wholesale shift to organic farming. Künast was not going to get her way.

More or less as a sop to the reformers, Fischler told the German current affairs magazine *Der Spiegel* that tiny farms could have a flat-rate subsidy of 1,250 euros a year, to save them filling in the forms to obtain land or cattle subsidies. But the 'barley baron' subsidies would be unchanged. In an almost con-temptuous snub, the EU Commission promptly announced a 5 per cent increase in the agriculture budget for the forthcoming year, a direct negation of the Berlin agreement, where reforms had been finalised on the basis of a progressive reduction of subsidies. Thus, whether attacked by Nick Brown, Tony Blair himself or the devil incarnate, the CAP was going to roll along much the same as before.

The essential wickedness of all this was that, in terms of the 2001 general election, farmers had been disenfranchised. No matter what the political parties had said in their manifestos, there was no prospect of change in agricultural policy until 2006. Since governments are elected for five years, any changes could only be negotiated by the following government. Agriculture was firmly off the agenda. Even if it had been on, voters would not be given an opportunity to select their policy-makers. We do not have an agricultural policy in this country. That is determined by the EU. The role of the British government is confined to that of supplicant. We get to elect our negotiators, nothing more.

Powerlessness

Nothing more illustrates the powerlessness of our government than the performance of New Labour, which, prior to the May 1997 election, had pledged CAP reform. Armed with a massive majority and its commitment to a 'constructive, engaged and positive' approach to 'Europe', the newly elected government – soon to take over the presidency of the EU – was determined to honour its commitment. Within a month of the election, the new minister of agriculture, Jack Cunningham, was declaring that farm subsidies had to be scrapped and replaced with EU aid to 'rejuvenate rural areas, encourage jobs and protect the countryside'. Speaking before opening the Royal Show at Stoneleigh that year, no less than Britain's premier agricultural show, he said that the government had made reform of the CAP a 'major objective of its European policy'.

By September that 'major objective' was running off the rails, with reports of 'clashes' with Germany, which was opposing sweeping reform. Jochen Borchert, its agriculture minister, could not have made his country's stance clearer. 'The reform is unacceptable to us in its present form, and it will have to be changed considerably if we want to reach a consensus.'[6] Effectively, by January of the following year, it was all over bar the shouting.

Despite John Prescott, the deputy prime minister, having reaffirmed reform as a 'key priority' in the Queen's Speech debate the preceding May, and Blair, in his Lord Mayor's Banquet speech in November, having declared that Labour would 'change Europe where it needs changing', putting CAP reform at the head of a list of changes, the *Daily Telegraph* duly recorded, 'Blair abandons farm reforms.'[7] The Prime Minister – on assuming the EU presidency – had failed to include reform as a top priority 'because of stiff opposition from German farmers'.

Writing for the *Daily Telegraph* in March, Jonathon Porritt, a 'green' activist and member of Cunnigham's Agriculture Advisory Group, thought differently. 'There's a serious reform agenda in town, and it's starting to get to those who must once have thought they were beyond reforming .... The UK has to be able to punch its weight in Europe at ministerial level, especially as the UK is one of only three or four countries seriously engaged in trying to reform the CAP.'[8] But when agriculture ministers gathered in Brussels in February 1999, familiar 'deadlock' headlines began to appear. As farmers rioted in the streets, France and Ireland added their opposition to the reform agenda.

Cunningham, meanwhile, had been replaced by Nick Brown. Despite Porritt's enthusiasm, he was forced to witness the ultimate failure. After three weeks of tedious negotiation, Brown conceded a position which, far from saving money, increased CAP funding by nearly £1 billion. With considerable understatement, Fischler admitted that the reforms 'were slightly less ambitious than the Commission's original proposals'. Nevertheless, the position was ratified at the Berlin summit in late March after a twenty-hour negotiating marathon which had ended in 'exhaustion and fudge'. All that was left was for Tony Blair to emerge and announce a victory for Britain. But so badly had the reforms been bungled that the Commons Agriculture Committee warned that they would have to be renegotiated within two years. This was not to be.

A failure in waiting

Come the arrival of 2006, attention will be focused on yet another bout of CAP 'reform'. According to Mrs Beckett, the newly appointed head of the Department of Environment, Food and

Rural Affairs, Britain will, once again, be 'leading the pack' in pursuing reform along greener lines. But, from past experience, talks will be dominated by speculation as to whether the Germans, French, Dutch, Austrians, Spanish or Greeks will play ball with the Finns, Danes, Swedish, Irish or Portuguese, or any other combination imagination can construct. Crucially, we will also be entertained by the fraught question of EU enlargement, where CAP funding has become the sticking point which could bring the whole project to a grinding halt.

Already, the writing is on the wall. The Polish Prime minister, Jerzy Buzek, has insisted his country must receive the full aid package given to existing EU members should it join the EU. In particular, Poland wanted equal farm aid, despite having more farmers than the rest of the EU put together.[9] Germany – the main paymaster of the EU – has made it clear that it is not prepared to fund the Polish demands. France and the UK have done likewise. Without additional money, payments to Poland or the rest of the twelve aspirant states will have to come from subsidies paid to Italy, Spain, Greece and Portugal. But these 'Club Med' states are not willing to foot the bill either. Neither is Ireland, which remains a major beneficiary.

As a foretaste of the battles to come, Spain, during the course of the early part of 2001, started to block routine EU business to safeguard its national interests. Ireland, on the other hand, by voting in its referendum against the Nice Treaty, has signalled its opposition to enlargement and the possible dilution of its subsidies. Motivated by the need to maintain their own subsidy base, the Irish could also prove a formidable obstacle to CAP reform. And, come the real negotiations, any fundamental change in the Policy will require revision to the EU Treaties. That requires unanimity. Even little Luxembourg – with a population the size of a London borough – can exercise a veto. If either Ireland or Spain use their veto, reform will be dead in the water.

That is the reality of CAP reform. Brian Gardner, farm policy analyst at PRM Consultants in Brussels, put his finger on the problem when he said it would be 'persuading governments, who are still intent on maximising their own take from the agricultural budget'.[10] Every member state is willing to accept change, as long as its contributions are not increased and its receipts are not reduced. The system is trapped in perpetual gridlock. Thus, even if there were a general willingness to undertake a root-and-branch reform of the CAP, it would not happen.

Mansholt to MacSharry

When the 2006 attempt at reform fails, it will come as no surprise. No attempt at reforming the CAP has ever succeeded and, after each attempt, expenditure has increased. Yet, prior to each attempt, the rhetoric is alarmingly similar. When in 1969 the Commission produced its first substantive proposals for reform (known as the Mansholt Plan), it concluded:

> The Community is now having to pay so heavy a price for an agricultural production which bears no relation to demand that measures to balance the situation on the market can no longer be avoided ...[11]

That the Mansholt reforms – and the marginal reforms of 1977 and 1988 – failed is adequately demonstrated by the fact that, by 1991, there had been a 30 per cent increase in the CAP budget, there were twenty million tonnes of cereals in store, one million tonnes of dairy products and three-quarters of a million tonnes of beef, rising at a rate of fifteen to twenty thousand tonnes a week. The then Agricultural Commissioner Ray MacSharry in 1991 argued that 'the continuation of such a policy is not sustainable physically or from the point of view of the budget'. True to form, he then warned that 'the *status quo* cannot be defended or maintained'. But while his reforms of 1992 managed to reduce the surpluses, they neither stemmed the escalating costs of the CAP – which increased from 30 to 40 billion euros in ten years – nor addressed the structural problems of agriculture. By those measures, MacSharry failed, as did the Agenda 2000 reforms before they even got off the ground. There can be no dispute that the only consistent feature of the CAP reform process is that it always fails.

The tragedy of modern farming

The tragedy of modern farming is that nowhere will you see in the literature from the main UK parties an acknowledgement of this reality. Nor will you see an admission that the UK does not have an agricultural policy of its own; that it has to rely on the common policy determined collectively by the member states. Nowhere will you see spokesmen admitting that significant changes must be agreed unanimously. Nowhere is it conceded that UK demands will not necessarily be agreed (and, in fact, are unlikely to be agreed), so policy formulation will be constrained by what is acceptable to the rest of the EU member states.

All that is on offer is 'denial', an absolute refusal to confront reality, a perplexing, irrational attempt to maintain the charade that we are still in control of our own affairs. Thus we see in the Conservative manifesto[12] the claim that:

> We will also fight for a fair deal for consumers, by intro-ducing honesty in labelling and requiring the country of origin and method of production of the main ingredients to be stated on the label of all food products.

Yet when in 2000 Tory backbencher Stephen O'Brien tried to do just that by introducing a private member's Bill, he was rebuked by the Minister of State for Agriculture, Joyce Quinn. She coldly informed him that his bill was an 'abuse of the Parliamentary process' because the proposition was contrary to EU law. What price Mr Hague's wonderfully misleading slogan 'In Europe but not ruled by Europe'?

Nevertheless, 'denial' is not the sole province of the Tories. All three main political parties are locked into the myth that, somehow, their dreams and aspirations can be realised by the process of reform. This is a fantasy of such crass vacuity that it is scarcely possible to believe that grown adults could be so dis-mally stupid as to even consider it, much less speak it out loud. But then we are talking about politicians.

They are the real culprits. The EU with its CAP is not actually the villain. Looking at it dispassionately, very few policies are wholly good or wholly bad. For a time, for some member states, the CAP had its uses and performed a positive role for some agri-cultural economies. But not even good aspects of a policy can be good for all time and, when they have had their time, they become bad. The essence of good policy-making – like good farming – is flexibility, the ability to respond to changing circumstances. Therein lies the central flaw of the CAP. It requires the assent of all parties – fifteen disparate member states – before any fundamental changes can be made. So frighteningly inflexible has the policy-making machine become that the only agreement that can ever be reached now is an agreement that the parties to the policy will never be able to agree to those changes.

But British agriculture desperately needs change. To quote the Lib-Dem manifesto, reform is long overdue. That reform has not happened is a major contributor to the decline of British agriculture. Yet, rather than admit there is no realistic mechanism for reform, politicians posture and prance, pretending they can do something that simply cannot and will not happen, deluding themselves and the nation. Agricultural policy has thus been paralysed, locked in a time warp from which there is no escape.

By that measure, the true destroyers are our own politicians, those, self-satisfied denizens of Westminster who venture into the real world only at election times, and then retreat in alarm as they discover the degree of contempt in which they are held. In the real world, which they so assiduously avoid, variously up to 52 per cent of the British population has expressed a desire to leave the EU. In that world, it is readily acknowledged that, before the fate of farming can be decided, the issue of our membership of the European Union must be settled. It must be recognised that the real choice for farming is between a limited, inadequate, tardy and wholly unsatisfactory sham 'reform' which solves nothing and creates still more problems, or a 'clean sheet of paper' exercise that could only be implemented on our withdrawal from the EU.

Maybe those politicians and others who support the fantasy of CAP 'reform' do not have blood on their hands through the act of plunging their daggers in the body of agriculture. But in cravenly supporting the lie than there can be any progress as long as the UK is locked into the CAP, they bear direct responsibility for the decline of agriculture. Those who continue to subscribe to the fantasy, despite multiple and continued evidence of failure, are dangerous. It is their fantasy which has paralysed the body politic, staving off that which is glaringly obvious to anyone not trapped in the rosy-hued bubble of self-deception – that reform is simply not an option.

4. Murder on the Fontainebleau Express

Despite the 'Maffia', and the self-deceiving politicians who continue to hold that CAP reform is the answer to agriculture's woes, being firmly in the frame these two culprits alone could not have accounted for the mortal wounds of so proud a beast as British agriculture. There is a much larger conspiracy. In the hunt to expose the additional conspirators, a logical place to continue is in the grimy world of politics, taking the advice given to Woodward and Bernstein, the *Washington Post* reporters of 'Watergate' fame – follow the money. Such a stratagem is eminently logical. If anything is killing agriculture, it is – in the final analysis – money, or lack of it. Agriculture is a business and cash is its lifeblood. Anything that causes it to ebb away has to be a prime suspect.

Actually, the decision to follow this line was less inspirational than it was coincidental. The strongest clue that agriculture was being deprived of its life blood emerged not from any direct investigation of the possibility but from discovering an almost casual observation in a European Parliament report on young farmers. There, it was explained that the reason for lack of support given by Britain to its young farmers was that 'UK agricultural policy has been dominated by the Treasury seeking to minimise the use of the EAGGF in order to maximise the rebate'.[1] The EAGGF is the European Agricultural Guidance and Guarantee Fund, the actual fund used to finance the CAP. The bland statement that the UK government was minimising its use of this fund had massive implications. Virtually every agricultural industry in the developed world, and all our EU competitors, attracts considerable state subsidies, both through the CAP and through national support programmes. Therefore, it is a matter of simple deduction that the financial health of British farming must be determined by two factors. The first is the level of state funding our industry receives, relative to its competitors. The second is the level of access to our markets afforded to our immediate neighbours and the rest of the world.

If our competitors get more subsidies than our own industry and have free access to our markets, their lower cost base will enable them to offer lower prices while maintaining their own profitability. For British farmers to compete in this environment, they must match those prices and, with higher costs, must either increase productivity or reduce their incomes – or both. It is as simple as that. Just as simple is the proposition that, if the relative subsidy disparity is too great, productivity gains will be insufficient and incomes will be squeezed. In this context, we already have evidence that British farming incomes have collapsed to dangerously low levels. Could it be that the collapse was due to tinkering with the subsidy payments?

The European scene

Following this trail was difficult as the evidence could only lie in the records of CAP funding and the structure of that funding is nothing if not labyrinthine. Nevertheless, it was possible to determine that there are three general categories of support: non-discretionary, discretionary (both coming within the EAGGF) and – for non-eurozone members – the 'agrimoney' compensation scheme.

Non-discretionary payments comprises the main tranche of agricultural subsidies. They are made up of direct aid to producers, and market support. Producer aid is currently by far the largest type of assistance and includes 'area aid' – fixed sums awarded per acre of arable land farmed – and livestock subsidies, paid on a headage basis. Market support includes export refunds (which are paid to exporters who send certain products outside the EU), storage aid and 'intervention', taking out surplus product when preset prices are not reached. Under the current regime, when farmers comply with the EU rules for receiving production aid, payments must be made by member states. They then reclaim the full amounts – plus administrative fees – from the EAGGF. Similarly, the bulk of market support is non-discretionary.

Even in this non-discretionary area of expenditure, however, there are disparities which are difficult to reconcile. Britain appears to do well. It produces 8.4 per cent of the EU's agricultural goods yet claims 10.1 per cent of the EAGGF budget (1995-98). However, Ireland, our major competitor in beef and milk products, does much better. Accounting for only 2.1 per cent of total EU production (but 6.9 per cent of the beef, exactly the same as the UK), it draws down 4.5 per cent of the budget – effectively 70 per cent, pro rata, more than Britain's farmers.

If both country's EAGGF receipts were exactly linked to their percentage of EU agricultural production, Ireland's drawings in 1998 would have been 0.8 billion ecu (approximately £0.56 billion), instead of the 1.7 billion ecu it actually received. To maintain financial equivalency, the UK should have drawn down 6.3 billion ecu, rather than the 4.4 billion it actually received, a comparative shortfall of £1.4 billion a year.

This, however, is an historic disparity. Currently and in the future, disparities are being magnified as a result of the Berlin Summit agreement. The basis of this agreement was that producer aid and market support should be reduced (although there is little sign of this happening) and more funds should be channelled into discretionary schemes such as rural development. These are intended to promote farm modernisation, assisting young (under forty) farmers to start up, and compensation for less favoured areas.

Unlike the non-discretionary producer aid and marketing support, these schemes require 'matched funding', with member states making direct contributions. Furthermore, member states can decide, within limits, how much money they allocate.

The current rural development programme covers the seven years 2000-6, for which member states have already made commitments. Significantly, the Irish – with a population of under four million – have set up schemes costing an average of £500 million per year. The Irish government's contribution is 55 per cent, the balance being made up by the EU. Germany has committed to £1.1 billion a year, taking up 16 per cent of the Community's rural development budget, while France leads the field with £1.2 billion a year, calling on 17.5 per cent of the budget.

The UK government, on the other hand, has a record of parsimony when it comes to matched funding schemes. This is indicated by its uptake of the scheme for encouraging young farmers, by way of cheap loans and development funding. While the French gave assistance to 11,952 young farmers between 1990 and 1997, the Spanish 6,005 and Portugal 2,365 – between them spending 249 *million* ecu – the British assisted a mere twenty-seven, committing a paltry 152,000 ecu.

Thus, the clues began to emerge. In comparison with its EU 'partners', Britain has remained reluctant to commit serious money to rural development in the current expenditure round. With a population similar to that of France, it has drawn down a mere 3.5 per cent of the budget, allocating the paltry sum of £230 million a year. This is a fifth of that devoted by the French to their schemes and less than half that allocated by the Irish government, whose farming industry produces a quarter of British output.

Crucially, our main competitor in the livestock field (beef and milk products) is Ireland. It is with Ireland, therefore, that equivalence is important. To maintain competitiveness, the UK would have to match the Irish funding commitment. On a population-adjusted basis, from a population of nearly sixty million against less than four million in Ireland, that would bring the British rural development fund commitment to £7.5 billion a year, more than three times the amount of total support currently provided under the EAGGF.

Comparison on a population-equivalent basis is probably unrealistic. Ireland is still mainly an agricultural community, with farming contributing significantly more to its economy than is the case in Britain. Parity might thus best be measured in terms of the relative sizes of the industries. Since British total output is four times that of Ireland, a four-times multiplier would seem more appropriate. On that basis, the UK government should be funding rural development to the tune of £2 billion a year, instead of the £230 million allocated.

So far, therefore, it can be seen that the UK government has been handicapping its own industry in two specific areas: an historic (and probably continuing) disparity in EAGGF payments, compared to one of our nearest and most important competitors, and by limiting payments of rural development funds. But there is a third major area of disparity – currency fluctuations.

As a result of the UK opt-out from the eurozone, the weakness of the euro (and the ecu before it) has meant that the British government has been paying its EAGGF contributions to the EU in hard currency (pounds sterling), about half of which are then paid back to farmers in a devalued currency – the euro. To compensate farmers for the reduced value of the euro, a top-up scheme exists – known as 'agrimoney' – to which the UK has to contribute. But the bulk of monies have not been paid. In the four years 1997-2000, the National Farmers Union estimates that British farmers have been short-changed by £1.2 billion – or £300 million a year, more than the annual amounts allocated to the rural development fund.

The true impact of the shortfalls under these three headings – producer aid disparity with Ireland, miserly rural development funds and the 'agrimoney' deficit – can be measured in terms of loss of competitiveness. Under the EU's single market regime, British farmers have to compete with unrestricted imports from member states such as Ireland, whose farmers benefit from the higher levels of support. Despite calls from British farmers to reduce imports from our EU partners, the government cannot respond. It would be illegal for it to do so.

The roots of parsimony

Why government should be so careless of the needs of British farmers – and so cynical in its attempts to conceal the real issues – has, until recently, remained a complete mystery, even to those closely associated with agricultural economics.

To understand the reason for the government's parsimony, it is necessary to delve into the structure of EU funding. The key is the way that individual member states' contributions are and have been calculated and the way payments were made, originally mainly from the CAP (EAGGF), which in the early days accounted for more than 90 per cent of the EEC budget.

The system that was in place prior to the UK's entry to the (then) EEC depended on direct contributions from the member states. Then, in 1971, two years before Britain's entry, a system of 'own resources' was introduced. Funding now came from two sources, customs duties and agricultural levies, which were to become known as the Traditional Own Resource (TOR), and levy on VAT (which was not actually introduced until 1979).

When the UK joined the Community in 1973, it adopted the TOR system. But because our agricultural sector was relatively smaller and structurally different from those in other member states, the UK did not benefit fully from CAP funding. On the other hand, because a larger proportion of food was imported from outside the Community, our TOR payments were higher than those of other member states. As a result, a budgetary imbalance was created.

In 1979, the situation got worse when the (then) EC finally introduced its levy on member states' VAT income. This, combined with an inability to contain CAP spending arising from the accession of Greece and Spain, meant that the UK's budgetary imbalance increased. Thus, as the Commission observes, 'Persistent complaints on the part of the UK ... became a feature of the budgetary disputes that were prominent during this period'.[2]

After much posturing and politicking, a temporary resolution of these difficulties was secured at the Fontainebleau Council in June 1984 when the then Prime Minister, Margaret Thatcher, negotiated a reduction in the UK's net contribution, amounting to a 66 per cent rebate of the imbalance. Additionally, a 1.4 per cent cap was placed on the VAT 'rate of call'. But tied up in the small print was the establishment of a 'correction mechanism' for dealing with the continuing budgetary imbalances. Its complexity was such that, according to Hugo Young,[3] it was 'outside the comprehension of every normal European citizen'. Even in the dry terms of Commission-speak, it '... inhibited transparency in the financial relationships between the Member States and the Community budget'.[4]

In 1988, at the Brussels summit, further revisions were made to the funding system where what became known as the 'Own Resources Decision' was made. This provided for a reduced role of VAT in funding the Community and a new system of payment based on each member state paying a proportion of its Gross National Product (GNP). This, in turn, created new distortions and required a new mechanism to calculate Britain's rebate. How it worked was explained in a subsequent document produced by DGXIX of the European Commission, the directorate responsible for the Community budget. Taking our cue from Hugo Young, it is instructive to review that explanation.[5]

... the shares of the Member States in the VAT and GNP bases are not equal and the introduction of the GNP resource favoured some countries relative to others. The countries which desired to reduce further the role of the VAT resource, failing to obtain a reduction in its maximum call rate, obtained a reduction indirectly through the UK rebate mechanism. It was, in effect, decided to calculate the amount of VAT theoretically necessary to finance the UK rebate and not to call a corresponding amount of VAT.

The provisions of the *Mode de Calcul* determine an amount (called the '*gross* equivalent' and which is actually larger than the UK rebate) that must be left aside for the notional financing of the UK rebate. The percentage of the EU VAT base necessary to generate this amount (called the '*frozen* rate') is deducted from the maximum rate foreseen in the Own Resources decision to obtain the yearly rate of call. This rate of call changes every year depending on the size of, and shows the same high variability as, the UK rebate.

This situation creates additional complications every time the amount of the UK rebate is revised. An upwards or downwards revision of the UK rebate provokes a change in the opposite direction of the rate of call of VAT and in the amount to be called (or that [which] should have been called). Given that the size of the budget to be financed remains the same, a change in the amount of VAT called must be compensated by a corresponding change of opposite sign in the amount of GNP called. Since Member States have different shares in the bases of the two resources, these changes are not neutral (this effect of the rebate on the VAT and GNP contributions of the Member States is usually called the '*indirect* effect'). If the amount of the UK rebate must be revised, it becomes necessary to compensate the Member States for the incorrect amount of VAT and GNP contributions that have been called. This calls for complicated calculations for each revision of the UK rebate and its budgeting in two different chapters ... *which produces the somewhat surprising result that the United Kingdom appears to participate in the financing of its own rebate* [my emphasis].

Clear?

While the Commission actually suggests that the amount of self-financing involves 'very small amounts', the cumulative effects of the Brussels 'adjustment' and the Fontainebleau accord resulted in a situation such that, whenever CAP funds are drawn down by the UK, over and above the threshold level determined in 1984, the Commission – through its 'correction mechanism' – is able to claw back a substantial proportion of the funds paid. Currently, this is of the order of 71 per cent.

For matched-funding schemes like the rural development fund, when the UK's contribution is taken into account the net cost to the Treasury is not the 50 per cent or so that other member states have to pay, but 85 per cent. With agrimoney compensation also, the UK government has to find some 85 per cent of monies paid to farmers, leaving only 15 per cent to be paid out of Community funds. Crucially, with the UK's net contribution to the EU being a highly sensitive issue, the additional sums clawed back show up in the UK's budget as an increased contribution to the EU. Increased CAP funding, therefore, is politically unsustainable.

National support

So far, all that has been considered is EU-originated support schemes, funded from the EAGGF budget, with or without member state contributions. The disparities identified have their greatest effect on competitiveness with Ireland and, in terms of the rural development programme, with France.

Nevertheless, the situation is not uniform throughout the Community. The Netherlands, for instance, fares relatively badly out of the EAGGF, producing 7.7 per cent of the EU's agricultural goods yet claiming only 3.5 per cent of the budget. This is largely due to its specialisation in intensive egg, poultry and pig-meat production which, together with seeds, accounts for half its agricultural output. None of these sectors attract support on anything like the scale of the beef, milk and cereal regimes. Despite this, Dutch produce is highly competitive and is often able to undercut British produce. Yet farmers in The Netherlands have been able to avoid the catastrophic cut in incomes which has so affected their British counterparts.

One of the reasons for this stems from the peculiar geographical situation of Holland, and the buoyancy of the overall economy. These factors have enabled many farmers to take on second jobs outside the industry. Thus, against the EU trend, there has been a dramatic increase in the number of Dutch farmers who work part time. In 1990, nearly all were fully employed in agriculture yet, by 1997, just over 65 per cent were thus engaged. This is attributed to a very low unemployment level and good mobility arising from the country's relative small geographical size and the excellent public transport system.

If this is a natural advantage – although one magnified by higher government spending on the transport infrastructure – there are other significant advantages accruing to Dutch farmers arising from national support measures, entirely outside the CAP.

For instance, young farmers are offered up to £40,000 in grants on investments in pig farms – often paid when they take over existing farms from their parents. Through a variety of schemes, most agricultural land is exempt from municipal taxes and from capital transfer tax. And, in a country where 30 per cent of agricultural land (accounting for approximately 50 per cent of holdings) is leased, there are rent controls which keep prices down. Additionally, there are fiscal reliefs for start-ups, a wide range of nationally funded subsidies for nature management, landscape development, control of damage by game and other things, and other 'financial and social measures'.

This information was obtained from the report produced by the Directorate General for Research at the European Parliament, devoted to 'The future of young farmers in the European Union', and – although not covering agricultural support in general – it gave an insight into areas which are otherwise notoriously difficult to identify, what are essentially hidden subsidies.

But not everything which aids our competitors is a subsidy, as such. Another of the major advantages enjoyed by Dutch farmers is the way the industry is organised. Every sector has its own representative organisation, known as a *produktshap*. These control production through quotas and levies, and organise marketing, advertising and industry intelligence – including many of the functions carried out in this country by MAFF. Each *produktshap* also funds and promotes research, and co-ordinates disease control measures – for which it is able to tap into government funds.

A typical example of this sector organisation is the *Produktshap voor Pluimvee en Eieren* (PPE) which deals with the egg and poultry-meat sector. Based at Zeist, just south-east of Utrecht, it is funded from compulsory levies on breeders, hatcheries, parent stock farmers, egg packing stations, egg processors and slaughterhouses. There is no direct equivalent in the UK. The *produktshap* system is regarded by the Dutch as the secret weapon which maintains the profitability and the health of their agriculture.

Elsewhere in mainland Europe, there are other nationally funded support mechanisms which confer considerable advantages on our competitors. In Austria, the taxation applied to farming is based on an approximation system in which income is calculated on the basis of values one-tenth of actual market values. As a result, only some 40 per cent of full-time farmers pay income tax, and those at a reduced rate. Generous reduced-interest government loans are given to Danish and Finnish farmers while, in France, a whole raft of grants, cheap loans and other support is available. Furthermore, French agricultural co-operatives – which market the bulk of agricultural produce – do not pay corporation tax on profits until these are withdrawn from the co-operative.

Germany also has schemes that enable farmers to pay reduced income tax, not least by assessing only 75 per cent of their income when calculating tax liabilities. Greece, similarly, provides tax breaks and subsidised loans. Italy has a policy of 'tax neutrality', easing the transfer of land between generations, and provides a wide range of grants and tax breaks to aid investment and modernisation. As for Ireland, this country too has a number of grant schemes, tax breaks and other measures which improve the financial lot of farmers. But, as in the Netherlands, there are other aspects of the economy which provide an income stream, independent of the agricultural aid system.

For anyone who has enjoyed a freewheeling driving tour of the Emerald Isle, an example of this support can be readily recognised in the superb farmhouse holiday scheme, promoted by the Irish Tourist Board. Farmers (and others) have been given generous grants to convert suitable houses to bed-and-breakfast standard, which are then actively promoted, right down to individual signposts in towns, directing guests to the specific locations. Income from rooms provides a valuable supplement to farm businesses, and also provides opportunities for secondary incomes from selling recreational activities such as horse-riding.

While it is difficult to attribute specific – or even relative – values to all the national support schemes (bearing in mind, for instance, that UK farmers do not pay uniform business rates on agricultural land), the European Parliament report referred to earlier remarks blandly that there are no special support measures for UK farmers. Although this report applies to young farmers, this is also the case for mainstream farming. Thus, any added value conferred by support given to our competitors is likely to increase the disadvantages which beset UK agriculture.

The single market effect

The other half of the equation is the single market. Under this regime, our borders have been opened to all the other member states, and our farmers are expected to compete against imports from other member states – and third countries which have concluded trade deals with the EU. The killer here is that many of the products coming from other member states earn for their producers more than British farmers gain from the same produce, relieving them from the same pressures on profitability and incomes. All pigs are equal, but some are more equal than others.

Quite how devastating this effect has been is barely realised even by our own farmers. Any traveller in rural parts will almost certainly encounter a sign positioned in a roadside field, enjoining the passer-by to support British farming. Invariably the sign will depict a stylised 'little red tractor', the NFU's logo for its much-treasured 'British Farm Standard'. By reference to this, when it is depicted on packaged food, we are able to determine whether the food has been produced in Britain – in theory at least – and thus support domestic production. In fact, to the eternal embarrassment of Ben Gill, the NFU President, the logo is a charade, deceiving both farmers and consumers. It no more certifies British-produced food than does the oval stamp on EU-produced food bearing the mark 'UK'.

The clue to the deception lies in the careful wording used: British Farm *Standard*. What the logo attests to is that the food is produced to standards approved by the scheme organisers – the NFU. But any foreign producers who comply with the standards are entitled to apply the mark to their foods. To prevent them so doing would be deemed to give UK producers an unfair trading advantage, contrary to EU law.

Exactly the same applied to the 'lion' egg scheme adopted by the British Egg Industry Council (BEIC) in the wake of the salmonella-in-eggs scare, a measure designed to restore 'consumer confidence'. Originally used by the British Egg Board, the 'little lion', stamped on the egg, had been the trademark of British eggs. But when the BEIC tried to use the symbol as a British designation, it was blocked by the EU Commission. The industry could use the 'lion' designation but not the 'British'. Furthermore, any foreign producer who met the standards imposed by the BEIC could also market Lion eggs.

All of this stems from the desire of the founding fathers of what was to become the European Union, who, in pursuing their ambitions for an integrated European state, sought to diminish the importance of national identities. To do so, they effectively vetoed the use of national designations. They were happy to see regional identities maintained, however, which means that Welsh and Scottish producers – coming from 'regions' rather than countries in the community lexicon – can identify the origins of their products. And there is nothing to stop the canny Danes marketing Danish bacon. They had the foresight to trademark the word 'Danish' so that it became a brand-name rather than a national designation under EU law.

Nothing is quite so dispiriting, however, as the laments of farmers about the import of foreign meat and their calls for its prohibition. Such calls intensified during the foot and mouth crisis, not least when it was realised that supplies of beef for the British Army were being obtained from South American countries where the disease was endemic. It is dispiriting for one important reason: once again, under the single market rules, the dead hand of the EU makes a mockery of our aspirations. We are not permitted to ban imports if their home countries have con-

cluded trade agreements with the EU and individual producers
have been approved.

As regards meat, the system is straightforward. Any foreign
producer from a country which has an export agreement may
apply to the EU for approval of any of its plants. Here, our old
friend directive 64/433/EEC kicks in, and still applies to third-
country operations. Veterinary inspectors from an organisation
called the Food and Veterinary Office, based in Dublin but
responsible to DG SANCO (the directorate dealing with food
safety and consumer protection), will inspect the plant. Provided
the plant complies with the provision of the directive, it will be
awarded with an 'establishment number' and a coveted 'oval
stamp'. Once the approval has been given, it is illegal for any
member state to refuse entry to the product.

As regards a made-up product using imported meats from
third countries, the situation is even worse. Should it be
imported by another member state, it will be inspected at an
approved port of entry – known as a 'Border Inspection Point'
(BIP) – where documentation checks will be carried out. Once
admitted at any point into the Community, no routine border
inspections may be made if it is then transferred to any other
member state.

But the real gem comes if the imported food is then used as
a raw material in a product processed in the EU. Once so incor-
porated, the material loses its identity and the finished article
acquires the 'establishment number' of the processing plant.
Thus, Botswanan beef imported into Holland which subsequently becomes part of a frozen spaghetti bolognaise
manufactured in Dortmund acquires German identity.
Similarly, should Thai chicken be imported into Italy, and subsequently used as a ready-meal ingredient in a factory in Milton
Keynes, the finished product will bear a UK establishment
number.

As regards the Army, much has been made by the NFU – and
agricultural trade magazines such as *Farmers Weekly* – of a campaign to persuade the Ministry of Defence to purchase British
meat. Outraged farmers have even gone to the extent of refusing
the Army access to their properties for training. But the campaign is to no avail. The Ministry of Defence, like any other
public sector organisation in the UK which makes substantial

purchases, is bound by the EU's procurement directive. Tenders for contracts such as the supply of food to troops must be advertised throughout the member states in the *Official Journal* and bids must be accepted from any qualifying supplier. Equally, the Ministry is obliged to buy from the cheapest bidder. To do otherwise would be to break the rules – and British produce simply cannot compete on price.

A cause of decline

Thus, here is revealed a major cause of British agriculture's decline. As regards Fontainebleau, it is indeed the case that UK agricultural policy has been dominated by the Treasury seeking to minimise the use of the EAGGF in order to maximise the rebate. What started out as a personal triumph for Prime Minister Margaret Thatcher in 1984 has become a disaster for British farming.

While all EU member states are funded under the same regime – i.e. the *Common* Agricultural Policy (CAP) – the funding is far from uniform. Key competitors receive a greater share of EU funds than do British farmers. In fact, not only is EU support catastrophically lower in the UK than is the case in the rest of the EU, it is actually falling. And, where EU support is not forthcoming, member states support their agriculture to a greater extent than does the UK, which has shown a lamentable lack of enthusiasm in this area.

Thus, the Fontainebleau accord, that lack of enthusiasm for national support schemes, and a single market which forces the UK to open its markets to better-funded competitors, all combine to put our farmers at a terminal disadvantage.

To 'level the playing field' in order to put British farmers on the same competitive footing as our EU 'partners', thus restoring farming incomes, our government would have to balance the financial equation. To equalise just the three areas explored in this chapter, the additional bill could be as much as £3.5 billion a year. That is the measure of the handicap under which agriculture labours. Far from being 'feather-bedded', as is the common perception, British farmers have been seriously underfunded for many years.

Farmers' leaders, politicians and others may bleat about them having to be 'globally competitive', but the government – by act and default – has ensured that the only league tables in which farmers can excel are those relating to suicide and bankruptcy.

5. Red Tape and the Mad Officials

If the British government comes top of the list of those responsible for the troubles of its own agriculture, for robbing farmers of the ability to compete on level terms with the rest of the EU and other countries which have been given access to their markets, it also has to come a close second for failing to address the burden of regulation on farming, 'red tape' as it is so often called, and for its failure to deal with the officials who implement and enforce its regulations.

Red tape

In our book *The Mad Officials*, Christopher Booker and I gave many examples of 'red tape', not least of which was the 'bureaucratic chaos' caused by the introduction of the revised farm subsidy system on the back of the so-called 'MacSharry' CAP reforms. This was the Integrated Administration and Control System, or 'IACS' for short.

To illustrate the absurdity of the system, we described how in Exmoor in 1993 two hill farmers, John Edwards and his son Oliver, had been forced to commission the Ordnance Survey (OS) to measure every inch of their farm. In common with 300,000 other farmers, they had been given six weeks by MAFF to fill in a complex form, with the 'aid' of a seventy-nine-page explanatory booklet, giving the exact cultivable areas in hectares of each of their fields, to two decimal places. Areas occupied by footpaths, hedges, ditches or electricity pylons had to be subtracted.

For several weeks in April, tens of thousands of farmers had to queue at OS offices to obtain large-scale maps in order to provide the necessary information, but for John and Oliver Edwards, and hundreds of other farmers in the more remote areas, the problem was even worse. They had discovered that the OS had not yet mapped their areas to the required scale. Faced with dire penalties if they failed to complete their forms on time, they had to pay £800 for their own survey.

At the time there were many such complaints about the system and most were entirely justified. Its introduction was rushed, it was unnecessarily complex and, worst of all, MAFF was extraordinarily (but typically) high-handed, penalising honest mistakes yet refusing to take any responsibility for its own errors.

However, many years later the volume of complaints has diminished and the system has settled down. Farmers still grumble about the bureaucracy, but many farmers are major beneficiaries of the system. Some receive cheques in excess of £1 million. For that sort of money, filling in a few – albeit complicated – forms is an extremely modest impostition.

The problem is that the IACS forms are the least of the red-tape burden. Most arable farmers produce grain and most are locked into the 'Assured Combinable Crop Scheme', a quality assurance programme which, although not government run, is virtually mandatory if the best prices are to be gained from grain sales. Participation requires the keeping of extensive records and conformity with lengthy and expensive procedures.

Then there is the 'co-responsibility' levy – through which grain growers fund the export restitution scheme – with its own crop of paperwork. Vegetable and fruit growers must provide considerable amounts of data for the Intervention Board, and sugar beet growers must deal with a formidable layer of bureaucracy to establish their quotas and deal with the processor.

But it is not only the arable sector which has to fill in forms. Shepherds must complete their Sheep Annual Premium forms and obey complex rules. Beef producers have a variety of subsidies for which they may claim, such as the Suckler Cow Premium or Beef Special Premium, and have to keep on the right side of the government's cattle passport scheme, which requires all calves to be registered at birth and all movements recorded. But notification to the passport office does not remove the need to keep separate movement books. And, if a census every ten years is too much for some, all livestock keepers have to fill in an animal census each June.

Milk producers, as well as the passport scheme and other demands, share with arable farmers the requirement to participate in assurance schemes, in their case administered by the dairies. A typical scheme has over sixty separate requirements which are effectively mandatory, milk purchases being conditional on compliance, among them keeping a whole range of records, from bulk tank and milking machine inspection reports to animal health records and feeding plans. Supporting documentation, such as feed receipts, must be kept for three years. Full details of milk production must be kept for the Intervention Board, to enable compliance with milk quota restrictions to be checked.

Farmers in Less Favoured Areas (LFAs) have a separate tranche of bureaucracy to deal with, while those who have the misfortune to have some or all of their farmland designated Sites of Special Scientific Interest (SSSIs) virtually have key aspects of their farm management decided for them by phalanxes of officials. Those farmers who opt for special environmental payments have to go through the hoops of the Countryside Stewardship Scheme or the Environmentally Sensitive Area scheme.

Those in Nitrogen Sensitive Areas have to keep special records on their use of fertilisers, while those in the EU-designated Nitrogen Vulnerable Zones must keep even more records. Even the use of natural 'muck' has to be recorded, and the limits on application are so stringent that, in some of the areas designated, not only will it be impossible to keep intensive poultry, but also free-range egg production will be outlawed, unless the chickens are issued with nappies to stop them doing what comes naturally. And those intensive livestock keepers who escape the NVZ net must brave the rigours of Integrated Pollution, Prevention and Control (IPPC).

All farmers have to carry out 'health and safety' audits and COSHH (Control of Substances Hazardous to Health) assessments of any dangerous chemicals kept. Medicines books have to be kept, to record drugs administered to animals. Those who produce their own feed have a formidable set of rules with which to comply, to say nothing of the copious records which must be completed. Many own and operate heavy goods vehicles, for which there is an additional layer of bureaucracy and record-keeping.

Then, if farmers take advantage of the duty-free concession on diesel, there is a price to pay. Full records of purchases and consumption must be kept and, if any quantity is stored, petroleum storage regulations apply. Many farmers have shotguns and they must be licensed. Stringent storage conditions for the guns and ammunition apply.

For farms with footpaths – most of them – there are rules to be observed. There are rules for the burying of dead animals, rules for the disposal of waste, rules for spraying pesticides and fungicides, welfare rules for animals, rules for using medicines, rules and rules. Those who decide on 'organic' status have to face a complex and detailed registration process – for which a substantial fee is payable – abide by yet more rules and fill in copious records, all of which must be kept available for inspection.

All of this is in addition to the normal bureaucratic burdens which any business must face. If farmers have employees, they have payrolls to manage, and have to deal with the increasing burden of employment law, in addition to which they have to deal with their own particular bureaucrats in the Agricultural Wages Board, which sets pay scales for different workers, their overtimes rates, holiday allowances and other details. They also have their tax returns to complete, both personal and for the business. Since many of the farms are valuable properties in their own right, they must keep a weather eye on highly complicated matters such as capital transfer tax, death duties and the like, should they want to hand their farms down to their children.

Then there is the little matter of diversification to take into account. Farmers who respond to government entreaties to broaden their interests then open themselves up to an almost infinite range of red tape. At the most basic level, those who dip their toes into direct marketing and open a modest farm shop immediately confront packaging and labelling rules, food hygiene requirements, and trading standards legislation – including the metrication laws.

Those who are slightly more ambitious and also sell produce not grown on their own farms have to contend with planning laws and, if they manage to pass through these hoops, will often find themselves having to deal with the intricacies of the Highways Acts and the rules for site access from public roads – compliance with the requirements often proving more expensive than the rest of the project. And if anything more than a 'class 2b' advertising sign is wanted, it's back to the planners.

Even to provide holiday accommodation, the often arcane conditions for being included on the listings of the various tourist boards must be read and inwardly digested. There are fire regulations to understand and obey, building regulations to comply with and, of course, planning requirements. Then, if turnover exceeds even a modest level, the unfortunate farmer must learn to cope with making VAT returns.

And woe betide those who go into food production, especially such traditional activities as making unpasteurised cheese, slaughtering Christmas turkeys or curing hams. In each case complex laws apply, with considerable additional bureaucracy.

Officials galore

Late one afternoon, I passed a petrol station on my 'patch' as a young public health inspector (before the title was changed to environmental health officer). It was due for an inspection of the food area so I popped in and introduced myself, asking to look round. To my surprise, I was met with a torrent of abuse. Nonplussed, but seeing no value in a confrontation, I advised the man I would return and left the premises. I had gone no farther than a hundred yards when the man came running after me, apologising profusely. He did not mean any offence but I had been the eleventh inspector that day.

If this man thought he was hard done by, pity the benighted farmers. Depending on the precise nature of their businesses, they can suffer the attentions of well over twenty different official and semi-official bodies.

MAFF officials, of course, may be the most frequent visitors, but they come in many different guises. Veterinary officers may inspect animal facilities, and the animals themselves, or a local private vet may be appointed by the Ministry to do the work; regional office inspectors may verify IACS, SAP (Sheep Annual Premium) or BSP (Beef Special Premium) claims; Intervention Board officials may check details of milk production. For egg producers, there is even the Egg Inspectorate. Animal records can be inspected by Cattle Passport Scheme officials, but records can also be checked by local authority trading standards officers. If any irregularities are found or suspected, a MAFF investigation officer may be called in.

Pollution affecting the neighbourhood may bring out an environmental health officer. This particular officer, a specialist or a technician, may inspect certain food operations like farm shops. Dairies, however, are inspected by dairies inspectors contracted to MAFF. If turkeys or chickens are slaughtered, this will involve licensing visits by vets from the Ministry. Slaughtering may be supervised by an 'official veterinary surgeon' and/or a 'meat hygiene inspector' from the Meat Hygiene Service. Animal feed production may be inspected by Ministry vets but, if drugs or any medicinal products are added, even fairly innocuous coccidiostats for poultry feed, a separate inspection may be made by an official from the Royal Pharmaceutical Society.

Police may call at any time, but a firearms officer will inspect any guns, rifles or other small arms, and their associated storage facilities. Various officials from the Environment Agency may inspect any of the farm facilities for pollution control, leakages into watercourses or related issues. Customs and Excise officers can inspect all vehicles – including private cars – to see whether 'red' (tax-free) diesel is being misused. Officials from the Health and Safety Executive can check safety provisions. Fire officers may follow in their wake. Ministry of Transport officials can check heavy goods vehicles and any maintenance arrangements. If the operation is VAT registered, a VAT inspector may call, as indeed may an inspector from the Inland Revenue.

Footpaths are checked by 'footpath inspectors' from the county council (or unitary authority). Holiday accommodation may be inspected by tourist board officials, and the rating officer will also want a look-in. Conservation officers may also call if there are any listed buildings, and it is not unknown for planning officers to visit farms just to make sure there have been no unauthorised developments. Officials from English Nature can inspect to ascertain whether there are any flora or fauna of interest, or any protected species. Then there is a whole raft of inspectors employed – usually as contractors – to monitor compliance with the various assurance schemes.

Supermarkets may send their own inspectors to check 'due diligence' arrangements, a provision in food law which allows a defence against prosecution if adequate precautions have been taken. They often cause considerable aggravation as inspectors from different groups often seem to be in competition, vying with each other to see who can apply the most rigorous standards. A particularly pernicious stratagem employed is the misuse of 'due diligence', whereby the supermarkets 'dump' responsibility for complying with standards on growers.

Mad officials

Like any sector of humanity, officials come in all shapes and sizes. Some are intelligent, experienced and sensitive, some are simply 'jobsworths'. Others, at the far end of the spectrum, are clearly moronic. One supermarket inspector, for instance, insisted that strawberry pickers, working under the baking sun, should wear white coats and latex gloves, while a mobile toilet and washroom should follow them along the field. Fortunately for the farmer, he did not need the supermarket's business. He escorted the inspector off the premises.

At the Royal Welsh Show, held in Buithwells, Mid Wales, one summer, show secretary Peter Guthrie noted that the course due to be used for equestrian events was extremely dry – presenting a risk to both horses and riders. To soften up the ground, he asked for a tractor to bring water in a bowser from a nearby lagoon, and spray it over the ground. As the tractor driver was doing the work, two Customs and Excise officials arrived and asked to sample the diesel in the tractor's tank. Predictably, as it was a farm tractor, 'red' diesel was found in the tank. The officials immediately told the show secretary that this diesel could only be used for agricultural purposes. Equestrian events – even at an agricultural show – were not deemed to be agricultural, so he was guilty of an offence. But when the officials turned up formally to charge the show secretary, the show chairman intervened. He told the officials that, if they wanted to live, they should leave immediately. The officials departed in some haste and nothing more was heard from them.

This incident was an exception. Unfortunately for most farmers, getting rid of officials is not that easy, especially if they represent official bodies and are armed with statutory powers. When confronted by a person from the wrong end of the spectrum, they must bite their tongues and suffer.

One luckless farmer was confronted by an official from the Environment Agency who, some days previously, had taken a sample from a nearby stream. He alleged that the stream had been polluted by run-off from a manure heap on the farmer's premises. Apart from the fact that the manure heap was dry, after weeks of sunny weather, chemical analysis of the pollution showed it to be of a different composition from liquor from the heap, and ten thousand times more dilute – but exactly matching the composition of domestic effluent. Examination of the stream showed two overflows from domestic septic tanks discharging just upstream from the official's sampling point. Amazingly, despite this evidence, the inspector insisted on prosecuting and, in front of a judge who had previously been a local authority prosecuting solicitor, managed to secure a conviction and a hefty fine. The jubilant official was later seen proudly adding a photograph of his latest victim to his collection pasted on the inside of his car boot lid.

In another pollution incident, an egg producer, washing down his hen-houses, inadvertently allowed soiled water to escape from a house, whence it ran into a dry stream bed and soaked into ground which later produced a fine crop of nettles. The water had, in fact, drained down a clay conduit housing a three-phase electricity cable, installed by an electricity board engineer without the farmer's knowledge. Nevertheless, the ever-vigilant Environment Agency took the case to court and notched up another fine. It was less keen to act, however, when a farmer complained of raw sewage, toilet paper and other detritus flooding over his fields where sheep were grazing. The source was traced to a public sewerage system, which had surcharged because a pumping system had failed. Pollution was allowed to continue for some days until the pump was fixed, with the full knowledge of the inert agency.

Slaughter most foul

Remembering the carnage attendant on the foot and mouth epidemic, with tales of panicky beasts being shot at random by MAFF slaughtermen – under conditions that, if they had occurred in more normal times, would have warranted prosecution – it is instructive to recall what sort of things did go on in 'normal' times.

For instance, before His Honour Judge Charles Harris in the crown court in Oxford during May 1995, Mr Anthony Barclay, owner of a deer farm at Nuneham Courtney in Oxfordshire, appealed a decision of Thame Magistrates' court, handed down in October 1994. There, Barclay, Major Patrick and Mrs Joanna Maxwell had all been found guilty on four counts of 'causing unnecessary distress to livestock' under Section 1(1) of the Agricultural Miscellaneous Provisions Act 1968 and fined nearly £6,000 between them.

The three had been organising a deer cull on the farm on the morning of 29 October 1993. On that day, Major Maxwell had corralled a group of twelve deer in a paddock, in which a shooting point had been set out in one corner. He had shot eight of them, without difficulty, when an authorised meat inspector for South Oxford District Council, Mr Malcom O'Hare, had turned up to check some refrigeration. As the meat inspector arrived, he claimed to have seen Major Maxwell attempting to shoot deer which had been 'galloping' around the field at high speed, bizarrely estimating their speed at over thirty-six miles an hour. He also claimed to have seen the carcases of dropped animals.

But what actually happened was completely different. Until the arrival of O'Hare, the cull had been conducted properly and humanely, under the control of Major Maxwell, a skilled and experienced marksman. On his arrival at the farm, O'Hare had walked down the perimeter fence of the paddock, alarming the deer, thus 'blundering ignorantly into the cull while it was proceeding, precipitating the very events for which the defendants had been blamed and prosecuted'.

What also concerned the judge greatly was that, after the events had been reported by O'Hare to his superiors, and thence to the Ministry of Agriculture, no attempt had been made by the Ministry to interview any of the parties other than Mr O'Hare. No discussion took place with Mr Barclay or the Maxwells and written requests for a meeting were ignored. The prosecution thus went ahead on the word of a single official, bolstered by a number of expert witnesses, none of whom had been present at the time or had been to the farm.

The judge considered it 'highly unsatisfactory' that the prosecution should have been brought at all. 'It is to be hoped', he concluded, 'that a more civilised and responsible attitude will in future be displayed by the Ministry of Agriculture.' He ordered that the defence costs, amounting to over £50,000, should be paid from central funds but, conscious that full costs were rarely recovered by this means, ruled that the Ministry should make up any difference.

Double standards?

Compare and contrast this episode with an incident which was reported widely on 15 May 2001, headlined in *The Times* as 'Spooked cattle at large after cull backfires'. According to *The Times* report, MAFF had sent its slaughtermen to a farm near South Molton in Devon to kill two dozen Limousin bullocks infected with foot and mouth disease. These 'highly strung' cattle should have been sedated before being killed but they were not. Thus, as MAFF killers started work, nineteen of the animals panicked and escaped from their pens, stampeding across fields and dispersing to two neighbouring farms. A neighbouring farmer, Gordon Willmetts, described the scene: 'There were three of four marksmen taking shots and there were certainly more shots than the number of animals killed, but I have no idea how many were wounded.' Another farmer, Les Winslade, recounted how the animals had escaped after the slaughtermen had started taking 'pot shots' at them. 'The cattle were going berserk. I have never seen anything like it in my life. At least one was limping. It was obvious to everyone what was going to happen. Once you shoot one the rest smell blood and go wild.'

Whatever else happens – with the incident still recent at the time of writing – after a 'full investigation' by MAFF officials, no prosecution will be mounted. The official position was that the killing had gone wrong because Limousin cattle were 'highly strung' animals. Tell that to Mr Anthony Barclay, Major Patrick Maxwell and Mrs Joanna Maxwell.

Low-grade harassment

In fact, incidents rarely reach the courts, and still less frequently are the activities of the 'mad officials' so outrageous that they merit media coverage. More typically, officials engage in low-grade harassment of the type recorded by a farmer's wife who ran a farm shop in Oxfordshire.

Her problem arose from her trade in fresh chilled chickens, sales of which were very irregular. Since she never knew how many she was going to sell on any one day, on some days she was unavoidably overstocked. Birds left in the chiller after two days were taken off sale and frozen, following which they were offered for sale as fresh-frozen chickens. This admirable practice was wholly unexceptional and sensible, avoiding waste and loss of income.

But that was not what a visiting environmental health technical officer from the local council thought. On a routine visit, he promptly prohibited the practice. He confirmed this in a telephone call (after he had checked with his office), saying that 'it isn't good practice'. He demanded that any chilled chickens left should be handed out to staff or used in the family.

The point about this is, of course, that there was nothing wrong with the practice at all, and it was certainly not illegal. The official had no business prohibiting it. But that was not the only matter the official found exceptional. Whilst he was present, he saw a max-min thermometer in one of the fridges. Misreading it, he claimed that it was out by twelve degrees Centigrade and wrote a formal note advising the farmer's wife that the thermometer was 'unreliable' and should be replaced. Thus, a 'mere' farmer's wife found herself having to instruct the official on how to read the thermometer.

Such is an example of day-to-day relations with officials, all very minor, undramatic stuff, but what particularly upset the farmer's wife was the attitude of this official. He made her feel guilty, 'as if you were trying to poison the whole world and he was the only person standing in the way', she said. Altogether, she found the experience most unpleasant.

Regulation and farming

It is no exaggeration to say that it would be easy to fill a book describing the activities of the 'mad officials'. Christopher Booker and I did just that in our book, *The Mad Officials*, in 1994. We have since acquired more than enough material to write several more, of which the above is but a small sample. But while such accounts are at once both entertaining, in a macabre sort of way, and appalling, by their very nature they are self-selecting in that the subjects of the accounts allow their stories to be published.

To get a more balanced view of the effect of regulation and the depredations of the officials, it is necessary to take a more structured approach, to which effect I interviewed a large number of farmers to ascertain from them what they thought were their biggest problems. Although the exercise was not statistically valid, it did nevertheless provide a useful insight into the problems besetting agriculture. Their grievances were wide ranging.

One commonly recurring theme was the cost and uncertainty of getting planning permission for on-farm developments, and the distortions in the planning system which gave preferential treatment to supermarkets and out-of-town developments. An allied theme was the distorting effect of traffic laws, in particular parking schemes – yellow lines on main streets in rural towns. These had disproportional effects on small shop, vis-à-vis supermarkets, which hastened the closing down of high-street stores and thus limited the number of outlets to which farmers could sell locally produced goods.

What is known as 'urban encroachment' – residential development adjacent to farming – was also a particular source of aggravation. All too often, complaints would be forthcoming from the new neighbours of 'nuisance' (flies, noise, smells, etc.) which were taken up with enthusiasm by local officials and upheld by the courts. That the enterprises had been established long before the new developments afforded no protection. Activities that had sometimes been carried on for decades were summarily shut down, with no compensation.

The 'right to roam' issue also featured strongly amongst complaints – not that many farmers objected in principle to giving access to their land. The bone of contention was the excessive costs in providing and maintaining footpaths and rights of way and damage from walkers – as well as vehicles. Of concern also was the presence of non-farming people who, ignorant of the realities of country life, all too often raised spurious welfare concerns on seeing animals in imagined distress, causing much time-wasting when officials called to investigate.

Welfare costs were a significant feature of complaints, such as the extra costs imposed on pig producers as a result of the removal of stalls and tethers. Again, there was no objection in principle – the problem was that the law had not been applied on the Continent. There, one man could look after 140 sows. Here, with the added welfare requirements, the ratio is one man per eighty to a hundred. Intensive egg producers also complained about the capital costs of cage size regulations, the uncertainties as to new laws that affected investment decisions, and the failure of other member states to enforce the regulations. The regulations relating to the welfare of animals during transport also came under attack, in particular the illogical restrictions which make live poultry transport very difficult.

One other welfare issue which was particularly of concern was the cost and difficulty of disposing of 'casualty' animals. One farmer observed that 'if your dog breaks its leg, you can put it in the car and take it to the vet – if a pig can't stand firmly on all four legs, you can't transport it to the slaughterhouse; you have to call in the knackers, for which a charge is made. In France, the government picks up the cost.' With the proposed ban on hunting with dogs and the possible abolition of hunts – which provide a highly valued service – the disposal of 'fallen stock' is set to become a major economic issue. And, if a sick animal has to be treated, British farmers are at a disadvantage. There have been increasing restrictions imposed on cheap remedies, and costs have increased owing to more rigorous licensing conditions. Drugs – which cost a small fortune here – can be obtained more cheaply on the Continent, but cannot in any event be used in the UK.

The disproportionate effect of all manner of regulations was a constant source of complaint. For instance, rigorous egg marketing regulations prevent small-scale egg producers selling their eggs locally without expensive and time-consuming grading. Hygiene regulations affecting Christmas turkey production impose considerable capital costs and make small-scale casual production uneconomic. Excessive Meat Hygiene Service inspection costs, in the context of the industry being 'uncertain' as to whether their competitors bear these costs, have a disproportionate effect on small abattoirs. General hygiene laws, applied far more rigorously in UK than elsewhere, have a disproportionate effect on retail food shops, markets and small producers, making it expensive and difficult to start small food businesses.

In terms of farming bureaucracy, the Nitrates Directive, with its 'Nitrogen Vulnerable Zones', has increased the costs of storage of slurry and limitations on spreading. The cattle traceability scheme (cattle passports) has increased paperwork and costs while IACS has added complex paperwork to the farming burden. The aggressive and unreasonable attitude of MAFF to mistakes is a constant aggravation.

The striking thing about these complaints is their variety, and the fact that many do not relate solely to farming. Not only do farmers have to deal with the demands which affect all businesses, they have their own additional burdens, which turn the running of a modern farm into a nightmare of bureaucracy.

Bludgeoned to death

The scale of regulation has a profound effect on the health and wealth of agriculture, but its effects manifest themselves in a number of ways. Up front, one important effect is the loss of competitiveness, both internationally and, in respect of the smaller farms, domestically. In the first instance, where we have more regulations, or regulation is more rigorously enforced than in other countries – particularly where our EU trading 'partners' are involved – British agriculture is at an economic disadvantage. Thus, the disastrous effects of less financial support for the industry are exacerbated by added costs which are not borne by our competitors.

This effect is magnified in small enterprises, both directly and indirectly. The small, often family-run farm is less able to cope with or afford regulatory requirements, yet the costs – as indicated in the 'complaints' list – often fall disproportionately on the smaller operation. Indirect effects can be just as damaging. Small shops, for instance, which provide small farmers with their outlets, find equal difficulty in meeting regulatory costs and, as their demise is hastened, so the small farms find it harder to make a living.

Effects can be, and often are, more subtle and corrosive. The 'red tape' is so daunting that farmers – who are better known for their practical approach to life than their bureaucratic skills – find difficulty in coping with it. Generally, however, specialists can cope with the paperwork of schemes which apply to them and come to terms with it. The greatest difficulty confronts the small mixed farmer, with perhaps a few sheep, cattle, poultry, and a variety of arable crops. This is, perhaps, the idealised farm, but it is this type of farm which is exposed to the whole range of bureaucracy, having to deal with far more paperwork than do the specialists, for less reward.

Thus, the hidden effect of regulation and its attendant red tape is to discourage generalists and to reward specialists, in effect driving monoculture when popular demand is for diversity. Furthermore, because of the rigidities inherent in the various sectoral schemes – and quota restrictions, where they apply – it is sometimes extremely difficult to switch farming activities. This limits the ability of farmers to respond to market changes and economic trends. Red tape and regulation prevent farmers from diversifying quickly, precluding them from capturing new markets. Planning and other restrictions can mean that, by the time a farmer is in a position to exploit an opportunity, the market has peaked or changed.

These factors, in themselves, are sufficient to spell death to farming. All agricultural economists, farmers and politicians should heed the advice given in a respected farming textbook, first published in 1924:[1] 'No rigid farming scheme can be expected to produce maximum profit over any long period of time, and since neither economic changes nor technical developments can be predicted with assurance, flexibility is an important objective in farm planning.'

But the greater and most damaging effects are the least obvious. These are encapsulated in the response from the farmer's wife running the farm shop in the Oxford area, after her encounter with the visiting environmental health technical officer: she found the experience most unpleasant. People go into farming, and remain in farming, for a variety of reasons but the main reason is that they enjoy it. For these people, farming is more than a job – it is a way of life. The steady encroachment of red tape and regulation destroys that enjoyment. When the practical work of farming is done and the farmer – or, all too often, his wife – then has to confront a mountain of paperwork, or when the working day is punctuated by a procession of 'jacks-in-office' demanding attention, farming is no longer fun.

More to the point, the children – who would traditionally inherit the farm and take over its running – look at their parents, working harder for less, wearing themselves out for something they hate, harried by officials and baffled by incomprehensible and ever-changing rules. Not for them, they decide, and often move on to other jobs. That is why the average age of farmers is fifty-eight and rising. The youngsters simply do not want to know. The farms, for want of new blood, are sold off when their ageing occupiers finally give up the unequal struggle. The farmhouses become bijou second homes for 'townees', or residences for wealthy commuters, and the land gets amalgamated with other holdings to become one enormous 'agribiz' enterprise.

Farming, as we know it, already bleeding to death from numerous wounds, is being bludgeoned to death by regulation.

6. The Deregulators

As a result of our own columns and other activities in the media, and the publication of our book *The Mad Officials*, Christopher Booker and I would like to believe we were part of the movement which forced over-regulation onto the political agenda during the last Conservative administration. Certainly, 'deregulation' became a buzzword when, at the 1992 party conference, the then Prime Minister John Major invited his deputy, Michael Heseltine, to take on the role of Tarzan, 'hacking back' the 'jungle of red tape'.

But in subsequent meetings with ministers and officials, I implored them not to use the word 'deregulation' as it invited negative connotations and gave sustenance to those who believed regulation was an unalloyed good. In fact, as is demonstrated in this chapter, deregulation is neither a useful nor even an effective mechanism for getting rid of over-regulation. On the contrary, 'deregulation' is a necessary part of the regulatory cycle and a precursor to greater regulatory activity. What we were (and are still) suffering from, was the 'wrong type of regulation'. We needed a complete rethink about how certain activities were controlled, not least in farming, where the regulatory burden was particularly stifling.

But in the same way that they failed to understand the underlying dynamics of food scares, ministers also completely failed to understand what was needed to 'hack back the jungle'. As a result – albeit under a different administration – we now suffer a greater regulatory burden than in any time in our history, with perhaps the exception of the Second World War period. Thus, it is not only those who have deluged the industry with red tape and regulation who are helping to kill off British agriculture. Equally to blame is the succession of British ministers – past and present – who did not and do not understand the mechanisms and pressures which give rise to over-regulation, and thus have failed, and are failing, to control the leviathan.

The essential problem

The essential problem confronting Conservative ministers, when they tried to deal with 'deregulation', was one of perception. The large element in society that believes regulation to be an unalloyed good believes it to be the bastion between good and evil, the upholder of law and order and the protector against chaos. So limited and distorted can this perspective be that those who complain about regulation are seen in stark terms, as defending the forces of evil and advocating descent into anarchy.

In this context, it should have been unsurprising that the Conservative administration's focus on 'deregulation' would eventually be seen as 'anti-regulation'. Equally, in the scare-ridden climate of the time, it should have been equally unsurprising that 'deregulation' would be blamed for the many ills of society. But in their pursuit of their policies, ministers failed to see the trap they had created for themselves.

Thus, when BSE reared its ugly head, it was inevitable that a prime candidate for its cause should have been 'deregulation'. The target of choice, in this case, was the rendering industry which, it is claimed, as a result of 'deregulation', reduced processing temperatures for meat and bonemeal and allowed the infective 'prion' to survive, thus causing BSE.

Yet, far from being an example of 'deregulation', the so-called 'low temperature' process was a major technological advance in an industry which had changed little for decades. It heralded a move from the relatively inefficient 'batch' process to one of continuous processing which produced a more consistent and safer product. The 'deregulation' was simply a matter of MAFF adjusting codes of practice to permit the new system to be used.

In the batch process, large chunks of material are boiled in a retort at atmospheric pressure, reaching 100°C, but crucially, from the perspective of the 'deregulation' myth, the 'low temperature' continuous process actually works at a higher temperature. What happens is that the process involves a low-temperature water separation phase, from which it takes its name. But with the bulk of the water removed, further heat is applied and the temperature climbs to 130°C or more for the remainder of the process. And since continuous processing requires a smaller particle size, heat penetration in this latter phase is much more assured, a fact readily demonstrated by the far superior microbiological results obtained.

Such is the power of the myth, however, that when this was patiently explained to MEPs and others at the European Parliament Committee of Inquiry in 1996, delegates still chose to believe that 'deregulation' was at fault. People such as these see the world in black and white terms and cannot accept that it is possible to argue against specific regulations without being against regulation in principle. Even the doyen of free-market liberals, Friedrich Hayek, saw no conflict between his principles and the state controlling weights and measures, or preventing trading fraud and deception in other ways.

But at the heart of the Conservatives' problem was a simple failure to realise, much less understand, that the motivation of regulators was not benign. While there can be no doubt that much of the regulatory output was well meant, produced to address what us authors perceive to be real problems, the use of regulation had significant political overtones. For the Opposition, it was a mechanism for exerting control, exercising power and thereby shaping the world in a fashion desired by its authors. In the post-socialist world, it was a way of controlling free enterprises which, hitherto, governments had sought by means of nationalisation. Latterly, they had found that state ownership was not necessary: control could be exerted by regulation. From this perspective, the regulation of agriculture has become *de facto* nationalisation. Thus, 'deregulation' was more than a process of reducing regulation. It became a direct challenge to what was, effectively, a crypto-socialist agenda.

The payroll vote

Aiding and abetting the regulatory ethos was a vast army of civil servants and public officials whose wealth, career prospects, status and wellbeing depended on a never-ending flow of regulations for them to enforce or implement. This 'payroll vote' inevitably favoured more and more regulation, and was able to exert its power to promote greater state control.

But crucially for any 'deregulation' policy, the power exerted by the 'payroll' servants of the state was not exercised by them individually but within highly structured organisations – the bureaucracies. These organisations run 'Brussels', Whitehall, the town halls, the 'quangos' and all the other apparatus of modern societies. They have a life of their own, beyond the easy reach of politicians of whatever ilk – and certainly beyond the reach of the 'deregulators'.

So powerful had they become that they were able to pursue their own agendas, promoting more and more regulation. Thus, for the Conservative 'deregulation' initiative to have succeeded, it would have had to have addressed their power. This the Conservative administration manifestly failed to do, mainly because it failed to understand how bureaucracies behave.

One of the most illuminating examples of how they behave arose from a study of an American institution,[1] the Tennessee Valley Authority (TVA). This was set up to deal with some of the effects of the US depression in the 1920s and '30s, primarily by redistributing land to small farmers. But as it carried out its work, it met powerful opposition from established landowners, with strong political support. With its very survival under threat, the TVA changed tack and ended up supporting the status quo, the very opposite of what it had been set up to do.

From this study came the term 'self-maintenance', a phenomenon applying to bureaucracies, by virtue of which their most important function becomes self-perpetuation. This takes precedence over all other requirements, including the very functions for which they are set up. Thus, the politicians, who in their innocence create organisations to do their bidding, end up slaves to ravening monsters which demand of their former masters more and more resources devoted solely to their own sustenance. Thus it was with the 'deregulation' initiative. Like lambs to the slaughter, Conservative politicians rolled over and created more and more regulation to serve their new masters.

Breaking down the controls

If the 'deregulation' initiative failed to deal with bureaucracies as they existed, other developments were to make the situation inestimably worse when the Conservative government removed a key constraint on their growth.

That essential constraint was funding. As long as regulatory activity was directly funded by the taxpayer, and elected representatives determined the proportion of tax income devoted to specific regulatory activities, normal budgetary controls imposed some restraint on the growth of regulation. If they had sufficient courage and determination to refuse increases in funding, politicians could check the growth of bureaucratic power.

But that was to change with the creation of 'Next Steps Agencies', devised by the third Thatcher government. They were introduced to improve management of the Civil Service by creating identifiable, 'free-standing' operational units to carry out specific functions – analogous to private companies. As semi-autonomous units, with their own chief executives, they had their own budgets and were financially accountable. Their performance could thus be measured, as their accounts were no longer buried in larger departmental accounts.[2]

But while organisations like Her Majesty's Stationery Office or the National Weights and Measures Laboratory were turned into single 'cost centres', other organisations, which were not simple trading entities, also acquired agency status. Among these were components of the Environment Agency, the Veterinary Medicines Directorate and the Meat Hygiene Service (MHS), about which we will learn more in Chapter 13, all of them regulatory agencies.

Their 'Next Step' agency status did much more than introduce financial accountability. For instance, with a staff of over a thousand and an income of £50 million, funded almost entirely from fees charged to the industry for its compulsory 'services', the MHS became a 'regulatory business', living off those it regulated.

These 'regulatory businesses' were a completely new development. They were not 'quangos' but self-financing regulatory agencies, or 'sefras', defined not so much by their structures as by their powers. Their defining characteristics were their ability to enforce regulations on businesses or other forms of organisations; the power to charge fees for compulsory registration or licensing; in many instances the power to charge fees for inspections; the power to impose penalties for non-compliance – fines, closure or withdrawal of licences; and the power to act in effect as their own arbiters – i.e., there was often no statutory appeal against their decisions.

Within their general and very often widely framed powers, sefras were able to circumvent – or reduce the effect of – normal political controls. They were no longer reliant on taxpayers' money, the disbursement of which needed the assent of ministers. Instead, they could survive and prosper by charging fees from those they regulated. Unwittingly, perhaps, the Conservatives paved the way for a new, more vigorous bureaucracy.

Frustrating the process

Another trap in the 'deregulation' process – into which ministers fell with unfailing regularity – was that, to identify deregulatory targets, the politicians turned to the same people, the officials, who had created the legislation in the first place. Attempts to use outsiders did not succeed as they lacked the in-depth knowledge of the system and were frustrated by those with greater knowledge, i.e. the officials. Where, as was often the case, staffing levels were threatened, as in the salmonella-in-eggs scare, the officials adopted what is known as the 'shroud waving' ploy, warning of dire consequences, deaths and injury if a particular instrument was abandoned, or funds were not made available. The former Director-General of the Health and Safety Executive, John Rimington, recognised this ploy, writing, 'Any regulator of harm soon realises that the commodity in which he deals is fear, and fear is the shapeless and emotional aspect of the human condition.'[3]

Fear opened up the purse-strings and wrecked the deregulation initiative. Added to this was the role of interest groups, identified by two researchers who argued that

> ... the *source* of the demand for regulation is any interest which sees a possible advantage in obtaining a particular regulation. In other words, the market for regulation is best understood as part of the competitive process. Regulation therefore occurs because there are well-organised interests which expect to benefit. Trade organisations lobby in Parliament, in the press, through public relations activities.[4]

David Willetts, MP, former Director of Studies at the Centre for Policy Studies, took a slightly different view. Writing for the Social Market Foundation in 1993, in a pamphlet entitled

'Deregulation', he drew the distinction between big and small businesses, stating that: 'Big businesses may be quite relaxed about regulations – they are a useful barrier to entry, keeping out small new entrepreneurs ...'.

But it was not a question of being relaxed. Big businesses are a central part of the regulation-making process, not forgetting professional groups, government agencies and the rest.

Mind games

It was here that 'mind games' began to prevail. Regulation is always prone to fail, but such failures were seen as demonstrating a need for yet more regulation. On the other hand, when problems arose which might have been addressed but the regulation had been removed (or not introduced) because of 'deregulation', difficulties could always be blamed on that process.

Not only was this stratagem successfully employed with BSE, it came in handy with a variety of other problems. Thus, after the world's largest fatal *E. coli* outbreak in Lanarkshire, which began in November 1996, enforcement officials immediately claimed that the failure to license food premises – which had long been advocated by their professional body – was partly responsible for the catastrophe. Not from them was there any hint that, as the subsequent Fatal Accident Inquiry determined, the officials themselves had been partly responsible. They had failed to detect a large number of obvious and serious defects in the butcher's shop responsible for the outbreak. Their answer was more regulation. Christopher Gill, former Member of Parliament for Ludlow, summed up the dynamic. Writing in his new role as Chairman of the Freedom Association, he observed:

> In spite of all the regulations and in spite of all the inspections, when something goes wrong there are no prizes for guessing where the buck stops – in precisely the same place it has always stopped but, equally predictably, far from being censured for failing to prevent the incident occurring or to be in any way held responsible, the bureaucracy simply turns round and demands more legislation and more inspectors.

And the Conservative government fell for the blandishments of the officials in the *E. coli* episode, aided by Professor Hugh Pennington, a microbiologist who had prepared a singularly ill-judged report on measures needed to prevent further outbreaks. Supposedly committed to deregulation, the government launched into a new round of regulating butchers' shops and permitted even more draconian controls to be implemented in slaughterhouses, which had not been implicated in the outbreak. Through their own failures, the officials thus achieved a long-cherished ambition.

Deregulation – a precursor to more regulation

This phenomenon was very much in evidence in the late 1980s and early 1990s in the UK, when, after attempts to remove 'burdens on business', there was an explosion of regulation, including the Financial Services Act, the Environmental Protection Act, the Children Act, the Dangerous Dogs Act, and the Food Safety Act. It even has international dimensions. After the Reagan deregulation initiatives in the United States, the Bush administration managed to increase the Federal Register, in which all regulations are published. The 53,376 pages in 1988 – President Reagan's last year in office – grew to 67,716 in 1991, the highest total ever.

That is the tragedy of 'deregulation'. The net effect of every deregulation initiative is always a reactivation of the regulation phase. But as each new cycle starts from a higher base, the overall effect is an inexorable increase in regulation, the so-called ratchet effect. In a very real sense, deregulation is indeed a precursor to more regulation. This is what Conservative ministers completely failed to appreciate, and what subsequent administrations have not even bothered to learn. One of the first moves of the newly installed Labour government was to abandon any pretence of deregulation and install Christopher Haskins – chairman of one of the largest food processors in the country – as head of the Better Regulation Unit. Under his leadership, regulations climbed to record levels.

The nature of regulatory models

What was entirely missing from all of the government's activity was any attempt to rethink the fundamentals of regulation. After centuries of regulating society, it seemed as if politicians, and their officials, had completely lost sight of what they were trying to achieve.

But what we had seen had been a quantum leap in the way society was regulated. Historically, the law was more simple, aiming only to 'ring-fence' individuals. Inside that 'fence', the individual was allowed freedom of action, and choice, as to whether to observe or defy the law. Societies, or their representatives, acted only when the law was transgressed, i.e. when individuals failed to conform, by extracting penalties.

It is true that, in the past, those penalties had often been quite savage and sometimes disproportionate to the seriousness of the actual crime, but not always so. But if there had been a lack of proportionality, it may have been explained by the law having a dual role, as a deterrent but also an instrument of revenge against the transgressor – the biblical penalty of 'an eye for an eye'. This has always been an accepted function of penalties imposed by society – to regulate the conduct of its members.

The 'eye for an eye' regime is what is known as the 'penalty' model of regulation. It may have been a harsh doctrine, but it was also a strictly limited one. Society set up behavioural norms and penalised failure to observe, or divergence from, those norms. By definition, these failures or divergences became crimes. And, to an extent, this basic regulatory model remains established in our legislative code. Murder is a good example. Society does not tolerate the unlawful taking of human life but takes no specific steps to prevent citizens murdering each other. Each individual, with numerous opportunities and the means to break the code, is free to choose whether or not to obey it.

The 'intervention' model

While vestiges of what is known as the 'penalty' model have survived for specific offences – usually those recognised as 'moral' offences such as burglary, rape, affray and the like – postwar governments increasingly began to rely on a different form of regulation. This transition was facilitated by a move away from what is known as 'primary legislation' – Acts of Parliament – to 'secondary legislation', technically known as 'statutory instruments' or, more simply 'regulations'. The changeover was in part a result of the increasing willingness of Parliament to delegate the legislation process to ministers – who, of course relied on their civil servants to frame the 'instruments' – and partly because of the torrent of new law emanating from the EU, where traditional law-making processes simply could not cope with the sheer volume.

But, underlying this change was also a paradigm shift in the way law was framed. In contrast to the traditional law-making process, the civil servants – who had become the real masters – were increasingly no longer content to make laws and wait until people broke them, relying on the courts to penalise them. Instead, they sought either to prevent 'non-compliance' or to reduce the means or opportunity for transgression. More and more they aimed to intervene, defining regulations which were aimed not at punishing law-breaking but at preventing it. This is what is known as the 'intervention' model.

The development of this 'model' can be seen in the way the meat industry was regulated. Up until 1963, official meat inspection was optional. Traders were simply punished if they sold unfit meat. Post-1963, a relatively relaxed – but nonetheless effective – regime was introduced, with modest charges for inspection. But with the advent of regulations implementing Directive 91/497/EEC, not only have the inspection standards been tightened but the inspection regime has become both intrusive and cripplingly expensive.

The crime of selling unfit meat survived but regulation was developed to such an extent that there was a massive increase in the number of offences which could be committed. But all the additions were aimed not at penalising the sale of unfit meat but at penalising slaughterhouse owners for not taking the prescribed steps to prevent unfit meat reaching the market. To cap it all, the owners were then forced to pay the officials for standing over them, to make sure they complied. It was as if all motorists had to pay a policeman to follow them in order to prevent speeding, and then pay the fines when they went over the limit.

Returning to the example of murder, the parallel is similar – the state refuses to countenance even the possibility of unlawful killing and stations a policeman in every house to guard against the possibility of any such offence, whilst still retaining the penalty for actual murder.

If the analogy is to be developed to its fullest extent to bring it into line with the current regulatory model, the state would also make detailed rules prescribing forms of behaviour which might precede – or have been known to precede – murder. These might include swearing, drunkenness, adultery, and even singing and whistling. The state might even prohibit serving burgers with pickles.[5] And, of course, in the nature of the full-blown 'intervention' model, the state would then appoint inspectors to ensure compliance with these rules and would extract penalties for failure to conform – as well as charges for the inspectors.

As murders continued, as indeed they would – no doubt including in their number some of the 'anti-murder' inspectors – the state would 'learn' from each incident, prescribing yet more and more rules, each aimed at further limiting the opportunities for murder, with increased penalties for infractions. Eventually, the jails would become full, not with murderers but with those who had failed to take the requisite actions which the officials considered necessary to avoid the possibility of murder.

Failure not penalised

The perversity of this 'new' system, which again ministers failed to realise, was that it in no way increased public protection. For instance, in the sale of unfit meat example, it became possible to escape conviction for an offence simply by claiming 'due diligence' – that all reasonable measures had been taken. But since the officials now took responsibility for inspecting meat before it left the slaughterhouse, we saw instances where defendants succeeded in 'not guilty' pleas precisely because officials had been responsible for the inspections. And, in many cases, the penalties for not complying with supposed preventative measures were greater than the fines imposed for the non-compliance which the rules were supposed to prevent. By this means, fines for running an 'unhygienic' shop – where no food poisoning had been caused – were often higher than those handed down for causing quite serious outbreaks of food poisoning.

The worst of it all is that the official controls are based on what is known technically as the 'predictive model'. They rely on the imaginations of the bureaucrats to define the controls necessary to prevent a problem, the controls which they 'predict' will prevent the problem. However, not least because of the limitations of the bureaucrats' imaginations, the 'models' have rarely been defined with any great accuracy or with any certainty of success. Thus, when it comes to the highly expensive and intrusive meat inspection requirements, it has long been proven that the single most important source of contamination of meat in the slaughterhouse is the meat inspector. Yet the system still survives, to the ridiculous extent that, in New Zealand, where a more scientific inspection system applies, 'high purity' meat can be produced with a long shelf-life yet, if it has to be subjected to the EU type of inspection, it can only be sold frozen. The bacterial contamination is so high that it spoils before transportation in a chilled condition is complete.

As a measure of the fatuity of the system, one Yorkshire slaughterhouse owner, trading for over forty years in high-quality lamb – without a single complaint, such were his high standards – was forced to spend £500,000 'upgrading' his slaughterhouse to conform with EU rules. After he had completed his gleaming, 'hygienic' white plastic-clad palace to the vet's satisfaction, he was inundated by his butcher customers complaining that his lamb was going 'off' before it could be sold.

More is less

So it was that the Conservatives' 'deregulation' initiative failed, partly because ministers had failed to understand the nature – and limitations – of prescriptive legislation, partly because of regulatory pressure from the EU, partly because of their lack of political courage in resisting the blandishments of their own civil servants, and partly through the creation of the 'sefras'. The failure was all the more inexcusable when ministers had the perfect example of how regulation could fail to work, given to them by Lord Robens when, in 1972, he was asked by an earlier Conservative administration to review health and safety legislation. In his report, he noted:

The first and perhaps most fundamental defect of the statutory system is that there is simply too much law …. [which] may well have reached the point where it becomes counter-productive.[6]

He warned that regulation became irrelevant to the prevention of failure, but took on a life of its own, independent of the problems it addressed, remarking that:

> People are heavily conditioned to think of safety and health at work as in the first and most important instance a matter of detailed rules imposed by external agencies.

Nevertheless, the Robens message was ignored. And it was not as if the message was so complicated that it was beyond the limited wit of politicians. More than twenty years later, during John Major's administration, Christopher Fildes, a columnist on the *Daily Telegraph*, commented on the controversy over the Nolan Committee recommendations on a code of conduct for MPs. He cited Sir Christopher Hogg, chairman of Reuters, who said:

> There is an alarming tendency abroad in the land to think that progress will be assured simply by following an agreed process. It won't. All that happens is that the process becomes an end in itself.[7]

Even to a journalist, it was obvious that there was a danger that businesses were becoming more concerned with obeying regulations than with avoiding failure. But still ministers failed to stem the torrent of legislation.

The Robens report led to the Health and Safety at Work Act 1974 – which broke new ground in setting out general responsibilities and duties of care, seeking to avoid masses of detailed, prescriptive legislation. It is a measure of the failure of the politicians to heed Robens' message that the Act has since been augmented by COSHH (Control of Substances Hazardous to Health) Regulations, the CHIPS (Chemical Hazard Information and Packaging for Supply) Regulations 1994, plus the EC-derived safety regulations known as the 'pack of six'. These, and many more, specify in ever greater detail the duties of employers, but none adds to their basic responsibilities in respect of safety at work which were set out in the Health and Safety at Work Act. Nor indeed have they had any impact on the number of accidents caused.

Abject failure

Despite the clear messages to the Conservatives that their regulatory onslaught was going to cause massive problems for all sorts of businesses, they failed abjectly to grasp the nettle. After Heseltine's pathetic attempt in 1992 to 'hack back the jungle', the deregulation initiative fizzled into nothing. Even then, no lessons had been learnt. On 19 September 1995, Heseltine simply relaunched the same tired programme, with the publication of a White Paper. In it he claimed: 'Our aim is to release British industry from the shackles of unnecessary rules and regulations ....'

Yet he was only tinkering at the margins. The central features of the relaunch were the removal of '250 different licences', many of which had ceased to have any relevance and were barely enforced; the cutting of the number of government surveys; and what amounted to cosmetic changes in the National Insurance system. The lack of impact on the regulatory 'culture' was amply demonstrated by the fact that, within two weeks of the publication of the White Paper, the government had already proposed new licensing systems, one covering the production of animal feedstuffs and the other regulating adventure activity centres.

And, as we shall see, when concern over BSE erupted into a full-blown crisis on 20 March 1996 with a statement to the House of Commons by Secretary of State for Health, Stephen Dorrell, the government reaction was an orgy of prescriptive legislation. Just months later, after the world's largest fatal *E. coli* outbreak, Dorrell was to introduce licensing for butchers' shops, to be enforced by the very officials who had failed so spectacularly to prevent the outbreak.

Even now, the regulatory ethos remains. At the height of the foot and mouth epidemic, agriculture minister Nick Brown announced to the House of Commons that he was intending to introduce legislation preventing the use of swill for pig-feeding – on the entirely unproven assertion that foot and mouth disease had been spread to animals through improperly processed swill at Heddon-on-the-Wall. Additionally, he told the House he was going to impose a twenty-day limit on the movement of animals after their purchase from markets. The basis for this was that such a new law might help contain a future epidemic – notwithstanding that the real reason why the disease had apparently spread so rapidly was that it had been around many months before his officials had noticed (or admitted having noticed) it.

7. Mad Scientists and 'Killer' Eggs

Would that the list of suspects responsible for the near-death of British agriculture was now complete, but, alas, it is far from being so. In fact, there are still many other suspects to reveal. One group is better hidden than many, and all the more deadly for that as it conceals its true intent under a mantle of concern for the public good. This group comprises the scientists, the men in white coats who posture as the guardians of our safety. In particular, it comprises the corps of government scientists who, collectively, have done more damage to agriculture than can even be imagined.

The main reason why their uniquely damaging activities have been so well concealed is that they have so often been cloaked by highly visible phenomena, the 'food scares'. Therefore, any complete post mortem on British farming has to examine these phenomena, and the role of scientists in them. Their fingerprints are to be seen on all the major scares: salmonella in eggs, 'listeria' and BSE. Their role in the first of these deserves careful study.

Salmonella in eggs

The scare itself started in 1988 when, on 3 December, the then junior health minister Edwina Currie gave her notorious interview to ITN proclaiming: 'We do warn people now that most of the egg production in this country, sadly, is now infected with salmonella ...'. Those twenty words precipitated a wave of public and media concern – some say hysteria – about the safety of food which, in turn, was to precipitate a surge of ruinous legislation and devastate large sections of the British egg producing sector.

Two years after the start of the crisis, the egg industry had sharply contracted, from over 34,000 holdings and 31,000,000 birds to 28,227 and 28,000,000 birds in 1990. Hardest hit had been the small, often free-range producers, with flocks num-

bering twenty-five to a thousand birds. And at least four thousand people had stopped keeping hens altogether. Yet in some
regions, notably in the West Midlands, the number of large holdings actually increased. The effect of the salmonella scare,
therefore, was to decimate the smaller flocks, while accelerating
the concentration of egg production in larger holdings.

That phenomenon has characterised food scares. They start
with a wave of public concern – in which dominant themes are
revulsion towards 'intensive farming', 'cheap food' and the
effects of 'agribiz'. They end with a mass of new legislation and
controls that have a disproportionate effect on small producers
and drive many out of business. As a result, each affected
industry ends up in the hands of fewer, larger producers – the
very opposite of what the public wants or expects.

But while even to this day Edwina Currie is lauded for her
courage in bringing to public attention a serious threat which
had been concealed – according to public legend – variously by
the Ministry of Agriculture and the egg and farming industries,
the salmonella-in-eggs crisis was largely artificial. In the main, it
was engineered by one particular group of government scientists
pursuing their own agenda. The net effect of the crisis was to sac-
rifice a large number of egg producers to sate the ambitions and
aspirations of a scientific group entirely unrelated to the farming
industry.

To understand how and why this happened it is important to
appreciate that, while the public phase of the scare effectively
started on 3 December, the 'eggs' issue had been building up for
some time. Edwina Currie's actions did not come 'out of the blue'
but were part of an endgame that took months of planning and
scheming.

Genesis

Before these events can be explored, it is necessary to go back to
the Second World War and the birth of an obscure organisation
called the Emergency Public Health Laboratory Service
(EPHLS). Strangely, this is the key to events that were to happen
nearly fifty years later.

The EPHLS was established shortly after the outbreak of war
to deal with the epidemics which were expected in the aftermath

of the mass bombing of cities, and to assist in the treatment of victims of biological weapons, should Hitler choose to use them. In the event, although bombing was severe, the epidemics did not materialise – and biological weapons were not used.

In the absence of the feared disasters the EPHLS was largely redundant, and would have been totally so but for a fortuitous occurrence. As the war progressed, the country, for a variety of complex reasons – not least the import of large quantities of salmonella-infected powdered egg from the United States – was swept by an unprecedented wave of food poisoning. The incidence was sufficiently serious to interrupt the war effort, and would have had a devastating effect on civilian morale had its scale become apparent. The EPHLS was put to work to deal with the problem, and achieved some success in so doing. With its track record of success, and nationalisation and public service in vogue, EPHLS was formally reconstituted in 1945 to become the Public Health Laboratory Service (PHLS), an organisation which remains today.

Outwardly a benign organisation, the PHLS now monitors communicable disease, providing laboratories for that purpose, and supplies 'medical detectives' to search out and eradicate new diseases. It is staffed by skilled, hard-working scientists, doctors, technicians and officials, all dedicated to public health and the protection of human life.

But in the early to mid-1980s, the PHLS was faced with a serious threat. Under the Thatcher spending reviews of the time, it was confronting a major cutback in funding and there was also the possibility of privatisation. This had been picked up by the *Guardian*'s then science correspondent Andrew Veitch (now working for Channel 4 News), who, in May 1987, wrote a piece headed 'Backdoor manoeuvre to "rationalise" health tests'.

In his piece he outlined how the government was looking for £350 million savings in its annual bill for pathology services and, without making a public announcement, had appointed a firm of management consultants to advise on where to cut. Its gaze had fallen on the PHLS, where there was '... already concern amongst professional bodies that it had too few staff to cope with the AIDS epidemic which was dominating the headlines'. Fears were being voiced that the review, 'organised in such secrecy', had been designed to cut costs rather than improve services.

This problem intensified by the end of the year, when Andrew Veitch again wrote in the *Guardian*,[1] reporting 'Staff exodus hits public health laboratories'. Detailed was a catalogue of woe. 'Vital health screening services in the disease-monitoring network are threatened by an exodus of staff ... Low pay, poor career prospects, and uncertainty over privatisation are to blame.' And it got worse: 'Funding changes to be implemented by the NHS management board in April mean that health authorities will have to pay the PHLS directly for its services. Mr John Moore, the Social Services Secretary, is expected to tell hospitals soon that they must put laboratory services out to tender, seeking quotes from private companies wherever possible.'

For any public sector organisation, there is no greater threat than the withdrawal of funds, other than, perhaps, the threat of privatisation – which was regarded with horror by many public sector workers. The response could have been predicted. Owing its very existence to the emergence of a serious food poisoning problem, the PHLS returned to its past glories and started work on increasing public concern about this disease. It may seem remarkable but, at that time, figures for annual food poisoning were routinely published only two to three years after the year to which they applied. But very soon PHLS officials were to offer journalists weekly briefings.

The PHLS was largely aided in its self-appointed task by a cyclical change in the nature of salmonella food poisoning affecting the community. As happens with some regularity, the established strain – then a type known as *Salmonella typhimurium* – was being supplanted by a different strain, actually a more benign if less familiar type known as *Salmonella enteritidis*. The emergence of this type as the dominant strain coincided with a periodic upsurge in food poisoning notifications, which increased from 8,634 in 1970 to 15,312 cases in 1987, about 86 per cent of which were salmonelloses.

These data provided the PHLS with all the material needed to counter threats to its existence. By manipulating the statistics and increasing media access to them, it 'talked up' food poisoning and, over a period of a few years, turned a scientific curiosity and minor public health problem into a major crisis. In effect, it created a threat to counter a threat, inventing an epidemic to justify its continued public sector funding.

That in turn led to another dynamic. Having talked up the increase, it became politically necessary to come up with some idea of the cause. But while there appeared to be an underlying increase in salmonella food poisoning, no one had any real idea what was causing it. Virtually every expert and expert group had its own explanation. As time marched on, the number of 'causes' increased, seemingly in line with the increased incidence. What few people appreciated was how primitive the surveillance system in this country was and still is. When it came to the actual causes, this system was simply incapable of finding out what was happening.

Into this situation came yet another dynamic, familiar to most in academia and the sciences. Research, far from being a leisurely pursuit in ivy-clad towers, is a vicious rat-race, far more competitive than industry. There are reputations to be made and glittering prizes to be won for the first to discover the miracle cure, the structure of DNA, the way to achieve cold fusion – and the cause of the increase in food poisoning. In 1987 the race was on in a big way, with the PHLS at the forefront.

Without the evidence needed to track down the real cause of the increase in food poisoning, in the context of a system that lacked the capability to acquire it, the PHLS did the only thing it could – it created the evidence.

Initial inspiration

After a number of false starts, when suspicion fell on failures of pasteurisation in bulk liquid egg, an apparently novel possibility came from the United States. There, a paper was published on food poisoning arising from fresh-shell eggs[2] suggesting that *Salmonella enteritidis* was infecting the ovaries of laying hens and, in turn, infecting yolks before shells were formed.

The story was covered by most of the UK media. On 16 April 1988, the *Today* newspaper announced 'It's no yolk!'. It used a photograph of an egg to form the 'O' in 'yolk'. 'Britain's favourite breakfast – the egg – is not all it's cracked up to be. Egg heads in America say it could be a killer,' it declared. *The Times* announced 'US scare threatens soft-boiled eggs', citing a DHSS spokesman saying, '… there is no reason for any new advice about preparing eggs and chicken, beyond observing normal hygiene and ensuring both are thoroughly cooked'.

But it did point out that salmonella was occurring *inside* the egg. This was something different, although far from new – one of Louis Pasteur's students had noted the phenomenon. Nevertheless, a number of senior scientists in the PHLS, probably for the first time, started to believe that fresh-shell eggs – as they came to be called – could be a plausible cause of their food poisoning 'epidemic'. Armed with this new belief, they set about gathering the evidence they needed to support the thesis.

Ottringham – a golden opportunity

A golden opportunity came on 29 April 1988 when a salmonella outbreak occurred at a Conservative party fund-raising event in Ottringham, East Yorkshire.[3] Crucially, the event organiser owned an egg farm and, by the time investigators had finished, the outbreak had become a *cause célèbre* in the scientific community. It was widely cited as the key case which proved that eggs were being infected and poisoning the population. But how those investigators behaved demonstrated just how anxious they were to prove their point.

Described by its organiser as a 'Bridge and Pâté Party', the event had been attended by seventy-two guests and seven to eight helpers, many of whom had been ill. Several different foods had been served, including – as would be expected – a variety of pâtés. Among those had been chicken-liver, venison, pheasant and mackerel, plus an 'ordinary' pâté made either from pig or calf liver. Then there had been sweets, which had included a mousse, rum-and-raisin ice cream and home-made vanilla ice cream. Of all the foods eaten, only the vanilla ice cream had contained fresh-shell eggs – from the event organiser's farm. It was this which became the focus of the inquiry.

From the start, however, the investigators had some difficulties. This was not an ordinary outbreak from a commercial kitchen. The food had been produced by volunteers in their own kitchens, delivered on the day and served buffet style. The ice creams had been made by separate people and the pâtés, with the exception of the 'ordinary' pâté, had been made by the event organiser's wife. All of them had contained an amount of chicken liver, used as a filler, obtained from a local broiler producer. Significantly – although never admitted by the official investigators – it had come from a plant in Lincoln where birds had been found to be infected with *S. enteritidis*, exactly the same type which had affected the event guests.

Under ordinary circumstances, the liver would have been a prime suspect for the food poisoning. However, the PHLS had eggs 'in the frame'. One of its staff epidemiologists arrived on the scene on 10 May, so long after the event that speculation around the small Yorkshire village as to the cause had been rife. Almost everyone was convinced the chicken liver was to blame, but not the epidemiologist. To everyone's surprise, he told a local official, who picked him up from the station in Hull, that the outbreak had been caused by eggs. Later, when the event organiser's wife ventured that the pâté might have been the cause, the same epidemiologist told her 'I'm almost a hundred per cent sure that it was eggs.' He then started his investigation.

Scientifically, the investigation did not proceed well. Nothing was left of the sweets, other than a small amount of rum-and-raisin ice cream. No salmonella was recovered from it. No pâtés were left and nothing remained from the original batch of chicken liver. Undeterred, the investigators found a different batch of liver and tested it anyway, finding a different type of salmonella from that which had affected the villagers. On that basis, the PHLS epidemiologist confidently eliminated all of the pâtés from his enquiries. After he had interviewed the people who had been at the event, he pronounced that, of those who had not eaten the pâté, the majority had been ill. Yet many of those who had eaten pâté had suffered no symptoms. To say that the event organiser and his wife were puzzled by this is an understatement. The event, after all, had been a 'pâté party' and nearly everyone had eaten one or other or the pâtés available, in most of which there had been chicken liver as an ingredient.

Nevertheless, despite the original certainty of the epidemiologist, when he later wrote to the event organiser, all he could say was that eggs were the 'likely' source of the outbreak, although this was 'impossible to prove epidemiologically'.

But the story did not end here. A Ministry of Agriculture vet had been sent into the egg farm owned by the event organiser, to take samples of hen faeces and dust. They yielded the same type of salmonella found in the outbreak. This, the investigators admitted, could have been a coincidence, but the vet persevered.

Dead birds were obtained from the farm, and salmonella of the outbreak type was recovered from half-formed eggs extracted from the decaying carcases.

Controlled tests on eggs from live birds on the farm failed to yield any infected eggs. Neither did sister birds from the same pullet grower and the same parent flock. Nevertheless, results were rushed into print in the letters page of *Veterinary Record*. These highly selective findings laid the foundation for what became the predominant theme throughout the egg crisis – that parent birds had been infected by contaminated feed which, in turn, had produced infected eggs, so infecting the commercial laying birds. These birds had then gone on to produce their own infected eggs which were infecting humans.

Meanwhile, having offered the event organiser a highly equivocal explanation of the cause of the outbreak, the PHLS epidemiologist reworked his original data, which had included three people who had eaten the ice cream made with raw eggs and had not been ill. These people did not appear when the new results were produced. When published in a prestigious medical journal, they demonstrated unequivocally that the Ottringham outbreak had been caused by eggs.

By this means, a myth was born. It subsequently became reinforced by a series of highly suspect investigations of what became known as 'egg associated' outbreaks. Cowed by the inherent authority of 'government scientists', the egg industry was unable to contest the claims, while the media accepted the data uncritically and published it with relish.

The real problem

That said, there is no question that there had been a real – if exaggerated – increase in salmonella food poisoning, and eggs had been partly responsible for the problem. No one could seriously doubt that there had been a problem with eggs. The *Salmonella enteritidis* that was causing the increase in food poisoning notifications was found in hens and chickens. And it was also the case that this type of salmonella was different. It had what was termed 'invasive' characteristics – that is, unlike many other types of salmonella, it could penetrate the gut and enter the bloodstream. By this means, it could infect eggs laid by hens.

But salmonella affecting poultry and travelling to hens' eggs was by no means new, even if there was good evidence that invasive *S. enteritidis* was causing a new cycle of infection. This cyclical effect had been observed, with different salmonellas, at roughly ten-year intervals ever since the war. But the PHLS was single-minded in its belief that 'infected eggs' were *wholly or mainly* responsible for the increase in food poisoning which it had identified. Despite this, it had nothing even approaching proof, and there was no shortage of alternative explanations.

One of the most plausible alternatives was cross-contamination from raw poultry in commercial and domestic kitchens. This, in itself, was not new, but there were significant differences in the way *S. enteritidis* affected broiler chickens, i.e. meat birds. The disease had the unusual property of causing an enlargement of the heart sac, the liquid contents of which became filled with an almost pure culture of billions of *S. enteritidis*.

Owing to the rapid, mechanical processing of broilers in industrial plants – brought about in part by the implementation of EU poultry-meat hygiene regulations – these infected sacs were very often ruptured during evisceration, spreading the bacteria onto the machines and thence over the birds in very high numbers. With the arrival of *S. enteritidis*, therefore, there had been a massive leap in the infectivity of broiler carcases, magnifying the effects of cross-contamination, and dramatically increasing the chances of food poisoning in the context where – in mass catering and the home – cross-contamination was the rule rather than the exception.

To appreciate the significance of this, it is important to understand that, with more 'conventional' salmonellas, contamination on a poultry carcase was usually, numerically, very low – no more than a few hundred organisms. These presented no problem if carcases were well cooked: thorough cooking easily destroyed the bacteria. The main problem was cross-contamination, occasioned when an infected raw carcase was placed on a surface, and either the cooked bird, or other food, touched the same surface. Sometimes the process was indirect, when the same utensils or tools were used on both raw and cooked food, without intervening cleaning and disinfection.

Normally, this presented relatively little problem. There was a considerable dilution effect when bacteria were transferred and the dose of salmonella required to make a healthy person ill is very high – in the order of 100,000 to 100,000,000 organisms. Unless contaminated food was held at room temperatures for quite a long period – allowing the salmonellas to multiply – no infection would arise. Therefore, typically, for infected poultry to represent a threat, three things had to coincide: a cross-contamination event; holding the contaminated food at temperatures at which the organisms could multiply; and retention for a considerable period. But *S. enteritidis* changed all that. For the duration of what amounted to an epidemic of the disease in broiler birds, there had been a quantum leap in the *level* of contamination in meat birds, increasing the potency of cross-contamination.

This was ignored by the PHLS. The cause of the increase in food poisoning had to be novel, something different, and cross-contamination was too obvious. Nor would such an explanation have found much favour with Currie. It would have placed responsibility for the increase in food poisoning firmly within the remit of her department, and complicated her dealing with NHS hospitals, as we shall see in Chapter 8.

In pinning the blame so firmly on the humble egg, all the 'experts' missed, or chose to ignore, yet another crucial phenomenon. Over the years preceding the crisis, for a variety of reasons, cooks and caterers had been progressively reducing the amount of vinegar used in home-made mayonnaise, a product made with fresh-shell eggs. With a high level of vinegar in the traditional recipe, salmonella in the product actually died. But with reduced vinegar, a formerly safe product became a potent medium for salmonella growth.

The effect of this change became apparent in a large food poisoning outbreak in a sandwich bar in the City of London during July/August 1985. Some 140 were affected by sandwiches in which mayonnaise had been used as a filler, and investigators attributed the problem to the low level of vinegar used in the mayonnaise. Unfortunately, the outbreak was not publicised and the significance was not appreciated. It should have been. Up until then, outbreaks involving mayonnaise had been extremely rare. There had been one reported in 1945, on board an American Liberty ship, and another in the 1960s originating in a pub in Sleaford, Lincolnshire. Thus, the City of London outbreak, because of its rarity and scale, should have acted as the 'tripwire'. The very function of surveillance authorities like the PHLS is to note the unusual, and to draw inferences which might assist in devising prevention and control strategies. But the outbreak passed unremarked.

There was then another major outbreak at the Gatwick Hilton Hotel in April 1988, again involving home-made mayonnaise. That should have rung alarm bells too, as again investigators noted that very little vinegar had been used. Then there was an outbreak in the House of Lords in May, once again involving mayonnaise – some of which had been scraped off diners' plates and returned to the 'pot'. In the same month, Leeds City Council had also experienced a major mayonnaise outbreak in a restaurant in its area. Yet again the alarm bells should have rung, as they should have in November when Spanish health officials wrote to the *Lancet* noting increased food poisoning from *S. enteritidis* attributable to home-made mayonnaise. But the 'watchdogs' didn't bark.

When details of forty-six outbreaks accounting for 1,342 cases alleged to have been 'egg associated' were submitted by the PHLS to the Agriculture Committee in January 1989, fifteen outbreaks and 618 of the cases involved the use of home-made mayonnaise made with fresh-shell eggs. Had the mayonnaise problem been highlighted, these outbreaks might not have arisen and the impact of the egg scare would have been very much diminished. There may well have been no scare at all. That would not have suited the PHLS. And mayonnaise would not have suited the Department of Health. For both, the problem had to be eggs. They were indeed 'killer' eggs, but their victim was British agriculture.

8. Hysteria Rampant

The reason why changes in the way home-made mayonnaise had been made could not have been acceptable to the Department of Health as an explanation for some of the increase in food poisoning – and even less, cross contamination in kitchens – arises from the way responsibilities for the food chain were split between Health and Agriculture. Basically, between farm and fork, the division came after primary processing. Food on the farm, in the vegetable sheds, in the egg packing plants and the slaughterhouses came under MAFF. From there on, as food went through manufacturing, distribution, catering and retailing, the DHSS took charge.

With power came responsibility. On where in the food chain the food poisoning problem occurred would depend whether Health or Agriculture was blamed. Mayonnaise came under Health. Eggs came under Agriculture. The Department of Health was determined that the blame for increased food poisoning – when it came – would be firmly attached to MAFF. Thus, when the PHLS offered 'infected eggs' as the explanation for the increase in food poisoning, it was a highly desirable proposition.

Unfortunately, when Edwina Currie came to make her statement on 3 December 1988, to the effect that there was a problem relating to a primary agricultural product – and thus a responsibility of the Ministry of Agriculture – its revelation by a health minister was taken as evidence of a cover-up by MAFF. Denounced as the 'farmers' friend', MAFF took much of the blame for the crisis. It was forced to take damaging countermeasures – including the compulsory slaughter of three and a half million laying hens – to prove its consumer credentials, those measures being far more draconian than would have been necessary had a calmer atmosphere prevailed.

Thus, while Edwina Currie undoubtedly believed she was championing the consumer cause, her department was involved in a devious game of 'pass the parcel'. Whatever else happened, the blame for any problems had to be laid at the door of Agriculture rather than Health. The transfer of blame resulted in another mortal blow to agriculture.

But there was another agenda. The Department had a much bigger problem than just the increase in food poisoning. Barely perceived by the public was the emergence of a particularly nasty form of food-poisoning caused by a little-known bacterium called *Listeria monocytogenes* – better known simply as 'listeria'. Here, the underlying agenda was the good old-fashioned 'cover-up'.

Two things about the bacterium particularly concerned the DHSS. Firstly, listeria was mainly associated with prepared foods – which brought it within the Department's remit. Secondly, and more importantly, the organism had a peculiar ability to multiply at much lower temperatures than was normal for food poisoning bacteria, even being able to replicate under refrigerated conditions. It was thus associated with chilled foods – and chilled foods were the key to Currie's plans to rejuvenate and improve hospital kitchens, and with that the reputation of the NHS, which had suffered over the years from damaging press as a result of its appalling record on food poisoning.

Why chilled foods should have been so important to Currie is simply explained. After a spate of highly embarrassing scandals involving food poisoning in hospitals – which had led to the resignation of her predecessor – and the removal of 'Crown Immunity', whereby hospitals had been exempt from the law, ageing and unhygienic hospital kitchens needed to be replaced. But, under the Thatcherite regime of the time, there was a snag. Currie had to do this without increasing public expenditure.

The solution was to move away from making meals in the hospitals themselves to a new system of preparing all the meals for groups of hospitals in vast central kitchens. They would be cooked, chilled and then distributed direct to the hospital wards, where they were to be reheated in special equipment. The system was called 'cook-chill' and was to be financed by the labour savings gained from its greater efficiency, thus bringing NHS catering kicking and screaming into the twentieth century without asking the Treasury for an additional penny.

But to Currie's consternation, listeria's ability to multiply at low temperatures – combined with an unexplained and worrying increase in the incidence of listeria food poisoning – had been linked by an obscure scientist to the growing use of cook-chill systems, both in hospitals and in commercial food production, especially the lucrative 'ready meal' market.

That obscure scientist was none other than Professor Richard Lacey, a clinical microbiologist at Leeds University, who had been fronting a campaign to get the listeria threat recognised. Variously described as a 'bogus professor' by parliamentary critics, a 'prophet of doom', a 'sensationalist', 'simplistic and alarmist' and even a 'charlatan', Lacey liked to see himself as the outsider, the brave lone voice speaking up on behalf of the oppressed, the victims, those at risk, who were being ignored, poisoned, killed even, by the heartless forces of big (agri-)business and government. Although in early 1988 he had yet to become a media star, his influence in the specialist area of cook-chill was profound, causing health authorities to rethink their plans to convert to the new system, thus putting Currie's plans at risk.

All this had to be seen against a background of the unexplained increase in listeriosis (the disease caused by *Listeria monocytogenes*) which represented a far more serious threat to public health than salmonella. Identified only in 1926, the disease had initially been so rare that it had remained a scientific curiosity through most of the twentieth century. But in the mid-1980s its annual incidence – which hitherto had been fairly static at twenty to forty cases a year – started rising. There had been 107 cases in 1986 and 259 in 1987, three times the level for the previous year and seven times the average for 1967-77. Moreover, the average fatality rate was 30 per cent of reported sufferers.

From the perspective of the late 1980s, while there was no obvious explanation for the rise, there was considerable concern amongst health professionals, not least those dealing with food safety, including myself, who suspected that the increase might be associated with food.

Our suspicions were well grounded. There had been an outbreak in 1981 in Nova Scotia, Canada, involving coleslaw, affecting forty people, and a hospital outbreak in Massachusetts, USA, in 1983, affecting forty-nine patients who had drunk pasteurised milk supplied to the hospital. In 1985 there had been another outbreak, this one in Los Angeles and Orange Counties, USA. Some 142 people became ill after eating a 'Mexican-style' soft cheese. Thirty infants died, before or immediately after birth. Then there had been a major outbreak from Swiss Vacherin Mont d'Or cheese in 1987, which had killed thirty-one people. During November 1987, the DHSS learned that the Swiss government had withdrawn the cheese from public sale. It issued a formal warning to the public not to eat this cheese.

Despite growing concern and increasing media interest, the DHSS refused to accept that there was a link between the rising tide of listeriosis in the UK and the consumption of food. Frustrated by this, Lacey brought the matter to a head in an interview with *New Scientist* magazine on 21 July 1988, claiming that hospital caterers were causing the listeriosis epidemic. But the DHSS stuck to its guns, arguing that no deaths had ever been traced to food in the UK. It pinned the blame on 'human contact with living animals', accusing Lacey of suffering from 'listeria hysteria'. The Department was to regret using that phrase.

Adverse publicity continued, mainly inspired by or centred around Lacey. The *Guardian* on 24 August 1988 reported a claim by Lacey that: 'Cook-chill preparation method places hospital patients in danger'. A few days later the PHLS pitched in with a letter in the *Lancet*, pointing out that listeria had been identified in Britain in frozen poultry, and ready-to-eat foods such as soft cheeses, salami and continental sausages. The authors also noted that two cases of listeriosis in the UK had been definitely linked to foodstuffs, one a French soft cheese and the other a British goat's cheese, concluding that: 'Listeriosis is an emerging public health problem, and a concerted diagnostic and research effort by clinicians, microbiologists and epidemiologists is required.' The net was closing round the DHSS, its protestations of there being 'no food link' looking increasingly vacuous.

In its September edition of *Which?* magazine, the Consumers Association also had a go, telling its readers that 'one in four hospitals are serving cook-chill meals which are putting patients at risk from food poisoning'. This was picked up by national newspapers and by Southend's *Evening Echo*, where a new cook-chill system was about to be introduced in the local hospital. The paper asked: 'Are hospitals cooking up a virulent new killer?' This was definitely publicity the DHSS could do without.

Then, on 9 October 1988, the *Observer* published a full-page feature on food poisoning, entitled 'Food poison plague hits

Britain'. Eggs were mentioned but most space was given to Lacey, claiming that listeria was killing three hundred people a year and linking the problem to the growth of cook-chill in hospitals.

To the relief of the DHSS, however, this flush of publicity subsided without making any great public impact, leaving Lacey brooding about the DHSS's denials. But, in late October 1988, he learned that a local woman had miscarried as a result of listeriosis. He rushed to her home and found a pre-cooked chicken portion in her dustbin. Back in his laboratory, he recovered listeria bacteria from the chicken. That was the proof he needed to demonstrate that listeriosis was food borne. He pushed the news out and it was covered extensively by local media.

To Lacey's great disappointment, the issue then died again. He was particularly worried by the lack of national TV interest, without which his stop-start campaign was struggling to get off the ground. His ultimate objective, the banning of cook-chill, remained as distant as ever.

Meanwhile, on 19 November, Lacey had received a call from the BBC *Watchdog* programme, asking him to appear on the slot scheduled for transmission two days later. But his excitement at finally breaking through into national television was tempered by an inconvenient fact – his views on listeria and cook-chill were not wanted. The programme was after his views on eggs. Nevertheless, Lacey agreed to give them. On the programme, alongside food campaigner and then director of the London Food Commission Tim Lang, he claimed that MAFF had conspired to 'cover up' the details of the growing egg 'peril' from the public.

Having tasted the fruits of television fame, Lacey then took to the eggs issue with zeal. Throughout the early days of the egg scare, he acquired the mantle of media 'guru', his particular contribution being to advocate the cause espoused by the journal *Veterinary Record*[1] that the increase in *S. enteritidis* in poultry had probably been due 'to birds receiving contaminated feed and then subsequently spread by site contamination and infected parent flocks'. For the Department of Health, eggs were a gift. For the time being, it completely neutralised Lacey and other cook-chill critics, diverting attention to salmonella and farming.

Listeria hysteria

Despite the success of the Department of Health's diversionary tactics, listeria was never going to escape media attention completely. Its turn came on 11 January 1989 – some weeks after Currie had resigned – when the *Daily Mirror* carried a page-four lead headline, 'Shock warning over killer bugs in chickens'. Bristol's environmental health department had been looking for listeria in cooked and raw chicken meat and had found that 'one in every fifteen cooked chicken products was infected'. Sixty per cent of fresh chickens 'were also found to harbour the bug'. The *Mirror* called the organism the 'meningitis brain bug', which '... kills nearly a third of those it strikes'.

The next evening, Lacey – who had made no secret of the fact that his primary target was listeria – fulfilled his wish for more publicity on this issue. Thames Television followed him through a number of Leeds supermarkets, buying up chilled ready-meals to test for the presence of listeria. He found it in 'a quarter', and then announced that microwave cooking often failed to kill the bacteria. The programme had the Department of Health claiming that twenty-three people had died from listeriosis in 1987, but Lacey put it at 150 – to take account of 'under-reporting'.

The *Daily Mirror* ran a page-one report the following day, headed 'Stores fury as TV prof brands cooked meat a killer'. According to Lacey, listeria was now killing 'up to two hundred people a year'. The paper followed up with a page-seven lead, white out of black, asking, 'Food bugs – Who is telling the truth?' *The Times* ran with 'Fears over bacteria in pre-cooked chicken', while the *Daily Telegraph* picked up the microwave slant with 'Microwaves fail to kill bacteria in chilled meals'. The *Sun* was on the case as well, with the headline 'Danger in TV dinner – brain bug warning', having Lacey claiming 'up to one hundred and fifty deaths a year'.

The next day, the *Daily Mail* had an exclusive – or so it thought – with 'Food alert as baby girl dies' in a banner headline taking up most of the front page. A newborn baby, about to become one of the most famous dead babies in modern history, had been 'the latest victim of deadly listeria bacteria'. Her mother had been ill herself, after eating soft cheeses and pre-cooked chicken – 'the type of food linked to listeria'. By Sunday, 15 January, the mother who had previously asked not to be named had lost her anonymity, appearing in a photograph on the front page of the *Sunday Times*. She was the photogenic Sally Anne Bourne, pictured holding her surviving daughter Lilly. The picture caption was 'Mother who lost a baby to listeria'. Lacey's figure of 150 deaths from listeria had gone back to 'two hundred a year', and *The Times* reported the Department of Health as 'trying hard' to avoid an egg-style row over listeria. By now, though, 'listeria hysteria' was unstoppable. It was to run and run.

Indicative of the type of media coverage that was emerging, however, was a piece in the *Sunday Times* on 22 January. The 'Insight' column was devoted to an investigation of the Ministry of Agriculture's role in the 'listeria and salmonella scandals'. It was headed 'Whose side are they on?', and subtitled:

> Two outbreaks of food poisoning have highlighted a growing conflict between public health and private interest. The spotlight has been turned on the Ministry of Agriculture, Fisheries and Food. Do its ministers consider it important for individuals to know the full dangers of what they eat, or for farmers and food producers to be protected from damaging scares?

When it came to listeria, however, the reporters failed to understand the division of responsibility between Health and Agriculture, commenting that

> The Ministry of Agriculture, Fisheries and Food has a fundamental conflict: it has to protect the interests of farmers and the food industry, while policing them to safeguard public health. The Department of Health meanwhile has to act on any potential threat. But in respect of food production, it cannot warn the public unless it can prove to the Ministry of Agriculture that the dangers are real. It was precisely this minefield that Edwina Currie stepped into ...

A more distorted and ill-informed view would have been hard to find (although there was plenty of competition), but it expressed the general feeling of the time. MAFF was the culprit and, by implication, so was farming. And the pain was about to be increased. With 'listeria' having run in the media for nearly a month, the Department of Health's Chief Medical Officer, Sir Donald Acheson, was planning a devastating intervention – an admission that listeria was food borne.

He had for some time been intending to send out a warning letter to GPs on 'listeriosis and food', outlining the advice that should be given to patients. However, his concern had been that its content would be leaked, with the inevitable hue and cry. He thus decided to call a press conference for 10 February, to 'manage the disclosure'. Pregnant women and immuno-compromised patients, he told media representatives, 'should stop eating soft ripened cheeses such as brie, camembert and blue vein types, while ensuring that ready-made cook-chill meals should be re-heated until they were "piping hot" '.

If this was intended to dampen 'growing concern', as Acheson claimed, it failed dismally. Television and radio news led with his warning on all evening bulletins, with much TV debate following. The next day the warning ran countrywide, making front-page headlines in all the national dailies. But there was no criticism of the Department of Health. Instead, the media focused on cheese; typical was the headline in the *Independent*, which proclaimed 'Pregnant women warned against eating soft cheese'.

One of the results was an announcement by MAFF that it intended to consult on an unpasteurised milk ban in England and Wales, including a ban on its use in cheese, threatening the revival of craft cheese-making and putting the UK at odds with France. Significantly, the *Daily Telegraph* reported on the consequences of food scares: 'Small companies will be worse hit while diversity and massive investment protect the giants,' wrote Richard Bridges, a business correspondent.

Elsewhere in the *Telegraph* there was another interesting squib, reporting that France had 600 listeria cases annually, of which 180 proved fatal – compared with 291 cases in England and Wales during 1988, and 63 deaths. And on 16 February, the *Independent* reported a view from the Secretary of the UK Egg Producers' Association, Mr Keith Pulman, who declared that the listeria crisis had been engineered. After eggs, it was now the turn of cheese to take the blame. 'It is all a smokescreen to take the heat off cook-chill food preparation which is causing a lot of food poisoning,' he said.

Inevitably, the issue gradually slid off the front pages, but it did not go away. Saturday, 25 February saw Lacey back in the *Daily Telegraph* with the headline: '"Safest food in supermarkets is dog meat" says expert'. Described as a 'leading expert in food hygiene', he claimed that tinned dog food came under much stricter hygiene rules than many meals eaten by humans. 'A lot of the time human food is produced for convenience eating and that food is not produced under conditions which ensure safety,' he said.

On 16 June, with listeria almost a distant memory, *The Times* announced a reprieve for unpasteurised milk. The government had decided not to ban it. Then, on 29 June, the House of Commons Social Services Committee published a report, long in preparation, on the government's handling of listeria. It was a bombshell, summed up neatly by the London *Evening Standard*. It devoted its front page to 'Silence cost me my baby – Mother's anger as MPs reveal two-year delay in listeria warning'. The hue and cry spilled over into the next day's newspapers, *The Times* leading with: 'Government blamed by MPs for listeria deaths' and 'Mother condemns silence over listeria'. But the most trenchant comment came from the editorial in the *Evening Standard*, headed 'Infection in Whitehall'.[1] It ran:

> In answer to unanimous criticism ... the Department of Health feebly replies ... that chief medical officer, Sir Donald Acheson, issued his warning as soon as the epidemiological evidence warranted it. This statement is, if not downright dishonest, at least highly questionable. There is no evidence that listeriosis suddenly got worse in February of this year. Is it not curious that the epidemiological evidence should suddenly become overwhelming in the very week that the press began to report the widespread scare over listeria poisoning? In short, civil servants at the Department of Health are no longer to be trusted.

Perversely, it was all a one-day wonder. The Department of Health, in the minds of the media and the population at large, emerged unscathed. MAFF was still in the frame. But the best was yet to come.

On 12 July 1989, the Department of Health issued a press release, warning that listeria had been found in pâté. It advised pregnant women and 'other vulnerable people' not to eat the product. Once again, the media circus cranked into gear and it quickly emerged that there was something new. The pâté was Belgian, bought from a Gateway supermarket in Taff-Ely in Wales. Two sources were implicated: one a company called Sanpareil in Antwerp, and another called Mortier, in Veurne – both exporting under the Mattesson brand. On 11 July, the Belgian producers admitted problems in their factories, which they confirmed the next day when export from the Sanpareil factory was suspended.

The endgame

Once the dust had settled from this, post-incident reports started filtering through demonstrating unequivocally that the increased listeriosis between 1987 and 1989 had been food borne. The primary source had not been cheese, nor cook-chill, nor salads, nor any of the other foods highlighted in the run-up to the explosion of 'listeria hysteria'. It was something none of the experts had thought of – contaminated pâté, from Belgium. Yet the Belgian authorities did not pick up the problem; nor did staff at the factories. Only after *British* officials discovered it and the *British* Department of Health had asked the management of the factories to investigate did they find – or admit – they had a problem. When the *Belgians* cleaned up their act, epidemic listeriosis disappeared in the UK.

Prior to that, on 15 July 1988, at a press conference organised by the London Food Commission to launch its book *Food Adulteration*, Lacey had been a guest speaker. Denouncing British food safety standards, he claimed that 'Britain has the sick food of Europe', a claim that has been oft repeated, not least in the chamber of the European Parliament. But it was France that was reporting 600 listeria cases annually, and 180 deaths, while there had been 291 one cases in England and Wales during 1988, with 63 deaths. And when it came to adulterated food, the pâté picked up from Wales, and latterly throughout Britain, had been produced in *Belgium*.

That was the tragedy of it all. Despite the manoeuvring of the

Department of Health and its strenuous efforts to ensure that its cook-chill programme was not jeopardised, it had very little to worry about. Even without the Belgian connection, as early as 1988 it was known that *Listeria monocytogenes* was not a pathogen in the ordinary sense. What made it very different was that, unlike salmonella, most strains did not cause disease. The US, Swiss and, to a large extent, the UK cases were all being caused by a particularly virulent 'rogue' strain, which for reasons unknown seems to have emerged in the US in the late 1970s and had spread to Europe. Had the Department of Health concentrated on dealing with the problem, instead of playing 'pass the parcel', things might have been very different.

As it was, the salmonella and listeria scares, in quick succession, focused minds on food safety. Behind that came the regulatory onslaught, with dozens of new controls imposed on farming and allied trades, not least a new directive on dairy products which imposed a 'zero tolerance' on listeria in cheese, a measure which, in the fullness of time, was to make craft cheese-making on the farm a very uncertain business – still another blow to a reeling industry.

And Bovine Spongiform Encephalopathy, or 'Mad Cow Disease' as it was to become popularly known, had yet to make an impact.

9. The Politics of Incompetence

It is strange that, despite the torrent of words which poured out from every source imaginable, Mad Cow Disease, or Bovine Spongiform Encephalopathy (BSE) as it is more properly known, is still an enigma. Not least of that torrent was the report by Lord Phillips of Worth Maltravers, published in October 2000 after the inquiry commissioned by the incoming Blair government. Lord Phillips' brief had been

> To establish and review the history of the emergence and identification of BSE and variant CJD in the United Kingdom, and of the action taken in response to it up to 20 March 1996; to reach conclusions on the adequacy of that response, taking into account the state of knowledge at the time; and to report on these matters ...[1]

His endeavours, which expended what was estimated at £27 million of taxpayers' money, delivered sixteen volumes of leaden prose, possibly amounting to some five thousand pages – not that many bothered to count, much less read them. And when the media had finished picking the bones of the inquiry's press release (which saved them having to read the actual report), none of us was any the wiser. We could only conclude, somewhat ruefully, that never in the field of human history had so much been written about such a great disease, to so little effect.

Yet when the BSE inquiry was set up, in the aftermath of the euphoria following Blair's election in 1997, hopes were high that 'New Labour', committed to 'transparency', was actually going to deliver on its promise of a full, independent examination of the issues. There were some reservations when the terms of reference were published, setting a cut-off date of 20 March 1996. The inquiry was only going to cover the events up to when Stephen Dorrell, the then Secretary of State for the Department of Health, made his fateful statement to a packed House of

Commons. The official acknowledgement of a possible link between BSE and what was then called 'new variant' Creutzfeldt-Jakob Disease (CJD), the so-called 'human equivalent' of BSE, was to be the end of the chapter.

Those niggling reservations were, if not dispelled, then held in abeyance when the inquiry swamped the Internet with daily records of its proceedings and posted witness statements on its website, accessible to all those with a suitably equipped computer. This was 'transparency in action' and the pundits duly applauded the concession towards openness.

As the sessions droned on, however – with dark rumours (subsequently confirmed) that the inquiry was being 'nobbled' by ranks of lawyers representing key witnesses (at public expense) – it became clear that the inquiry was going to amount to nothing much at all. When its report was finally published, after years of delay, there was no real disappointment at its vacuous findings. It had long been expected that it would be a non-event.

Predictably, such blame as was apportioned to the players involved in one of the most cataclysmic series of events ever to affect agriculture was spread wide and thin. All Phillips and his team could offer was:

> In the years up to March 1996 most of those responsible for responding to the challenge posted by BSE emerge with credit. However, there were a number of shortcomings in the way things were done.

Crucially, in the first paragraphs of the report, Phillips also cautioned that criticisms of individuals needed to be read 'in their proper context', but it is the phrase 'proper context' which needs to be turned back on the inquiry team. They failed to look at BSE, as a whole, in its 'proper context'. That context was salmonella. What Phillips did not recognise – or perhaps did not understand – was the profound impact of the salmonella-in-eggs scare on the Tory government. For the first time in the history of any British government, a serving Prime Minister had been called to the dispatch box to defend her record on food safety. This was unprecedented – and resented.

Thatcher, hailed by many as the greatest Prime Minister since Churchill, had been dragged down into the gutter, having to talk about something she knew nothing and cared less about, *Salmonella enteritidis*. It was something she could not even pronounce, calling it – to the amusement of many – 'en-terry-dye-tis'. So deep did the humiliation go that, in her memoirs,[2] there is no mention whatsoever of eggs, salmonella or, in the index, of Edwina Currie. It is as if the cataclysmic events of December 1998 and the months following never happened.

Bernard Ingham, one-time press secretary to Thatcher, was more forthcoming. In his own book, he dated the decline of the Thatcher ascendancy from December 1988 when Currie 'scrambled her eggs with an excessive amount of salmonella'. After that, he noted, 'nothing went right for the government'. His own job had switched from being like that of the goalkeeper for Liverpool, who scarcely ever saw the opposing forwards, to that of goalkeeper for Halifax Town at the bottom of the Fourth Division.[3] Certainly, the salmonella scars went deep and words went out to ministers responsible for both Health and Agriculture. They were simple and unequivocal: 'never again'.

Privately, ministers at the time had no difficulty in admitting that the salmonella-in-eggs crisis was a scam, put up by scientists covering their own backs; and that Edwina Currie – with no technical background or understanding of the issues – had been persuaded to believe there was a serious problem. As a result, their response to the ensuing crisis had been governed not by the technical demands of the situation but the overpowering need to 'restore public confidence'. That imperative also drove the response to BSE, a politically inspired need directed at ensuring that 'Mad Cows' never provoked the same level of crisis as infected hens. Throughout the years from 1988 to the catastrophic announcement by Dorrell in 1996, public policy was therefore directed towards reassurance. Civil servants and government scientists took their cue from the top. If the politicians wanted reassurance, then reassurance they would get.

At the beginning, it was clear that damping down BSE was not going to be very difficult. Although – according to legend – the disease was officially identified towards the end of 1986, it excited very little interest and, even by the end of 1988, it remained the province only of a number of specialist journalists, such as James Erlichman of the *Guardian*. They could not even keep their editors interested, much less the broader public.

When the matter was first raised in the House of Commons, those great guardians of our interests and liberties – Members of Parliament – were neither concerned nor impressed. According to a parliamentary sketch by Andrew Rawnsley in the *Guardian* on 2 December 1988 – one day before Edwina Currie was to do her stuff – ministers had been quizzed the previous day about an 'outbreak of "bovine spongiform" which turns cows' brains into sponge and makes them appear drunk'. Dennis Skinner wondered whether humans could catch it. He had in mind the (then) Chancellor of the Exchequer, Nigel Lawson. According to Rawnsley, this 'spongibrain' taunt brought 'roars of laughter' from MPs. That was the first contribution from Parliament on an issue which, in 1996, brought more newspaper coverage than the declaration of war against Germany in September 1939.

Had salmonella and listeria not eclipsed it, it is perhaps possible that greater attention would have been given to BSE and the potential risk to man. Those with a suspicious nature and a penchant for conspiracy theories might even suggest that BSE provided a further dimension to the eggs scare, in that concern over salmonella in eggs – which just happened to start in earnest at the same time as a scientific panel was about to publish an interim report on the disease – was used to obscure a potentially greater threat, providing a convenient smokescreen behind which the problem could be quietly sorted out.

The early days

Going back to the origins of the 'discovery' of BSE, there is no early evidence of any conspiratorial intent on the part of the original 'players'. What does come out of the BSE inquiry, however, is a strange lack of curiosity. In this context, the person recorded as the first to notice something seriously wrong was a vet called David Bee. He encountered a puzzling disease in cattle at Pilsham Farm in 1984/5 yet did not consider submitting brain samples to the laboratory, to help identify what he called 'Pilsham Farm Syndrome', until the ninth animal had succumbed to what was latter identified as BSE. Similarly, another vet, Colin Whittaker, attending Plurenden Manor Farm, noted six cattle succumbing to the disease before he took similar action.

When I talked this over with a senior vet running a large

animal practice, he readily admitted that vets – like so many other professionals – tended to talk up their successes, the diseases and conditions they had identified, but seldom referred to their failures. He conceded that he had seen early cases of what, in retrospect, had been BSE but had diagnosed the affected cows as suffering from 'chronic staggers', a disease that does not exist. 'Staggers' is an acute disease of cattle arising from magnesium deficiency, from which cows either die very rapidly or recover quickly once treated. Although it can mimic BSE, the latter disease is characterised by its slow onset and long duration – hence the need to invent 'chronic' staggers.

When Bee realised he was dealing with something unusual, he sent samples to the Central Veterinary Laboratory (CVL) in Weybridge and received a report back in September 1985 – but took no further action. At the time he was first presented with the CVL report, he did not understand it. Some thirteen years later, according to his own evidence to the BSE inquiry, he still did not understand it. Had he been more curious, he could have asked more about it. He was not and did not. He could have enquired of his colleagues in the region whether they had noted anything similar. He could have written a letter to the *Veterinary Record*, with a similar request. Staff at the CVL might have done likewise – although they could not have acted without official approval, whereas Bee was a free agent. But Bee was a working vet, not a scientist. And he was not a conspirator.

Whittaker, the other vet involved in the early events, was perhaps more fortunate in that he had a firm diagnosis to go on. It took nearly ten months for the CVL to produce a definitive diagnosis, however, and that delay led to suspicions that the veterinary laboratory may have known more that it was prepared to admit and may have been engaged in an active 'cover-up'.

The truth is probably more pedestrian. CVL staff did not specialise in diagnosing spongiform encephalopathies – that expertise resided with a laboratory in Edinburgh, called the Neuropathogenesis Unit (NPU). Experts at that unit should have been called in but they were not, for what was probably a very simple reason. Under the same Thatcher-inspired public expenditure review that so threatened the Public Health Laboratory Service, the State Veterinary Service (of which the

CVL was part) was also under scrutiny. The CVL was actually marked down for possible privatisation and was being forced to assume a commercial attitude to its work. In this context, the NPU was a potential competitor. It was far better that the CVL should 'crack' the puzzle itself, putting it in a better position to 'scoop the pool' for any subsequent research funds. Thus, what should have taken weeks at most took months.

Nevertheless, by November 1986 there was considerable evidence that there was a BSE epidemic in the making. Four months later, MAFF commissioned field epidemiology. That delay, too, has raised suspicions but, by Civil Service standards, its response was relatively swift. Preliminary conclusions were reached in May 1987, again – by MAFF standards – a relatively quick outcome. Equally, there is no record of MAFF conspiring to withhold information from its political masters. Agriculture ministers were informed in June, which is again relatively fast for what was not, at the time, a major problem.

However, whereas agriculture ministers were advised, there is no record of health ministers being told at the same time. This suggests that – at least in the upper echelons of MAFF – there was no great concern about risks to human health. According to the BSE inquiry, it took until March 1988 before the BSE file was passed to Sir Donald Acheson, the Department of Health's Chief Medical Officer. This was the man who, for some years, had refused to accept that the increase in listeriosis was in any way connected with food and was subsequently censured by the House of Commons Social Services Committee for failing to take action to protect public health.

But if Acheson had failed to recognise the threat from listeria – his department's responsibility – he certainly saw a threat in BSE, the responsibility of MAFF. He told the BSE inquiry that he had written in his diary – at a time when a mere five hundred cases of BSE had been reported – 'We have another plague from Egypt'.

The Southwood Committee

At the very beginning of April, Acheson then did a very strange thing. Having decided on an evaluation of the potential human health issues arising from BSE, he did not speak to the experts in Edinburgh. Instead he called a former colleague, with whom he had served on the Royal Commission on Environmental Pollution – Sir Richard Southwood, Pro Vice-Chancellor of Oxford University and professor of zoology.

Acheson told him 'in great confidence' that 'this [BSE] was potentially a very serious disease', and asked him to set up a committee. 'Why me?' Southwood had asked. 'Because it is an ecological food problem and because I know you are an independent chap,' Southwood says Acheson told him. But was he appointed just because he was an 'independent chap' or because he was also 'sound', a chap who could be relied upon to 'do the right thing'?

Southwood acted with what *Star Trek* fans would describe as 'warp speed'.[4] As quickly as 20 June, he held the first meeting of his committee, with four members present, including John Wilesmith, the head of epidemiology at the CVL. He had carried out the epidemiology for MAFF on BSE. The head of MAFF's animal health division, Mr A.J. Lawrence, was also present. Crucially, for what Southwood himself later acknowledged was not an expert committee, the leading expert on scrapie – Alan Dickinson, formerly head of the Neuropathogenesis Unit in Edinburgh and the man who had pioneered strain typing of the disease – was not present. Nor was he ever consulted or asked to give evidence.

Members were, however, confronted with a MAFF briefing paper which did not pull any punches. It indicated that 'thousands/millions' of people could be at risk, and that – because of the long incubation period – it might be ten years before disease showed up in the human population. Southwood later told the BBC, 'I think our mood was very serious. We felt that we could here be on the edge of something which could have enormous implications.'

The mood of members was not improved when they were told by Wilesmith that cattle 'showing the symptoms of BSE' were entering the food chain, either human or animal. Later, Southwood was to tell the BSE inquiry, 'It was fair to say that we were all horrified.' The members had also been conscious that there were uncertainties in virtually every aspect of BSE. All they had to go on were analogies with an apparently similar disease in sheep and goats called scrapie, and the human diseases kuru and CJD. They also had to confront the prospect that the disease agent was out of the ordinary. It could be a long time before experiments on transmission could give results. Southwood wrote the very next day to the Permanent Secretary at MAFF. But he was not content with that. So concerned was he that he also faxed a copy, for which he had to make special arrangements, as facsimile machines were by no means as common then as they are now. The missive was received by agriculture ministers on 22 June, recommending that BSE-affected cattle should be removed from the food chain and destroyed, with compensation paid to farmers. Southwood also recommended the establishment of an expert working party to advise on research; that tests should be carried out to see whether, as Wilesmith had postulated, animal feed made from the remains of scrapie-infected sheep had caused BSE; whether scrapie could be transmitted via milk and muscle; and whether maternal transmission occurred in calves born to diseased cows.

Yet a mere six days later – after he had felt so moved by urgency that he had not trusted the ordinary post and had faxed the Permanent Secretary with his recommendations – Southwood allowed to be published an interim report from his committee. In stark contrast to the earlier alarm, it offered the anodyne conclusion that 'the risk of transmission of BSE to humans appears remote and it is unlikely that BSE will have any implications for human health'. The report did, however, add, 'If our assessments of these likelihoods are incorrect, the implications would be extremely serious ... with the long incubation period of spongiform encephalopathies in humans, it may be a decade or more before complete reassurances can be given.'

A joint MAFF/DHSS press release issued the same day left out the all-important qualifying clause. This 'official' version was broadcast by the BBC that night, thus omitting Southwood's caveat. Next day, in the *Guardian*, consumer correspondent James Erlichman also missed Southwood's caveat and followed the government's line that 'BSE presents no health hazard'.

If this interim report was merely buying time for a more thorough examination, holding off raising public alarm until the issue was better understood, this conclusion might have been explicable. It is also unsurprising at this stage that the government should want to avoid undue public alarm – hence its 'airbrushing' of Southwood's conclusions. But what is not easily explicable is Southwood's final report, issued in February 1989, while the listeria and salmonella food scares were in full swing. His conclusion was, to say the very least, curious. Remarking on whether BSE could be passed on to humans, he then advised that ' ... it is most unlikely that BSE will have any implications for public health'. Thus, in a space of seven short months – during which there had been an unprecedented level of public concern about food safety – 'unlikely' had become 'most unlikely', a phrasing which was reassuringly unequivocal.

To believe this change was coincidental – entirely unrelated to the succession of scares which had been tearing the government apart – one would also have to have a belief in fairies at the bottom of the garden and a conviction that pigs could fly. What is even more curious is the contorted line of reasoning by which Southwood reached his conclusion. Taking up Wilesmith's assertion that BSE had originated in cattle because they had been fed the scrapie-infected remains of sheep, he argued that, having passed to cattle – *because* it had passed to cattle – scrapie, in the form of BSE, could not pass to humans. The cattle were what were known as 'dead-end hosts'.

Yet it is one of the key disciplines in scientific writing that any conclusions offered in a report must be supported by the evidence adduced in the text. But Southwood's conclusion was entirely unsupported. For instance, the term 'dead-end host' appeared only twice in the body of his report. The first was in the context of transmissible encephalopathies appearing in some species such as rodents and mink, where the those species ' ... act as dead-end hosts' with '*no direct animal to animal* transmission' (my italics). It made its second appearance in relation to Southwood's estimate as to the eventual size of the BSE epidemic, which, he decided, ' ...will depend very largely on whether or not the cow is a dead-end host'.

In the first context, the term was clearly being used in relation to *direct transmision*, i.e. animal-to-animal spread, and in the second the context was *maternal transmission* – whether or not cows could pass the disease to their calves. But in his conclusion Southwood gave the term 'dead-end host' an entirely new meaning, in relation to species-to-species transmission, which was said not to occur. Turning to what was known at the time, one can refer to one of the leading books on medical microbiology then in print.[5] It refers to 'transmissible mink encephalopathies' (TMEs), and records:

> The agent of mink encephalopathy can be distinguished from that of scrapie only by its host range: the former can, it is claimed, be transmitted to rhesus monkeys unlike scrapie which will, however, infect mink.

On the basis that it had been suspected that a transmissible spongiform encephalopathy (TSE) had been transmitted to mink from scrapie-infected feed, it can be inferred that scrapie – in its original form – might not be able to pass onwards (using the rhesus monkey as a model). But once it had passed through the mink, it acquired new infectivity characteristics and the capacity to pass to other previously non-susceptible species.

Extrapolating that logic to the scrapie/BSE scenario, it could have been argued that scrapie, in its original form, was not transmissible to man. But once it had passed through cattle to emerge as BSE, it could have acquired new characteristics which then made it transmissible to man. In other words, what Southwood had offered appeared to be precisely the opposite of what may have been the real situation. Nevertheless, despite the slender evidence on which Southwood had based his conclusions, ministers seized upon his findings with zeal. The legend was born that, since scrapie had been around for over two hundred years and had not passed to man – but had passed to cattle – it was likely that the cattle were dead-end hosts and man was not at risk.

With the salmonella and listeria scares still running, one needs little imagination to predict what would have been the response had Southwood produced an 'alarmist' report. Instead of his having written that it was '*most unlikely* (my italics) that BSE will have any implications for public health', just suppose that – as his main conclusion – he had repeated what he had been told by MAFF. 'We could here be on the edge of something which could have enormous implications. Thousands or millions of people could be at risk, and – because of the long incubation period – it might be ten years before disease shows up in the human population.' The political fallout would have been immense. In the febrile climate of the time, the ensuing crisis might even have toppled the government.

So why did Southwood keep his counsel for so long? Years after the event, he told the BSE inquiry, 'We were trying to strike a balance between raising legitimate concerns and ringing in a clarion of large alarm about something which might not be enormously significant.' But the facts speak differently. They lead to the inevitable conclusion that his report had been 'sanitised' to prevent a further scare.

People don't eat cats

Although the BSE issue did not disappear with the publication of Southwood, the government's policy of 'reassurance' was largely successful. Publicity failed to reach the intensity of the 1988/9 scares – despite a German ban on British beef. That is, until 10 May 1990 when the sky fell in. MAFF announced that a Siamese cat called Max had died of the feline equivalent of BSE.

This was the first time a domestic pet had been reported as suffering from what became known as Feline Spongiform Encephalopathy, or FSE. There had been early warning in a *Daily Telegraph* article on 4 May in which it had been reported: 'Mad cow disease check as cat dies', but the news had now become official – 'Mad Max' had died of 'BSE'. The story ran on all major radio and television bulletins and, on 11 May, in all the national newspapers. What really blew the issue apart, however, was the coverage in the *Sunday Times* on 13 May, when Professor Lacey had the front-page lead, courtesy of editor Andrew Neil. The cross-page headline ran: 'Leading food scientist calls for slaughter of 6 million cows'. Lacey also wanted a total ban on exports, and, he said, 'We need to put the British Isles in quarantine before someone else does.'

On 16 May, partaking in a damage limitation exercise, then Agriculture Minister John Selwyn Gummer displayed his own kind of madness in a PR stunt which was to come to haunt him. The television cameras had followed him to the East Coast boat show in Ipswich, where – to camera – he condemned the 'amateurs' who claimed consumers were at risk from British beef. Then, in an extraordinary display of bravado, arranged the day before with the *Daily Mirror*, he offered a hamburger to his four-year-old daughter Cordelia. 'As you can see,' he said, 'my whole family enjoy it [beef] and I have no worries about my children eating it.' Every television news bulletin that evening carried the pictures of the reluctant child, unenthusiastically pecking at the meat and then rejecting it, uneaten, because it was too hot.

By 26 June, MPs were being told of the death of a fourth cat from FSE. With that news, the 'dead-end host' myth was itself dead and buried. Despite this, the government's chief vet, then Keith Meldrum, tried to hold the line, famously asserting that the deaths 'meant nothing'. With the directness for which he had become well known, he said 'People are not at risk – they don't eat cats.'

The mother of all scares

Although the issue was again to die, it never really disappeared from the media. In the words of one news editor, it bubbled away under the surface 'waiting for dead bodies to turn up'. When they did, and Dorrell was forced into an admission that there appeared to be a link between nvCJD and BSE, a 'dam-burst' effect took over and the crisis erupted.

The problem for the ministers who had so assiduously sought to prevent 'Mad Cows' becoming a crisis was that they had never understood why salmonella in eggs had reached crisis proportions. Following the 'dam-burst' about infected eggs, and then listeria and cheese, no post-mortem was carried out. There was no real inquiry, no attempt to understand the social dynamics of the scare. Instead, half-understood lessons were partly digested and all the wrong things were done. Little did they know it but ministers and their faithful civil servants, in their mindless pursuit of 'public confidence', were laying the foundations for what was to become the 'mother of all scares'.

Had they understood what they were doing, they would have realised that false reassurance simply conveyed the impression of a cover-up and bred distrust. When the government's already slender 'scrapie' alibi began to unravel, it was too late to change. Any divergence from 'the line' would have brought instant retribution in terms of a collapse in consumer confidence. Once they were trapped in the lie, ministers were forced to stick to it, until

20 March 1996 when even they had to concede it was no longer tenable. Then consumer confidence really did collapse.

What had started as political expediency became incompetence. The whole issue was then caught up in the dying days of a discredited Conservative government which, arrogant to the last, thought it knew the answers without putting the work in to find out what they really were, or understanding what they were dealing with. We had a 'know-all' government that thought it could 'manage' the situation. It could not. Through its own incompetence, it adds itself to the growing list of those who destroyed British agriculture.

10. The Department of Stealth

On 6 August 1989, when, in the wake of the salmonella and listeria scares, food premises registration was being considered for inclusion in a new Food Safety Act, columnist Norman McCrae wrote a piece for the *Sunday Times* headed 'How to make a little tummy ache lethal'. He argued against compulsory registration, which would allow the regulators to go through 'what the late Herman Kahn called the two familiar stages of "health and safety fascism" '.

The first was the bankrupting of small traders by imposing an excessive regulatory burden. The second

> ... almost invariably increases and disguises the few deaths from food poisoning that do occur ... Once it was running things, any regulatory body would want to hush up news about really lethal poisoning from one of its registered sites ... because the Daily Yahoo would crucify the inspector who had registered or permitted it.

The phenomenon McCrae was describing was, effectively, a form of 'regulatory capture'. This occurs when regulatory authorities become so involved in the processes they control that they identify more with the industries they regulate than the public they are supposed to be protecting.

This mechanism was to have an important effect on the course of the BSE crisis, leading to a situation wherby many farmers believe their industry was sacrificed to protect a much larger and more valuable pharmaceutical industry. The 'prisoners' in this case were officials and scientists in the Department of Health, responsible for regulating medicines. The suspicion was that, subject to 'regulatory capture', they put the interests of the industry they regulated before the more general interests of the country. While others were declaring 'open season' on beef in the months and years following McCrae's piece, the activities of this particular 'regulatory body' were to land yet another blow on British agriculture.

Medicines versus beef

The agenda of scientists and officials emerged very early in the BSE saga when media attention was focused on the potential danger of infected beef transmitting BSE to humans. A major distortion in risk perception was to emerge, the essence of which stems from a simple fact. Virtually from the point at which BSE was officially recognised, there were fears that it could spread to man and that there were two plausible mechanisms of spread. But instead of highlighting both mechanisms, officials sought to play down one while exposing the other to media scrutiny.

The first mechanism, which was to dominate the media headlines for over a decade, was consumption of meat and offal from infected animals. The other equally plausible way of passing on the disease was through injectable pharmaceutical products made from bovine materials, such as vaccines and hormone preparations. Throughout the build-up to the major BSE crisis in March 1996, the risks from medicinal products were scarcely mentioned.

Whether or not these products were, in fact, involved in the transmission of BSE to humans (which itself is still open to debate) is not the point. From the perspective of the mid- to late eighties, there was no possible way of distinguishing the importance of the diverse mechanisms. But if infection in meat could bypass the many defences of the gastroenterinal system to cause disease, it was equally plausible that the disease could be passed on when such material was injected directly into the human bloodstream.

If anything, there was every reason to suspect that 'biologicals', as they were called, could pose a greater threat than meat consumption. It is true that similarities had been noted between CJD and the disease kuru, which was said to have been acquired from cannibalistic consumption of victims of the disease by natives of the Fore tribe in New Guinea. But on the other hand, there was a well-recorded incident in the 1930s of 1,500 sheep having been infected with scrapie (the nearest animal equivalent of BSE), out of 18,000 which had been injected with a contaminated vaccine intended to protect them from a disease known as 'louping ill'.

Furthermore, in both the UK and France, CJD had occurred in some young people with growth hormone deficiency who had been given contaminated human pituitary growth hormone extract, obtained from cadavers. In France, about twenty thousand doses of the suspect hormones, taken from pituitary glands of dead bodies, had been given to children suffering from dwarfism between July 1985 and early 1986. About a thousand children had received the hormones.

Had both potential risks been discussed openly in public, it is a fair bet that when the hysteria erupted in 1996 attention would have been spread equally between beef and medicines derived from bovine material. That the focus was almost exclusively on beef owes much to the differing regulatory regimes applicable to the meat and medicines sectors, and the officials' responsibility for them. In this, the important difference between the two was that the manufacture and sale of biologicals were licensed by the government. Apart from basic production regulations – particularly those applying to slaughterhouses – meat sale was by no means as tightly regulated.

Given those differences, if BSE was transferred to humans and pharmaceuticals proved responsible, the government (and in particular the civil servants and scientists responsible for licensing) would have shared some of the blame. But if the disease was proved to be transmitted by meat, the trauma would perhaps be limited to the politicians. Blame would certainly not be attached to civil servants involved in the licensing process. Thus, while – at the very early stages of the BSE drama, when the risks were entirely unknown but either meat or 'biologicals' could have been responsible – precautionary measures should have been applied across the board with equal vigour, 'regulatory capture' ensured that officials treated the two sectors very differently.

In the meat sector, all stages of the slaughtering process were to be subject to an increasingly rigorous regulatory regime. Animal feedstuff regulation was also tightened up and substantial controls were imposed on rendering processes. From the very start, however, and throughout the whole of the growing BSE crisis, right up to and beyond the great crisis of 1996, no regulatory action was taken in the pharmaceuticals sector. What characterised the response to the potential risk from 'biologicals' was the informal nature of the action taken, the lack of urgency and the complete absence of regulation.

Crucially, the absence of overt official action, contrasted with the draconian and increasingly severe regime being applied to meat and livestock production, tended to reinforce in the public mind the potential dangers of meat. Regulation, far from increasing public confidence, tended to confirm suspicions that something was amiss.

The prisoners rattle their chains

The scene for a devastating blow on agriculture was effectively set as early as September 1987, when Department of Health officials admitted to being aware of a potential problem from BSE 'due to products for human use which contain an emulsion of bovine brain'. But, probably instinctively conscious of the effects of adverse publicity, they dismissed any prospect of a risk 'provided the brains are from clinically healthy cattle'. The culture of denial was so well established that this response could only have been expected.

Neither could the officials have been expected to pursue the issue with any particular drive. The concept of 'rocking the boat' was abhorrent to the Civil Service culture. Sleeping dogs were allowed to lie, and lie they did for over six months. It took until March 1988 for any sense of concern to percolate up to the rarefied rank of Chief Medical Officer, in the form of Sir Donald Acheson. This was the time when, on first being informed of BSE, he wrote in his diary, 'We have another plague from Egypt.' Perhaps he was thinking more about the 'biologicals', for which he and his department were ultimately responsible, than meat.

In any event, history recalls that he acted swiftly, immediately arranging a meeting with MAFF where 'particular concern was expressed at any possible risk from milk, biological products and bovine brain'. Then, when Southwood convened his committee, it was Acheson who insisted that it looked at 'material from cattle used in the preparation of biologicals'.

It was not until May, however – eight months after

Department of Health officials had been notified of a potential problem – that one of the government bodies which advised on the safety of medicines, the National Institute for Biological Standards and Controls, was asked for its opinion. The Institute, less constrained than the officials, was unequivocal in its advice. The only way their safety could be assured was if biological medicinal products were derived from cattle in areas free of the disease. It did add the caveat that BSE might pose no real threat to human health, but also noted that the information on which to base a decision was extremely sparse.

By this time the Southwood Committee was well advanced in its deliberations on the risks of BSE. A Principal Medical Officer at the DHSS who had been appointed to the committee secretariat, Dr Hillary Pickles, took up the theme of 'biologicals' and wrote to the department which ruled on the safety of medicines, the biologicals subcommittee of the Committee on the Safety of Medicines (CSM). Amazingly, the subcommittee had not yet formally discussed BSE.

Here, the much-maligned MAFF was well ahead of the game. By June 1988, the biologicals committee of the Veterinary Products Committee had already agreed to a set of guidelines for animal medicines. The CVL had recommended production of a paper on the use of pituitary glands, an urgent review of all products of bovine origin, and that the trade should be consulted about guidelines. By July, a letter to licence-holders about pituitary gland products was being planned.

By comparison, even in September – despite Dr Pickles's initiative – the Medicines Division had not responded to Southwood. Dr Pickles, a cautious civil servant, was moved to complain that BSE had only been raised informally, noting that the matter was being given low priority. She believed that the head of the Medicines Division, Dr Gerald Jones, simply did not consider the matter of 'pressing concern'.

Jones later told the BSE inquiry that he and his colleagues 'knew that there was this appalling mess in cattle with horrendous consequences for the cattle and agriculture', but their 'perception' was that the risk to human health from medicinal products was lower than the potential risk from eating meat. The potential risk from medicines was 'not regarded with the pressing concern of, for example, manufacturing defects with medicines, that could lead to the deaths of patients overnight' or 'serious adverse reactions'.

Faced with this inertia, Southwood had to take a hand, writing to Professor William Asscher, the head of the biologicals subcommittee. That was three months after Pickles had made her complaint. Although Southwood was particularly concerned about existing products, Asscher's reply was similar to that given by Jones. He and others on the medicine side were looking at hundreds of problems all the time, much more serious and pressing than BSE. Thus, by December, Pickles was telling Southwood, regarding Asscher's committee, 'I do not see anything in their recommendations that gives me any confidence that they will be taking any necessary action on existing products …'. In the third meeting of Southwood's committee, it was actually noted that the response from Professor Asscher had been 'somewhat complacent'.

While human health was treated with such leisurely disdain, progress continued on the animal front. The start of 1989 saw a meeting between officials from the CVL and the DoH to discuss a common approach for publicising guidelines on veterinary medicines, while concern was being expressed about the risks of obtaining bovine material for biologicals from overseas. It was recommended that MAFF set up a 'BSE-free Certified Herd Scheme'. However, that was for the future. There were already up to five years' supplies of vaccine made from bovine materials in stock.

It was here that the stark contrast between the attitudes to meat and medicines began to show. Perhaps alarmed at the unrestricted media speculation on the safety of meat, the officials showed their true colours. Any risk from medicines had to be played down. It was 'important', they said, 'to avoid raising public alarm that could impair vaccination programmes'.

Southwood by then was under considerable pressure to deliver his report, but he was still getting no co-operation from the CSM. He was thus forced to prepare draft conclusions and proposals without its opinion, including a provisional statement that the risk to man via medicinal products 'is remote', exactly the same view taken of meat.

With forty-three medicines using bovine products identified, all Asscher's committee could offer was a 'hope' that joint guidelines by MAFF and the Department of Health could be agreed and published. Once again, the main preoccupation was ' ...the impact on the supply of these important products whilst at the same time seeking to maintain public confidence in the vaccinations programme'. Draft guidelines made no mention of existing products.

Southwood's draft report, meanwhile, was being circulated to a tight group of officials, and it was then that the CSM finally responded, adding the comment: 'The CSM agrees with the Southwood Working Party that the risk to man from medicinal products is remote.' And it finally took some action, joining up with the Veterinary Products Committee to produce 'joint advice for manufacturers' as 'a purely precautionary measure', and 'for the sole aim of seeking to guard against what is no more than a theoretical risk to man'. Even then, Pickles had discovered that virtually none of the current essential human or animal vaccines could comply with the guidelines. She observed: ' ...and there may be several years of some vaccines in stock to make matters more difficult'.

By now it was early February, and the CSM's focus of concern shifted to the impending publication of the Southwood report. Officials were concerned that it was appearing to highlight the risk through medicines 'while relegating the qualification that any risk is remote'. Conveying the CSM's concerns, Dr Pickles told Southwood that 'public confidence in the vaccination programme must not be put in jeopardy'.

Through the evidence given to the BSE inquiry, we can now see into the inner workings of the machine. A careful solution was concocted to damp down any public fears. It was proposed that Southwood's report should state that the vaccine problem 'has been referred to the body with statutory responsibility in that area and leave it for the CSM to take appropriate action'. By any measure, a sinister fudge was in the making. And it was the potential damage, not to human health, but to the 'supply of important products such as vaccines and monoclonal antibodies for human use' which remained the main preoccupation of MAFF and Department of Health officials through early February.

Although publication of the Southwood report was imminent, Asscher's experts had still to rule on medicines safety – holding up production of the report. They finally delivered an opinion on

22 February by which time it was known that substantial stocks of potentially contaminated bovine-based vaccine were held, amounting to hundreds of thousands of doses, with up to fifteen years' supply in the pipeline.

But what the CSM's opinion amounted to was a recycling of Southwood's own words, words which had been entered as a 'stopgap' pending the CSM's own deliberations. Rather than offer its own opinion – for which it might subsequently be called to account – had it ducked the issue? The CSM had simply recorded agreement with the Southwood working party that the risk to man of infection by medicinal products was remote.

Despite Southwood's earlier entreaties, it was decided that no special action was required on any existing products. In accordance with the prearranged 'fudge', the plan was to establish a special working party to advise on the subject, thus deflecting any unwelcome attention from the media. Ministers took no part in this decision and, in subsequent meetings, appeared to have been unaware of it. Were the guidelines a 'figleaf', designed not only to fool the media but to keep ministers in the dark?

When, on 27 February 1988, the Southwood report was finally published, the sleight of hand became apparent, although unrealised. The risks from medicines appeared 'remote' and the working party recommended that the attention of the licensing authority, the Committee on the Safety of Medicines, be drawn to the emergence of BSE 'so that they can take appropriate action'. If the plan was to divert the media from focusing on medicines, it worked. The attention given to medicines and the risks posed was negligible.

Tyrrell and beyond

One of the key recommendations of Southwood was that a standing committee should be established to advise on research in relation to BSE. This was set up on the same day as the Southwood report was published, under the chairmanship of Dr David Tyrrell, then Director of the Medical Research Council's Common Cold Unit.

In mid-March, its first meeting had to confront the earlier paper produced by the National Institute for Biological

Standards and Control (NIBSC). This had stated that 'If BSE is held to be a problem, the only option is to ensure that bovine materials for the manufacture of biological medicinal products are derived from cattle in areas free of the disease'. The document was ignored.

Tyrrell's committee met again in April, and this time they considered Southwood's comments on medicinal products, in particular the proposition that there might be a remote theoretical risk of BSE being transmitted to patients through the use of injectable medicines derived from bovine materials. Additionally, the committee members had to consider the Committee on the Safety of Medicine's view that there was no reason to question the safety of existing products. Amazingly, as he later told the BSE Inquiry, Tyrrell 'felt it was a fair statement'. He may well have been influenced by the knowledge that complete replacement of bovine material was not possible.

Another member of the committee was Dr Richard Kimberlin, described as 'a distinguished virologist'. Formerly of the Neuropathogenesis Unit in Edinburgh, and 'being neither a medic nor a vet', he had been co-opted on the basis that he would bring an independent view to bear on the proceedings of the committee. Kimberlin was more forthright about the risks. He told the BSE inquiry: 'However you read the words "remote" or "theoretical", they were not sufficiently remote and theoretical that we did not need some guidelines for the protection of human and veterinary medicines.'

About this time, bowing to public concern, John MacGregor, the then agriculture minister, had proposed an extension of a recently introduced ban on offals most likely to cause infection in baby food, recommended by Southwood. On his own initiative, he had decided on a complete prohibition of their sale.

It was then that something quite extraordinary happened, something that was missed by the media then and passed unremarked when it was finally revealed to the BSE inquiry. The Department of Health actually opposed MacGregor's proposal. Its grounds for so doing confirmed to all those who cared to see it the underlying agenda of Department of Health officials. They felt such an action could 'refocus attention on bovine constituents of pharmaceuticals'. For all the opprobrium heaped on MAFF, which became the fashionable scapegoat for the whole of the BSE débâcle, it is hard to find a more blatant example of naked self-interest. Sensible precautions were being blocked for entirely cynical reasons.

A Department of Health official, Dr Jeremy Metters, who was working alongside Dr Pickles on the committee secretariat, put the issue in its true perspective. He told the BSE inquiry:

> The problem of pharmaceuticals was no different from the problem of food ... mainly that there were a very large number of people who would have already consumed pharmaceuticals, just as they had consumed food before any of the precautionary action was taken, and sadly, there was nothing whatever we could do about that, because the food had been eaten and the medicines would have been taken before any concern had been expressed.

But there was no way the officials wanted that sort of information to enter the public domain. For them, the absolute imperative was to keep medicines out of the headlines. And despite their worries about the MacGregor ban, they managed to hold the line.

Even then, cracks were appearing in the façade. In early July 1989, Southwood was apparently having second thoughts about his own report, for he wrote to Tyrrell stating: 'Personally I would have thought the possibility of human infection was moderately high if some medicinal products were made from tissues of infected animals and injected into humans.' Had he put those words in the published version of his report, there would undoubtedly have been mayhem. But he did not.

Nor was Southwood's letter passed to ministers. Kenneth Clarke, still Secretary of State for Health at the time, told the BSE inquiry that, had he known about Southwood's reservations, he would probably have ended up 'ordering withdrawal of all the batches that might be affected ...'. He was not told, and no action was taken.

So the die was cast. Despite the meat industry being burdened with massive statutory controls – and high level publicity – the pharmaceutical industry was treated with kid gloves. In September 1989, the first meeting of the CSM BSE working group agreed that companies which at present could not comply with the guidelines where cattle were UK sourced 'should be encouraged to do so as soon as possible'. Just what would have been the reaction had slaughterhouses merely been 'encouraged' to obey guidelines?

If anything, it got worse. Tyrrell's second meeting in January 1990 – by which time 10,091 cases of BSE had been declared – discussed the 'hazard-to-benefit ratio for the vaccines containing UK-sourced bovine material'. Without opening the discussion to the broader public, the assembled 'experts' decided that the benefits accruing from the continuance of the vaccine programme outweighed what had now become the 'very remote risk' to the population from the use of bovine material in these products. And entirely in keeping with the urge to downplay the risks, it was considered that 'negotiations should take place' to ensure that sources were changed as soon as possible and that existing stocks were replaced with new material 'whenever feasible'.

Interestingly, at the meeting was Bob Will, head of the CJD Surveillance Unit, the man who – with his colleague James Ironside – was to discover 'new variant' CJD and was to decide that the most probable cause was the consumption of infected beef. It was he who raised the alarm in 1996, which led Dorrell to his fateful rendezvous with the House of Commons. Also present was Dr Tyrrell. Both were parties to the decision to adopt a 'light touch'.

With that, effectively, debate on the safety of vaccines and other bovine-sourced medicines effectively disappeared. According to one official, 'there was [not] really much discussion either at SEAC[1] or elsewhere about industry compliance or indeed industry views on compliance'. Dr Jones, of the Medicines Division, had his own comment. The pharmaceutical industry was not being threatened with anything. It was just told, please change as quickly as you can – re-source the supply.

In the ensuing months and years, as beef became more and more the focus of media attention, licensed medicines were hardly mentioned. The *Guardian* – at the forefront in the coverage of BSE – only managed a brief report on 11 January 1990, when its science writer, Nigel Williams, noted in a more general article on BSE, 'the pharmaceutical industry had voiced its concerns because cattle serum was used in vaccines and other medicinal products. The Medicines Control Agency was asked to investigate.' The cover story was holding and continued to hold. Farming took the fall.

Postscript

At the height of the salmonella-in-eggs scare, on 25 January 1989, Professor Richard Lacey was summoned to the House of Commons Agriculture Committee to give his views on the crisis. As part of his submission to the Committee, he called for the creation of a new body '... independent of specific government departments to ensure that the quality of our food is satisfactory'. He cited as models the US Food and Drugs Administration (FDA) and the Center for Disease Control (the American equivalent of the Public Health Laboratory Service).

Up until then, most of the calls had been for a reorganisation of MAFF, turning it into the 'Ministry of Food and Agriculture', although some wanted a separate ministry of food. That was the line taken by Tim Lang, then of the London Food Commission. But Lacey was out on his own. He wanted an agency.

The first contemporary reference to an agency in Parliament was on 16 February 1989, at the height of the listeria scare, during a general debate on food safety. The reference came from Mr Tony Banks, MP, later sports minister. He demanded that there should be an independent 'food safety executive'. Two days later, Robin Cook, then shadow health spokesman, demanded a 'safe food' agency, independent of ministers with its own budget. The idea was picked up by Neil Kinnock, then Labour leader, in a debate on 22 February. From that moment on, it became Labour Party policy.

MacGregor, then agriculture minister, was not keen on the idea. His successor, John Selwyn Gummer, rejected it completely. On 1 October 1989, he told the *Observer*:

I am not prepared to see a situation where, in a democratic society, the safety of the food of its people is not subject to parliamentary control. I am responsible for it. Members of Parliament would not be prepared to have a situation where the Minister is not there to be blamed.

He added that it would be quite wrong for him to be able to get up in Parliament and say he was sorry about the outbreak but the food agency did not come up with the right advice.

The idea was next put to the Lords, during the debate on the Food Safety Bill, in February 1990. The House decisively rejected it. But on 25 June 1990 the Consumers Association took up the theme, in the wake of the first major BSE scare. It decided that 'consumer interest' had been pushed to the bottom of the agenda and opined that '... calls for an independent food agency not beholden to farmers and producers must be heard and acted on.'

Then, on 9 September 1990, David Clark, then Labour agriculture spokesman, announced that his party, if it won the next general election, intended to set up an independent food standards agency. Although the concept had never even been debated in the House of Commons, the die was cast.

The project remained firmly on the political agenda and, just before the 1997 general election, Mr Blair asked Professor Philip James to work on a report outlining possible structures for a new agency. But he was not asked to consider whether it would be a good idea. Nor, from an evaluation of his report, published in April 1997, compiled using facilities provided by the Consumers Association, was it evident that this expert – in animal nutrition – had any clear idea of how the food safety system worked at grass-roots level. It is difficult to see how this could have been otherwise, in an exercise that took less than nine weeks.

In effect, a major policy change, what the incoming government promised to be 'the most radical shake-up of farming and food production since the war' – with profound implications for food producers, consumers and the safety of our food – happened by default. Patrick Holden, Director of the Soil Association, described it as ' ... a sort of bandwagon that once it started to roll, everyone was saying ... [it] is a good thing. It was like a mantra that people started to repeat.'

The bandwagon turned into a steamroller. Blair's new government lost no time in producing a Food Standards Bill, which was rushed through Parliament with only token consultation. This launched an independent 'Food Standards Agency', headed by yet another world-renowned food safety expert, a zoologist by the name of John Krebs – whose PhD thesis had been on the territorial habits of woodland birds. The key task of the agency was to take over and manage the food safety functions previously handled by MAFF, including the control of the Meat Hygiene Service. Crucially, the agency was to report to the Department of Health, cutting MAFF out of the loop.

In its incarnation as the Department of Health and Social Security – before Social Security was split off to form a separate department – the DHSS had been known to its many detractors as the 'Department of Stealth and Total Obscurity'. Having so successfully 'stitched up' MAFF on the salmonella-in-eggs issue, having escaped long-lasting opprobrium for its lamentable role in the listeria affair, and having kept bovine-derived medicines out of the limelight throughout the BSE crisis, in its new guise as the 'Department of Stealth' it had assumed control over the food safety agenda, packing the ranks of the Food Standards Agency with former Department of Health officials. Truly, the fox had taken over the coop.

11. The European Disease

As if the deadly effects of the BSE crisis were not bad enough, its dynamics were to become complicated by the involvement of a new conspirator, one that had not intervened to any great extent in the previous crises, the salmonella and the listeria scares – the European Union.

Thus, with BSE – in addition to combining the destructive effects of self-interested science, incompetent and arrogant politicians, and the calculated manoeuvrings of rival bureaucrats, all of which had managed to wreak their own havoc on the farming industry – there is an additional, international culprit to add to the list of those who have so damaged British agriculture.

Although there had been earlier EU involvement, particularly in relation to preventing attempts by the German Republic to implement its own unilateral ban on British beef in 1990, from the period when BSE first emerged until March 1996 the disease was largely a domestic issue, with other member states cast in the role of concerned observers. As far as the world was concerned, BSE was a British disease.

What turned BSE into a major political crisis, and gave it its crippling EU dimension, was the official admission by a senior government minister that, despite previous denials, the disease might have been transmitted to humans. That crisis was triggered by just twenty-four crucial words – four more than needed by Edwina Currie to trigger the egg scare. They were uttered in the House of Commons on 20 March 1996 by Britain's Secretary of State for Health, Stephen Dorrell.

As we now know, his statement was based on conclusions drawn up by two government scientists, Drs Bob Will and James Ironside, both of the Edinburgh-based CJD Surveillance Unit, conveyed to the government scientific advisers, the Spongiform Encephalopathy Advisory Committee (SEAC). Will and Ironside had been reviewing disturbing evidence of cases of CJD appearing untypically in young people and had concluded that the disease with which they had been affected was so dissimilar – and, to their eyes, novel – that it warranted the description 'new variant'. Without anything even approaching hard evidence, they immediately associated this apparently novel finding with the continuing cattle epidemic and advised their SEAC colleagues accordingly. With only hours to prepare what was to be the most important speech of his political life, Dorrell took his scientists' opinions at face value. 'While there is no direct evidence of a link' he told a packed House, 'the most likely explanation is that these cases may be linked to exposure to BSE.'

The entirely predictable effect of Dorrell's statement, in the neurotic health-and-safety-conscious mood of our time, was to unleash pandemonium. As Christopher Booker and I wrote in *The Castle of Lies*, it was like throwing a lighted match into a sea of petrol. In the first few days after Dorrell's statement, hysteria knew no bounds. Newspapers such as the *Observer* projected crazed, apocalyptic visions of Britain in 2015, with thousands of Britons dying every week from CJD, the Channel Tunnel blocked off and Britain totally isolated from the world. Apparently sober scientists solemnly agreed on television that the number of victims might well rise to half a million. Beef sales plummeted, not just in Britain but all over Europe.

It was that effect, whereby a British scare had broken out of its national confines and had caused serious damage to consumer confidence in other countries, particularly those closest to us, which brought a domestic issue onto the international stage. As one member state after another imposed bans on imports of beef from Britain, something which they were not entitled to do under EU law, the European Commission was forced to concede that the momentum was unstoppable.

On 26 March, the Commission's special 'regulatory committee', the Standing Veterinary Committee (SVC), imposed an EU-wide ban, extending to live animals, sperm and embryos, and meat from cattle slaughtered in Britain. It also included medicinal, pharmaceutical and cosmetic products. Of the fifteen members, the vote had been 14-1 for, only Britain voting against. Keith Meldrum, Britain's representative on the committee, condemned the decision as 'rushed, unscientific and completely disproportionate'. He was supported by Prime Minister John

Major, who announced that it was 'well beyond any action justified by the available scientific evidence'. Later, in a call to
Jacques Santer, the Commission President, he persuaded the
Commission to reconvene a meeting of EU officials to hear the
views of Britain's Chief Medical Officer, now Kenneth Calman,
and a leading expert on BSE.

But what had particularly shocked the British – and especially
many Conservative MPs – was that the EU ban extended not
only to trade with member states but also to trade with the rest
of the world. Although students of the EU were completely
familiar with its powers, it is a measure of the fantasy world in
which so many MPs lived that they had been unaware that the
EU actually had the power to do this. Their sense of shock and
outrage was palpable.

There was also confusion in Brussels. Within seventeen hours
of announcing its ban, the European Commission withdrew it,
having discovered that the SVC did not have the power to make
the ban. But the Commission readopted it that day, after hearing
Calman and other experts. A Dutch agriculture ministry official
at the talks, having listened to Calman, said 'There was very
little we hadn't heard before. There was no reason to change our
decision.' But the Commission did make provision for the co-
financing of compensation for eradication, promising a review of
the situation in six weeks. With some restraint, Meldrum said he
was 'very disappointed'.

'Disappointment', if anything, was a classic example of British
understatement. Agriculture minister Douglas Hogg now had a
very serious problem. Following Dorrell's announcement, he had
announced a raft of new controls which, he claimed, would further reduce the minimal risk which remained after the
implementation of the original controls in 1989 and subsequently, aimed at removing material which might convey BSE to
humans.

With that, the whole Cabinet, up to and including Prime
Minister John Major, had gone into 'damage limitation mode',
intent on reducing the economic damage and bringing the scare
to a swift conclusion. But with EU intervention, there was not
only the British public to reassure. There was also the
Commission and the Council of the European Union. And, as
long as the ban remained in place, this provided stark evidence

that there were still doubts about the safety of British beef. Those doubts would make it even harder for the government to convince domestic consumers that they should resume their normal eating patterns. On top of that, it was vital that Britain's beef exports should be resumed. Not only were they worth £550 million a year, they soaked up a great deal of surplus beef, which helped maintain domestic prices at healthy levels.

As it happened, only a week after the EU had imposed its ban, Douglas Hogg was due to visit Luxembourg for a routine meeting of the EU Agriculture Council, at which other EU agriculture ministers would be present. This was Hogg's opportunity to persuade them, face to face, that the ban should be lifted. To do so, Hogg and his officials came up with a plan that was to precipitate a new act in the unfolding tragedy, almost as disastrous as Dorrell's statement itself.

The plan was based on part of the advice the SEAC scientists had given Dorrell, to the effect that BSE was most likely to appear in older cattle. To be absolutely on the safe side, they had therefore recommended that meat from cattle over thirty months old should only be sold for human consumption after it had been taken off the bone and some specific tissues had been removed. Not for a moment had the scientists suggested that this meat would not then be perfectly safe to eat. In response, Hogg's officials had drawn up an emergency regulation under the Food Safety Act, ordering meat from such animals to be withheld from sale until arrangements were in place for its deboning and trimming in specially licensed cutting plants.

But such was the madness of the time that, on 25 March, the then President of the NFU, Sir David Naish, had informed Hogg that supermarket representatives had told him they had had 'no confidence' in their ability to sell meat from older cattle. They wanted meat from animals over thirty months old to be removed from the food chain altogether. Fatally, Hogg and his officials now seized on this as a way out of the mess they were in with the EU.

On 1 April, Hogg arrived in Luxembourg, looking woebegone in his shabby raincoat and fedora, for what turned out to be the most humiliating meeting with the European 'partners' any British minister had ever attended. He presented his officials' plan for the destruction of all thirty-month-old British cattle, proposing that their carcases should be rendered and disposed of, probably by incineration. Commission officials and the other ministers listened with barely concealed impatience, but agreed that, if this was what the British government wanted to do, they would accept it. Since the scheme would be hugely expensive – involving the destruction of an estimated three million cattle over three years, costing £2,400 million – they even agreed to 'co-finance' it.

Two weeks later Commission Regulation 716/96/EEC was issued, authorising the financing of Britain's 'Cattle Disposal Scheme'. Headlines proclaimed that the EU was generously 'coming to Britain's aid'. But the ghost of Fontainebleau was abroad. Much of the money paid would then be clawed back from Britain's budget rebate. In the end British taxpayers would be paying 85 per cent of the total, nearly £2,000 million.

The most astonishing aspect of all was that the scheme was only offered in the hope that it might persuade the EU to lift its ban. But it was regarded by the other member states as com-pletely irrelevant. Before they would even consider lifting the ban, they wanted a mass selective slaughter of herds in which BSE had been found – the so-called 'selective cull'. The plan to destroy millions of healthy cattle, most of which had been nowhere near BSE, was just a private sideshow.

Thus the unfolding tragedy moved into its third stage. It soon became apparent that the British officials had given no thought at all as to how to carry out their 'Cattle Disposal Scheme'. Astonishingly, they did not even have the legal powers to proceed with their plan. The Food Safety Act only authorised them to prevent food being offered for sale when there was a genuine risk to public health. The Animal Health Act 1981 only authorised them to kill animals when this was to control dis-ease. And the only purpose of this present scheme was to destroy perfectly healthy animals, posing no risk to the public, purely as a public relations exercise to 'restore consumer confi-dence' – shades of the slaughter scheme for laying hens, seven years previously.

Nevertheless, no MPs seemed to notice this startling fact, and amid scenes of indescribable chaos and confusion, the officials slowly put together a scheme which was in fact largely organised for them by a handful of large abattoir operators in the Federation of Fresh Meat Wholesalers. The task of slaughtering

25,000 animals a week was allocated to just twenty big industrial abattoirs, which were to be paid three times the normal commercial rate for killing the cattle.

Although after protests another twenty-one smaller firms were later added to the scheme, more than 350 of Britain's slaughterhouses were excluded, at a time when they were struggling to survive because of the loss of business caused by the BSE crisis. When the largest abattoir in Europe, Manchester Meat Market, offered to take part in the scheme at a third of the rate being given to the select few insiders, its offer was ignored. While the chosen handful of firms enjoyed an unparalleled bonanza – between them they were earning excess profits at a rate of £2 million a week – hundreds of their smaller competitors feared the BSE crisis would drive them out of business.

Inevitably, with such mountains of public money being thrown at it, this scheme gave rise to every kind of racket. But what was truly obscene was that, with 25,000 healthy cattle being destroyed each week, huge quantities of the finest and safest meat in the world were going up in smoke for no purpose at all. Although beef sales in Britain were recovering, particularly in country areas, there was no way in which the sight on television of this continual slaughter could help to 'restore consumer confidence'. Any idea that this might make a favourable impression on the Continent, where beef sales had fallen much farther than they had in Britain (in Greece the BSE crisis added half a per cent to the cost of living in a month), was the sheerest wishful thinking.

At the end of May, Mr Major suddenly gave vent to his government's growing frustration with the startling announcement that Britain intended to conduct a policy of 'non-cooperation' with the EU until it was prepared to make concessions on lifting the worldwide export ban. For four weeks, the rest of the EU stared in amazement as British ministers and officials solemnly vetoed every item of business which came up. The agenda of one meeting after another ground to a halt, as Britain put a stop to more than sixty-five proposals for legislation.

This so-called 'beef war' was intended to bring Britain's partners to their senses before the next summit meeting in Florence at the end of June. The hope was that they could be persuaded to abandon their proposal for the 'selective cull', which the British government insisted made no scientific sense, and to put forward a firm timetable for the lifting of the ban.

But when the prime ministers announced in Florence the deal they had arrived at, it became glaringly obvious that Britain's policy of non-cooperation had achieved nothing. The EU had forced Mr Major to accept the 'selective cull' of up to 147,000 cattle. These were mainly productive dairy cows, whose slaughter would have dealt a devastating blow to many of Britain's dairy farmers. In return the EU had given vague indications that, once this new mass slaughter programme was under way, further consideration might be given to a relaxation of the ban. Mr Major's 'beef war' had been nothing but petulant play-acting, which had made Britain's position in Europe more humiliating than ever.

Through the late summer months the unresolved dispute remained in a state of total impasse. The government already quietly realised that it would have great difficulty forcing through Parliament the new legislation required for any 'selective cull' scheme. The UK's European partners, led by the Germans, had, if anything, only hardened their position still further.

The only good fortune for the British government was that, thanks to an almost complete lack of interest the media, the British people still remained largely unaware of the shambles surrounding the Cattle Disposal Scheme, although many better-off households would be contributing hundreds of pounds in taxes to pay for the fiasco. The rendering plants were unable to keep up with the numbers. The backlog of hundreds of thousands of animals awaiting pointless destruction scarcely diminished, as thousands more cattle passed the thirty-month threshold every week.

Already this vast catastrophe had cost tens of thousands of jobs in and around the meat and dairy industries. It had forced thousands of businesses to the edge of bankruptcy and had already claimed more victims through desperate farmers committing suicide than 'new variant' CJD. But now the tragedy moved into its fourth stage with the approach of autumn, as the grass in the fields stopped growing. Throughout the summer, farmers had been able to keep vast numbers of animals out in those fields, waiting in the queue for destruction, kept alive by nature. But the moment was approaching when they would have to start paying to feed those cattle through the winter, at up to £10 a week for each animal.

When Stephen Dorrell uttered his twenty-four fateful words in March, Devon beef farmer Richard Haddock had a thousand animals worth £1 million on his 850-acre farm. Over the following six months, he would normally have expected to make £200,000 from sales. But because of the chaos surrounding the Cattle Disposal Scheme, only three animals had moved off his land. He now had to face the prospect of paying out £10,000 a week to feed his herd, when his income was nil and his bank manager could see no point in lending money to pay to feed cattle which were in effect worthless. Thousands of other farmers were facing the same crisis, many imagining that they would have no alternative but to leave their animals to starve to death in the fields.

So long as this hidden crisis remained unresolved, there was no way the British government could agree to the demand for another mass slaughter, which would simply pile more animals into a system already at breaking-point. In mid-September Hogg made another forlorn attempt to tell his fellow farm ministers that 'new research' had shown that BSE was dying out naturally, and by 2001 would have disappeared. They should 'rest on the science' and accept that their proposed cull was pointless. The EU ministers stared in disbelief, telling him politely they would 'consider' his new research. But meanwhile they rejected any prospect of their ban being lifted. On 19 September 1996, the British Cabinet decided it had no alternative but to call off the cull unilaterally.

The European Union Commission was immediately informed of this outcome, leaving the beef industry facing the possibility of an export ban until the next century. *Private Eye*'s 'New Muckspreader' observed that Major had little choice but to abandon the cull. With a backlog of more than 120,000 cattle over thirty months old, there was no spare capacity to deal with another 147,000 thrown up by the selective cull scheme. For whatever reason, Major's climb-down at Florence had been to no effect. The deal appeared to be dead in the water. Two days after the announcement, the *Daily Telegraph* published a report headed 'Farmer in BSE cash trap took own life'. After losing money on every head of cattle he had sold, Brian Elgar, fifty-three, had killed himself the day after attending a market. His body had been found in his car at a National Trust carpark near Godalming, Surrey. Mr Elgar had tied a plastic bag over his head and suffocated.

By the end of October, more than 600,000 cattle over thirty months old had been destroyed 'to restore confidence in beef', but this had failed to persuade the EU that Britain had gone far enough to ensure that British beef was safe. The UK's façade began to crumble. Hogg, after a visit to Luxembourg to see his EU counterparts, hinted that the British government would, after all, consider a 'limited' selective cull if it meant an end to the ban. Nevertheless, he stressed that the question of Britain going ahead with the full-blown cull was 'not on the agenda'.

In the event, despite well over a million thirty-month-old cattle being slaughtered, the Conservative administration was never able to achieve the resumption of exports. It took an incoming Labour government to reopen negotiations, by which time the ante had increased beyond all recognition. A database had to be kept, with details of all cattle in the UK, accompanied by a massively burdensome scheme of issuing 'passports' for all cattle. Each animal had to be 'double-tagged' with a bright yellow label in each ear. Then an 'extended' cull was introduced, conceding the full 147,000 cattle slaughter demanded at Florence, together with an additional 11,000 calves born to cows that had subsequently contracted BSE.

And a new phrase was added to the farming lexicon: the 'date-based export scheme'. Negotiations centred around lifting the ban only for animals born after 1 August 1996, when Hogg's additional BSE control measures had come into force. By early 1988, however, negotiations were drifting as it became clear that the 'restricted' cull was degenerating into a farce. Only 63,000 cattle had been specifically killed under the programme, with another 12,000 'understood' to be awaiting slaughter. But 49,000 cattle had 'gone missing' and a further forty-five suspect cattle were 'proving hard to track down'. Jeff Rooker, Labour's new junior agriculture minister, was nevertheless confident that the cull would be completed by the autumn, with a total of 80,000 cattle slaughtered – some 67,000 less than anticipated total of 147,000.

Even then, it took the European Union Commission until November 1998 to lift the ban, and it attached such draconian conditions that only a minuscule amount of beef could be exported. Not only were there the age restrictions, but farmers had to supply 'verified, positive, official evidence' that dams of the animals presented for slaughter had survived for six months after their calves had been born. Since there was no single database containing the evidence, gathering the necessary information was so cumbersome that less than half of the animals submitted could be accepted.

But that was the least of it. Abattoirs doing the killing had to be specially adapted and had to be dedicated exclusively to export slaughter. Ludicrously stringent and expensive veterinary checks had to be imposed. Unsurprisingly, only three abattoirs applied for the scheme – and then only under considerable government pressure – one each in Scotland, England and Northern Ireland. English farmers had to truck their cattle all the way to Cornwall to have them killed. So expensive were the slaughtering requirements that one company 'did the sums on processing 1000 cattle a week' and estimated their losses at between £0.5m and £1m a year.

To cap it all, despite the removal of the ban, the French refused to comply with the EU decision and continued to exclude British beef, thus depriving exporters of their most valuable market. The Commission, after some delay, referred France to the European Court of Justice. Then, before the case had been determined, foot and mouth disease struck the UK. With all meat and livestock exports banned, Britain once again was unable to export its beef.

Postcript

In June 1997 an illegal beef-smuggling operation was discovered in Belgium, through which some 1,600 tons of British beef had been sent to various countries, including Egypt, Russia and Germany. Then, in August 1997, German officials intercepted 600 tons of British beef with fake Irish labels. As a result, the EU Commission, on 12 November 1997, commenced against the UK 'infringement procedures', concerning its 'failure to maintain the level of veterinary control in meat plants and cold stores required by community legislation'.

The key to this was to increase supervision in order to reduce the possibility of smuggling, but the Commission justified its action in broader terms, adding, 'This inadequate supervision does not merely have consequences for the respect of the general public and animal health matters covered by EU legislation but also for the particular problem of enforcement of EU legislation concerning BSE – i.e., beef-smuggling'. Thus, because some firms which cut up meat (cutting plants) had been participating in a highly organised and secretive beef smuggling operation, the EU demanded that veterinary inspection of all cutting plants in the UK be increased.

One of those cutting plants was Graig Farm Organics, owned by Bob and Carolyn Kennard and based in Llandrindod Wells in Powys. It was started when they returned from ten years working in tropical agriculture in 1988. They say they were struck by the blandness of British meat, and appalled at some of the developments in intensive livestock farming in the UK.

Their initial plan was 'to produce chickens which tasted like chickens, and which were reared with compassion'. After some trials, they developed suitable systems and the chickens started to sell. Customers then started asking for similarly reared lamb, beef and pork. At this point, the Kennards concluded that the only standard which could not be debased was organic, and from then on this was the standard they used. As well as chicken, they started processing lamb, mutton, beef, and so the range grew.

As their business prospered, they had to expand beyond what could be produced on the farm, and the co-operative Graig Farm Producers Group was developed. Using locally killed meat, all the butchery and processing were carried out in new processing facilities on the farm, using a team of expert butchery staff 'to achieve and maintain our high standards'.

The official supervision at that time amounted to a veterinary surgeon from the Meat Hygiene Service (MHS) making quarterly visits to the cutting plant but, because of the Commission's action, it had to be increased. As an interim measure, the vet started calling weekly, but it was planned that daily visits would start as soon as the MHS could assemble the necessary manpower.

On the full regime, Kennard's fees were due to increase from a nominal £300 a year to a massive £20,000. Yet he handled only two carcases of beef a week. Effectively, he would be paying £200 a carcase for inspection, up from £4. When he wrote to protest, he received a standard reply from an official in the Welsh office, saying: '... the changes are being put in place to meet current legal requirements ...' and '... as the increase in supervision is a matter of National Policy I regret I am unable to make any exception'.

In a subsequent letter from the Welsh Office, an official wrote, 'This measure ... is essential if a European Court case is to be avoided, to improve control over meat in licensed cutting plants, and support the Government's efforts to lift the beef ban for the whole of the UK.'

Kennard was not on his own. All over the UK, meat firms were being subjected to an enormous regulatory 'blitz' to ensure that every last dot and comma of EU legislation was being observed. So sensitive was the government that it feared, with good cause, that any transgression would be seized upon as an excuse not to lift the export ban. For the privilege of allowing three firms to sell beef abroad at a considerable loss, the whole industry had to pay a very high price.

12. The Integrationalists

On 12 January 2000, to a crowded room of journalists in the heart of the European Union quarter in Brussels, consumer protection commissioner David Byrne unveiled with a flourish the much-awaited Commission White Paper on Food Safety. Included in its annex were no less than eighty-four proposals for new, and amendments to existing, Community legislation. Just one of those dealt with the establishment of a European Food Authority, and all of them, in combination, represented a major increase in the power of the EU.

While the Commission focused attention, through its press releases and its presentations, on the European Food Authority, few journalists, much less politicians, read the small print. Had they done so, they would have found that a key part of Byrne's proposals was seven specific measures aimed at tightening the controls on animal feedstuffs. So onerous were they that one feed manufacturer declared that the standards for producing animal feed would differ little, in substance, from those applied to food for human consumption. The cost implications were horrendous and threatened to inflate the price hard-pressed farmers already had to pay for their feed, and by an astronomic degree.

But what was even worse was that these provisions, ostensibly devised for the protection of public health, were anything but. Feedstuffs, in the wake of BSE and salmonella, were already tightly regulated. The additional provisions were in fact a cynical, populist demonstration of the willingness of the EU to respond to 'public concerns', thus proving the value to the 'citizens of Europe' of the 'European dimension' of food safety.

To legitimise its populist and self-serving gesture, the Commission was relying on particular events which in 1999 had shaken consumer confidence to the core in continental Europe, which, hitherto, had believed food scares were an 'English disease'. Those events, best known as the 'Belgian dioxin crisis', in addition to creating the climate for a massive lurch forward in regulation, were also to destroy the reputation of Belgian food and cost its industry some $1.5 billion.

Although explored by the Belgian Parliament, the real story has never been fully told to a British audience, its two-hundred-page report being available only in French and Dutch.[1] However, from this report, contemporary press accounts and interviews with some of the key players, emerges a tale of criminal conspiracy, corruption, official confusion and incompetence, all stoked by political opportunism. Little that should have been learned from the events was learned, and the Commission's attempt to grab more powers cannot be justified by what actually happened. Yet its actions were to qualify it as yet another contributor to British agriculture's decline.

The Belgian dioxin crisis

The events which were to have such a cataclysmic effect began some time between 19 and 26 January 1999, when a Belgian fat-processing firm, NV Verkest, situated near the city of Ghent, made at least four batches of material, described as 'animal fats', destined for use in chicken rations. But the material also contained an ingredient described as 'technical oil', which was actually used cooking oil collected by a firm called Fogra from sites around northern Europe. Though this was unknown at the time, it had been contaminated with transformer oil, containing both PCBs and dioxins, dumped – accidentally or otherwise, we will never know – into a vessel containing the used cooking oil.

One of the firms which received a contaminated batch was a feed compounder in the north-east of Belgium by the name of NV De Brabander. Its customers were large-scale poultry breeders, producing eggs from which table fowl were hatched, and it was for them that feed was produced containing the dioxin/PCB contaminants. Soon after the feed had been delivered, the breeders noticed reduced laying in their hens. Later on hens started to die and eggs failed to hatch.

Unusually, some day-old chicks which survived also appeared to be suffering from a nervous condition, so complaints were made to De Brabander. These were referred to the company nutritionist, Jan Van Ginderachter, who started looking for possible causes of the problem. All his early tests proved negative but, as the situation developed, the company insurers were notified and the destruction of all the day-old chicks coming from the affected companies was arranged.

By the end of February, despite intensive investigations, no solution had been found, so the insurers appointed a well-known veterinary surgeon, Dr André Destickere, to assist. But he also had a 'day job'. Dr Destickere was head of the local Institut d'Expertise Vétérinaire (IEV), the government agency which, on behalf of the Ministry of Public Health, inspected meat and poultry in slaughterhouses and processing plants and enforced hygiene laws. Thus Destickere, who was to play a crucial role in the developing crisis, was 'moonlighting'.

Despite Destickere's involvement, it was Van Ginderachter who made the first breakthrough when he found that some birds had received continuous doses of the suspect feed and were suffering from symptoms which could have been caused by wheat contaminated by disinfectants or pesticides. On 8 March, he contacted the Belgian Ministry of Agriculture, telling them of his concerns. The Ministry did not react.

Suspicions of dioxin

It was then that Van Ginderachter recalled a scientific article linking the condition he had observed with dioxin exposure. On 17 March he met a nutritionist working for another feed producer and found that this firm not only had the same problems but had also used material from Verkest. He resolved to send samples to a Dutch laboratory, known as the RIKILT,[2] for dioxin analysis.

The very next day, Van Ginderachter again contacted the Ministry of Agriculture, speaking this time to the director of a department called DG4. He told him that he suspected Verkest of supplying dioxin-contaminated material. But the Ministry was indifferent. It simply dismissed the problem as a 'commercial matter'. Nevertheless, responding to a request from Dr Destickere, DG4's director did tell his technicians to inspect Verkest. Amazingly, he did not take any other action.[3] Nor did he inform the head of DG5, the department of his own ministry which dealt with diseases in animals.

When the technicians visited Verkest, they took samples but

did not think to send them for dioxin testing. Instead, these were analysed in their own laboratory for a variety of other things. And while the technicians messed about, there was a 'ticking time bomb' in the making. Some of the contaminated poultry feed had been returned to the compounders where, instead of being destroyed, it had been remixed to make batches of pig feed. The circle of contamination was getting wider and wider.

Meanwhile, scientists at the RIKILT were at work, but such is the nature of dioxin testing that it took the laboratory until Wednesday 21 April to report finding dioxin, and two days more to notify the complete results. Dioxin levels were so high as to be almost unbelievable, so the laboratory retested. When the results were confirmed, their worst fears were realised. Between 781 and 958 parts per trillion of dioxins had been found in the samples – more than 1,500 times the legal limit. De Brabander immediately warned Dr Destickere and, on Monday 26 April, DG4 was told the bad news.

At last, the Ministry started to take note. After languishing in its laboratories for over a month, its samples were sent to the RIKILT for dioxin analysis and the director of DG4 was informed. So, for the first time, were the veterinary services at DG5. An action plan was drawn up, including a strategy to trace companies that might have received contaminated feed. But even then the first working list did not become available until 30 April, when work started in earnest – nearly six weeks after Van Ginderachter had warned the Ministry of his suspicions. Still no feed companies were closed down.

The 'Note Destickere'

Incredibly, neither of the Ministry of Health's two food safety inspectorates, nor the IEV, were told of the situation until 27 April. DG4 officials assumed that Dr Destickere would tell the IEV what was happening, and thus indirectly the other departments.[4] Crucially, however, the chief administrator of one of the inspectorates did receive on 28 April a 'note' from Dr Destickere. This 'Note Destickere' was to become a linchpin in the ensuing drama. It was also faxed to the Minister of Public Health the same day[5] but, despite being asked to send it on to the Ministry of Agriculture, Destickere did not do so.

The Note itself comprised a detailed history of the facts and Destickere's personal observations. He concluded that contaminated fats had ended up in laying hens and broiler chicks via their feed, that contaminated chicks had entered the food chain via slaughterhouses, and that their recycled remains were a secondary source of contamination. Destickere also reported that part of the fat had been included in feed intended for pigs.

Back at DG4, action was still being taken with glacial slowness. Instead of hitting the panic button, on 30 April the department decided to take official samples from De Brabander and Huys. Even with all the evidence flooding in, the director was still sceptical about dioxin contamination. Not until 4 May did he close down some of the companies involved. Then more samples were taken and two more companies were closed down. And, at last, the IEV started to work out a containment strategy. More meetings were arranged in the following days and faxes started flowing between ministries and departments. Almost incredibly, though, the IEV did not actually receive any lists from the Ministry of Agriculture of companies rearing laying hens until 17 May, and then they were incomplete and vague. Nevertheless, nineteen companies were closed during the period 17-21 May.

A turn for the worse

On 21 May, the growing crisis took another turn for the worse. The Ministry of Agriculture received from the RIKILT a positive dioxin result from its De Brabander sample, and three more on 26 May. These strongly indicated that the problem was more extensive than at first thought. Analysis showed high levels of dioxin in breeder hens and eggs. Only on that day were all the companies identified by the tracing operation finally closed down, a full two months since the Ministry had been warned of possible dioxin contamination.

Too late, the government departments were at last beginning to realise the scale of the problem. An immediate crisis meeting was called between the various ministry departments. Public Health took over tracing contaminated meat; Agriculture took responsibility for eggs. But then a fatal mistake was made. A press release had been prepared earlier, in which only feed contamination was mentioned. Jointly, the ministers for Agriculture and Public Health decided to publish it. The omission of any mention of contaminated meat fuelled, in the words of the parliamentary inquiry, 'suspicions that ministers were deliberately attempting to play down the growing crisis'. Those 'suspicions' reached fever pitch the next day when health minister Marcel Colla recommended the removal of chickens and eggs from sale.

In an attempt to remedy the fatal omission, two short, low-key press releases were issued, one from each minister. After saying that the removal of chicken and eggs from supermarket shelves was just a temporary safety precaution until the Ministry of Agriculture could absolutely guarantee they were safe to eat, the Ministry for Public Health sought to reassure consumers. But the releases, instead of reassuring, caused consternation.

Political exploitation

It was then that politics took a hand. A general election was looming and Belgium was ruled by a weak centre-left – and increasingly unpopular – coalition government headed by Prime Minister Jean-Luc Dehaene. It was expected to have a bitter fight on its hands against challenger Senator Guy Verhofstadt, head of the opposition Vlaamse Liberalen en Democraten (VLD) party. Conscious of the electoral implications of the crisis, Dehaene took personal charge. He cancelled a scheduled EU meeting in Luxembourg and instructed his two ministers to submit a full report to him. He personally contacted the trade federations in the sectors affected, asking them to draw up lists of companies which could be implicated in the crisis. With comparisons being made with the BSE scare, Dehaene then went on television, fighting to defuse a crisis which had reached epic proportions.

Amid the furore, the EU had been forgotten. It was not until 28 May that the EU Commission discovered what was going on – from the media. DGXXIV (later DG SANCO) officials contacted the Belgian government and asked for formal details, which were forthcoming later that day. Dehaene's action in cancelling the European meeting also had important repercussions. It indicated to the Commission that a very serious crisis had broken out.[6]

About to take centre stage, however, was Dr Destickere. Not

only was he a public official and head of the local IEV, he was also, as he later told the Belgian parliamentary inquiry, 'proud to be a member of a liberal union' and a member of the VLD. When, on 27 May, health minister Colla had published his press release, apparently seeking to downplay the dioxin risks, Destickere was said to have been 'very indignant'. Despite his official position, he indirectly faxed his 'Note' to Verhofstadt. It reached him two days later, the fax header having been removed.

With the Note in his hands, Verhofstadt waited until an evening press conference on Monday 31 May to ambush the agriculture and public health ministers. Then he discovered that Dehaene was unaware of the Note. He arranged a meeting and gave it to him. Dehaene was stunned. Given the previous events, this was entirely understandable. According to the subsequent parliamentary inquiry,

> The first sentence of the Note Destickere gives an account of a very serious case which indicated unquestionable dioxin contamination in poultry meat and finished products intended for human consumption, the rate being 1,500 times higher than the standard applicable to chicken fat. It is moreover clearly a question of a toxic product and Dr Destickere affirms that it is about a problem affecting the whole breeding sector.

Crucially, the inquiry noted that agriculture minister Karel Pinxten and health minister Colla had said nothing about these risks. But there was more to it than that. Many suspected that Destickere was exaggerating in order to divert attention from his 'moonlighting' and to promote his own research interests. Of Destickere, the parliamentary inquiry found:

> There was obviously a conflict of interest ... on the one hand between his obligation of notification as a public health official and on the other hand his duty of discretion as an expert. There also was conflict between the interests of the public health that the civil servant must defend the inherent financial interests of the insurance company.

It concluded:

The behaviour of Dr Destickere is unacceptable and clearly gave place to a certain number of infringements; additionally, it is manifest that there was confusion of interests.

The inquiry also noted:

Dr Destickere's note was disclosed to the media at a time when the public, not without foundation, believed that ministers had minimised the crisis.

The effect of the publication of the Note was to intensify the crisis, lending apparent credibility to claims of a cover-up. Verhofstadt admitted later that it had 'seriously harmed the general interest of the country'. In fact, purely electoral interests had encouraged him to make it public. But it was not only his interests which were advanced. The Green parties, with eleven seats in the Belgian Parliament, were looking to increase their numbers. They seized upon the issue with zeal, accusing the government of delaying action despite knowing about the contamination for about a month. Such was the outcry that, on 1 June, the health and agriculture ministers were forced to resign. In measured tones, the parliamentary inquiry reported:

The resignation of the two ministers had a manifest effect on the later management of the crisis. Their resignation clearly confirmed that there was a serious problem, which had been underestimated in previous months. The responsible ministers assumed the political responsibility for it.

The next day, acting EU farm commissioner Franz Fischler criticised the Belgian government for not informing the Commission of the problem as soon as it had known about it. The same day, the Commission extended the ban imposed by the Belgian government to the whole of the EU.

By 3 June, there was much speculation on the resignations. The French newspaper *Le Monde* accused Dehaene of acting because his ministers had badly underestimated the extent of the risk and, with the elections in the offing, of trying to protect himself. But most significantly, the previous day a 'weekly magazine' had condemned the two ministers and revealed that Colla had been about to suspend the licence of Destickere, 'the expert who had told the departments of health and agriculture of the risk of contamination on 26 April'. The cover-up legend was growing. Destickere, twisting the knife, told the media, 'I have the impression that the first goal of the ministers was not to inform the population.'

Predictably, the crisis continued to escalate. Dehaene – just five days before the election – was forced to hold a defensive news conference to reassure the public. His action was in vain. Known as the 'plumber' for his ability to fix problems, Dehaene was unable to fix this one. On 13 June 1999, two weeks into the crisis, his government suffered a massive defeat in the general election. He promptly resigned and a new coalition government was formed under the leadership of Guy Verhofstadt.

EU action

On 21 June the European Commission launched legal proceedings against the Belgian government for failing to inform its EU partners of the contamination as soon as it had been confirmed in April. The allegations of a cover-up had become official. And towards the end of July, the EU Commission was proposing a ban on the use of recycled fats in animal feeds. The regulators were moving in.

The irony was that there had been no significant health threat. Although high levels in animal feed had been detected, the dilution effect by the time animal products were consumed, combined with the limited dose, was such that consumer exposure had been minimal. Many people boycotted pig and poultry meat and substituted fish and fish products. However, because of industrial pollution in the North Sea, there are significant background levels of dioxins in these foods. Those who increased their fish consumption would have also increased their dioxin intakes.

But the final irony was that the dioxin contamination had only been picked up owing to the persistence of Jan Van Ginderachter and because his company, De Brabander, had retained samples of its feed, in accordance with 'good manufacturing practice'. Had the firm not kept samples, there would have been nothing to test and the episode would have been written off as 'just one of those things'. Furthermore, the dioxin contamination would have passed unnoticed if PCB/dioxins had not been used in feed intended for chickens. The poultry, very sensitive to dioxins, acted as 'biological sentinels'. If the contamination had been limited to feed intended for pigs, it would undoubtedly never have been noticed.

As to the Commission's proposed ban on recycled fat in animal feedstuffs, it is now clear that the whole incident arose from a single contamination episode, possibly a criminal adulteration of fats used for recycling and incorporation into animal feed, and was exacerbated by opportunist politicians seeking to gain electoral advantage, supported by the dubious – and illegal – actions of a public official. Added to that were the unnecessary delays in commencing the investigations, and the institutional incompetence of the ministries involved. A spokesman for the French feed-makers' association observed, 'Accidents or fraud can take place in any raw material. You can't stop them happening by banning reprocessed fats in feed.'

The Commission's action threatened the livelihoods of a number of well-founded and perfectly reputable fat processors. Furthermore, it created a disposal problem. Fats and oils – such as waste cooking oil from restaurants – which formerly had an economic value – were now a liability, incurring collection and disposal charges. And to replace the fat in animal feed, greater use would have to be made of fish oil meal, increasing pressure on a scarce resource and adding to overall food costs.

But the damage had been done. On 28 September 1999, David Byrne first suggested extending the list of prohibited substances used in animal feed. 'It is in the interests of everybody that agreement is urgently reached on stricter measures to limit or remove from the food chain substances and residues which are dangerous to human health,' he said.

What, in particular, emerges from the way the authorities handled the crisis is the lack of communication between departments. This must owe something to the fragmented structure of the Belgian food control system, which allocates responsibility for meat and meat products to one department and general food inspection to another department in the Ministry of Health, while the inspection of animal feedstuffs and animal health issues is dealt with by another two departments in the Ministry of Agriculture. Had the various departments been working more effectively (or been united), action could have been taken much earlier, and perhaps the public crisis could have been averted. Even then, had the IEV been acting effectively, the problem could have been picked up much earlier. Being responsible for meat and poultry inspection in slaughterhouses and processing plants, IEV officials were generating data on animals and poultry declared unfit and seized during production. Also, details of appearance, signs of disease and average weight were recorded. The monthly figures were collected by the local services and sent to the central administration, where, according to the parliamentary inquiry, 'these data were not treated in an adequate way on the statistical level'. Information was in fact under-exploited. Even a superficial analysis of the figures would have shown that there had been an increase in cases which could have been attributable to dioxin contamination.

All of this, however, escaped popular attention. The parliamentary inquiry held by the Belgian Chamber of Deputies reported only in March 2000. By 22 July 1999, Mr Bart Staes of the Green/ALE Party was telling the European Parliament, in words that were to be echoed during the British foot and mouth epidemic, that the crisis was:

> ... the result of a defective system, an erroneous Common Agricultural Policy that plunges farmers into a vicious circle of producing ever-increasing amounts ever more cheaply, investing ever more heavily, having ever larger scales of operation which must be farmed ever more intensively. Quantity takes precedence over quality.[7]

The 'beneficial crisis'

If the real cause of the crisis, apart from the initial criminal act of polluting the recycled cooking oil with transformer oil, had been the inadequacy of the Belgian authorities and their failure to inform others, nothing the Commission proposed addressed these problems. Nothing in the detailed analysis of its response to the dioxin affair suggests that it was even particularly concerned to improve food safety *per se*. Rather, it appeared to be exploiting the affair, a dynamic known as the 'beneficial crisis', whereby the Commission uses problems to its own advantage.

The Commission had already announced its intention to harness European institutions to the cause of political integration, to which effect it had identified food safety as a primary issue. In its own words:

> Political integration will become a reality as political leaders and citizens come to realise that their shared values of liberty, peace and stability, democracy, human rights, tolerance, gender equality, solidarity and non-discrimination can best be promoted through shared policies and institutions ... Real success is only possible if all institutions act in concert and if the public has confidence in Europe.[8]

The devastating effects of fulfilling this overarching ambition, it seems, are irrelevant. Farming was to be sacrificed to the cause of 'European integration', made possible, in part, by the 'beneficial' dioxin crisis. And, interestingly, a year after the crisis had broken, Dr André Destickere was still in his post.

13. The Harmonisers

The rationale for Britain's entry into what was then the Common Market in 1972 was that our membership facilitated international trade. With the removal of tariff barriers between member states, the Community became a single market, affording businesses equal access to what were to become 350 million consumers.

However, the removal of tariffs did not alone guarantee the free movement of goods and services. Each of the member states could still exclude their competitors' products if they did not meet national quality, safety and technical standards. By exploiting differences between these standards, individual member states – and their domestic businesses – became adept at protecting their own interests. The devices they used were known as 'non-tariff barriers'.

Inevitably, therefore, if the 'free trade area' (actually a customs union) was going to function efficiently, the problem of non-tariff barriers had to be sorted out. There were several ways of doing this. The most liberal and flexible would have been to require 'mutual recognition' whereby, once a product standard was recognised in one country, it would have to be accepted in all other member states. However, the chosen option was 'harmonisation', the compulsory adoption of common standards for goods and services. This was to be 'one size fits all' with a vengeance.

With the CAP being one of the first and most developed common policies, it was logical that agricultural products should be amongst the first candidates for 'harmonisation', and indeed they were. From this stable were delivered the 'straight cucumber', the minimum-size nectarine, the 'euro-egg' with its sizes 1-6 (removing for a time, the familiar 'large', 'medium' and 'small' designations) and the blemish-free yet tasteless apple.

What was particularly damaging about this enforced harmonisation was that it applied not only to export but also to domestic goods. Thus, while it was common for exporting countries to dispose of products which did not meet technical export-quality grades in their home markets – thus avoiding waste, providing a source of cheap produce for lower-income families and, in effect, subsidising the export market – this practice was forbidden under what became EU law. Thus, a small-scale egg producer could not sell eggs to a local shop without them being checked and graded in conformity with EU regulations.

But nowhere was this effect more pronounced than in the meat industry, or, to be more precise, the slaughtering sector. There, harmonising directives have caused – and are still causing – unprecedented damage, threatening the viability of small and medium slaughterhouses and the small-to-medium livestock producers who depended on them, as well as the small livestock markets. The particular instrument of torture is an EC directive on the marketing of fresh meat, 91/497/EEC, one of the raft of measures aimed at 'completing' the single market for its launch in 1992. Its application exemplified quite how deadly the whole of the EU's obsessive drive for common standards was.

Not least of its deadly effects stemmed from the fact that it was not new but a retread based on an earlier directive, 64/433/EEC. This had been 'done at Brussels' (the description on the signature block when directives are passed) some years before Britain had joined the Common Market. Its specific purpose had been to ensure that abattoirs producing meat to be exported from outside the Common Market to the Community, and those engaging in trade between member states (intra-community trade), complied with minimum standards of hygiene.

Thus, any British slaughterhouse exporting to the EC – even before the UK joined – had to conform with what was known as the 'EC export standard'. When Britain joined in 1972, more slaughterhouses started exporting to member states and the directive applied to them as well as when they were producing meat for export. Over several years this resulted in a two-tier restructuring of the industry. On the one hand were the large 'industrial' abattoirs which, albeit with the aid of many millions of pounds in grants, spent considerable sums on rebuilding their premises to comply with the directive. On the other were hundreds of medium-sized and small 'craft' slaughterhouses, most of which sold their meat only for local consumption. More often than not, their product was of a higher quality than that mass-produced by the large firms.

When officials began the negotiations in preparation for the single market, the existing directive was used as a basis for discussions. However, even in the late 1980s, it was widely acknowledged that the law was obsolete. In fact, it was loosely based on a German standard codified in 1890 by Von Ostertag, a contemporary of Louis Pasteur. But as negotiations progressed, considerable problems were experienced, to the extent that no agreement could be reached on a replacement. As it became ever more urgent that negotiations should be concluded in time for the commencement of the single market, officials abandoned any attempt to devise a new law. They simply re-enacted the original directive, added a few amendments and gave it a new front cover and designation – 91/497/EEC.

The key difference, however, was that instead of applying just to slaughterhouses involved in exporting, the 'new' directive would apply to all slaughterhouses in all member states, including the very smallest. Implementation was to hit the UK particularly hard for two specific reasons. Firstly, Britain had a much higher proportion of medium-size slaughterhouses than most other EC countries. These would now all have to spend up to £1 million rebuilding their premises to comply with the 'export standard', even if, as in most cases, they had no intention of exporting their meat. And, unlike the larger abattoirs which had already complied with 64/433, they would not be helped from public funds.

But the second part of the 'double whammy' was that slaughterhouse owners also had to pay for a new system of hygiene supervision carried out by vets. This was an important and devastating change which demonstrated quite how inappropriate the harmonisation process was. The problem was that British and continental traditions were completely different. In Britain, slaughterhouses had for decades been inspected by qualified meat inspectors and health officials employed by local authorities, under a system deriving from the great nineteenth-century hygiene revolution centred on local medical officers.

This system had given Britain meat as safe as any in the world. But in most continental countries a quite different system had evolved centred on vets, although those responsible for meat safety usually had qualifications specific to the task, unlike British vets, who had little or no training of this kind. Now, thanks to directive 91/497, it was decided to impose on British abattoirs a clumsy two-tier combination of both systems. Not only would they continue to use the existing inspectors, but on top of this they would also have to pay for supervision by vets without experience in public health inspection – which meant that charges to Britain's abattoirs would suddenly become much higher than anywhere else in the Community.

There were two reasons why MAFF's veterinary officials, who had taken over the task of licensing slaughterhouses from local authorities, were determined to implement the directive with maximum rigour. Firstly, it provided them with the opportunity for 'empire building', realising a long-held ambition of taking control of Britain's meat industry, thus enhancing their influence and status in the EU. Secondly, the directive gave them the excuse to replace the inspectors working for hundreds of different local authorities with a central inspection system, run by a new agency under the aegis of the Ministry itself.

Crucially, they were strongly supported by the owners of the larger abattoirs which, in the 1980s, had spent enormous sums on rebuilding to comply with the earlier directive. In many cases, they had taken the opportunity, while 'upgrading' their plants, to increase capacity, in the expectation of an export boom. When this did not materialise – not least owing to aggressive competition from the Irish industry – they had been left with underused capacity and excessive overheads. Not only did they therefore welcome the prospect of their smaller competitors being forced to spend huge sums on rebuilding, they openly offered their support for a measure which was attracting considerable opposition, in return for the Ministry driving their competition out of business.

'Food Sense – 1992 and You'

In every sense, the way in which the changes were implemented was dishonest and unprincipled. In essence, the programme got under way many years before the British law – what was to become the Fresh Meat (Hygiene and Inspection) Regulations – had been laid before Parliament. In fact, the Ministry vets started even before Directive 91/497/EEC had been agreed by the EU Council of Ministers.

Some years before – no one is quite sure exactly when because the initial approaches were made verbally by Ministry vets – slaughterhouse owners had been advised that new regulations were in the offing and that, if the standards were not met by 1 January 1993, their premises would be closed. Then, in 1991, a 'guidance' booklet was issued by MAFF to all slaughterhouses, entitled 'Food Sense – 1992 and You', setting out the standards which would have to be met. This emphasised, in capital letters, that 'premises will be prohibited from trading unless, by 1 January 1993, they have been licensed by agriculture departments as complying with EC requirement'.

Although the 'guidance' was accompanied by a 'health warning' that it was 'not an authoritative interpretation' of the directive, it was treated exactly as if it was. Owners were in disarray. Such was the extent of works required that many of them would have to apply for planning permission and arrange substantial modifications, which could take years to complete. Without access to regulations – which had not yet even been printed – they were unable to refer to any authoritative source and were thus obliged to treat the 'guidance' as if it was actual law. In this, they were further deceived by MAFF, which referred them to expensive consultants engaged by the Meat and Livestock Commission, which drew up plans incorporating all the 'guidance' requirements.

The real wickedness of this was that the guidance was not actually based on the directive but an amplification of it contained in an EC document known as the *vade mecum*. This document itself had a chequered history, stemming from a trade dispute with New Zealand which, in exporting to the EU, found that its meat hygiene regulations were more advanced. It thus discovered that its own producers were disadvantaged by having to compete with EU slaughterhouses operating to an inferior standard. Unable to negotiate the labyrinthine procedures required to amend the directive in time to avoid an all-out trade war, EU officials instead issued a more rigorous standard in the form of the *vade mecum*. This became the definitive standard, albeit without any legal base.

One 'requirement' which particularly baffled abattoir owners was that vehicles carrying live animals and those carrying meat must enter and leave the premises by separate entrances. In many instances owners spent tens of thousands of pounds on building new entrances, even though trucks leaving and entering would, within a few yards, pass each other on the road. Another 'requirement' which caused considerable problems was for loading bays to be completely sealed from the outside air, even though meat leaving the slaughterhouse might soon quite legally be wheeled on a barrow across the road. The new veterinary officials also had to be looked after, provided with a shower and an office which might not be used for more than ten minutes a week.

Nevertheless, no hint that the bulk of the more expensive requirements were not compulsory was given to harassed slaughterhouse owners. After many of them had calculated the costs of compliance, they simply ceased operating and shut their doors. This was the major reason why, between 1990 and the end of 1992, more than a quarter of all Britain's abattoirs, 205 in all, ceased trading. These included small traditional slaughterhouses producing some of the best-quality meat in the country.

With the approach of the January 1993 deadline, it became clear that a disaster was in the making. Large areas of rural Britain would soon have no local slaughterhouses left, robbing farmers, auctioneers and butchers of a crucial link in their local economy. But when this concern was voiced to ministers, the line from the officials was unwavering. Minister of Agriculture John Gummer and his food minister, Nicholas Soames, repeatedly denied any suggestion that the wholesale closure of slaughterhouses was any consequence of the directive. The official explanation, constantly repeated in ministerial speeches and letters, was twofold. Firstly it was claimed that closures were inevitable because there were more slaughterhouses than the market could justify. 'The industry', the officials repeatedly intoned, 'is suffering from forty-five per cent overcapacity.'

This figure was misleading, because it was based on the maximum capacity available throughout the year, whereas the meat trade is highly seasonal; even the most successful abattoir might well only operate at full capacity around Christmas. Furthermore, what the official figure concealed was that the overcapacity was confined to the large, new industrial plants already rebuilt to 'EC export standards', using millions of pounds of public subsidies.

Most of the smaller and medium-sized slaughterhouses being forced out of business by the cost of the new regulations had been working to full economic capacity. They had been profitable until the Ministry's new rules were applied. But Messrs Gummer and Soames had their own explanation: owners who shut down, they on several occasions explained, had 'taken a commercial decision not to invest in the future of their business'.

Temporary relief

The total disaster which threatened Britain's meat industry was actually averted, but only because of a growing campaign against the new directive – in the context of increasing Euroscepticism. This forced Gummer to apply to the EU for a 'derogation' – a temporary exemption. Abattoirs were thus allowed to hold a temporary licence and continue operating, so long as they pledged to complete the necessary rebuilding works within three years. More than two hundred took advantage of this, hoping they could somehow raise the money to survive or, at the very least, make use of their plants for a few more years before closing their doors.

But on 1 January 1993 came the second half of MAFF's double whammy – the arrival of the new 'official veterinary surgeons'. Initially contacted by the local authorities, owners had to pay up to £65 an hour for their unwanted services, in addition to the fees paid for the meat inspectors, who continued to check the meat. Stories abounded in the industry as to how unfamiliar many of these vets were with the technicalities of the meat business. Some could not even distinguish between the carcase of a pig and that of a sheep. Yet these officials had been given extraordinary new powers over the running of each slaughterhouse and, despite their frequent ignorance of the trade, they expected to be treated with deference and were not slow to show who was now in charge of operations.

The atmosphere of the meat trade changed dramatically. In the first week of the new system Christopher Booker and I reported on one abattoir in Farnborough, Hampshire, where no fewer than six officials were gathered to supervise the work of three slaughtermen. Larger firms were facing additional costs of thousands of pounds a week, and it was not long before the cost of paying for these new officials was driving a whole new swathe of abattoirs out of business. In February 1993, when Nigel Batts had to tell his seventeen employees that the Reading Abattoir was closing and that they were out of a job he told us it was 'the worst thing I have ever done in my life'. In the first year of the new system, 104 more firms closed their doors, a sixth of those remaining, reducing the national total to 543. The following year another forty-seven closed, bringing the total to below five hundred.

Typical of many smaller firms disappearing at this time was Wyndham Lewis's slaughterhouse and butchery business, run by his family for six generations in the South Wales village of Bedwas. It was a perfect example of the traditional rural economy, involving several families of the Lewis clan, who reared their own sheep and pedigree cattle, took them to the family abattoir and then, through their own butchers' shops, sold beef and Welsh lamb of quality as good as any in the country. But the exorbitant costs of the new veterinary supervision were more than the business could afford. As Mr Lewis said, the day he closed his doors in August 1994, 'the Government have been saying that they were going to step back from people's lives. But the burden of bureaucracy has increased. I am a lifelong Conservative supporter, but I could never bring myself to vote Conservative again.'

Mr Lewis certainly put his finger on one notable feature of this devastation the officials had unleashed on hundreds of responsible, efficient businesses; that it was being compliantly supported by Conservative ministers, representing a party which had traditionally stood for small businesses and against increasing the powers of bureaucracy and the state.

Even more remarkable, however, was that this destruction was being carried out in the name of a Brussels directive, when no other meat industry in Europe was being treated in the same way. Even Whitehall officials frankly admitted that hygiene requirements had not been a central concern when the directive was drafted. As the government's Review of the Implementation and Enforcement of EC Law in the UK put it, this lack of genuine concern for hygiene was 'one of the most striking features' of the negotiations behind 91/497/EEC, which were 'driven by other, wider issues'.

The report's authors noted, for instance, how 'Germany had already begun to use public health arguments to try to restrict access to its market', and how sensitive the French were to the growing impact on their home market of imports of British lamb. Undoubtedly such commercial considerations played a part in ensuring that, because of the peculiar structure of Britain's meat industry, it would be more seriously affected by the directive than any other in the Community.

But this in itself did not explain why Britain's own officials were then apparently so uniquely ruthless in the way they implemented the directive, firstly by adding so many requirements not called for by the directive, then in the way they seemed determined to close down so many of Britain's abattoirs for reasons which appeared to have nothing to do with hygiene. This was startlingly confirmed by a case in which Christopher Booker and I became directly involved in 1995.

Jim Law and the officials

In Bacup, Lancashire, pig farmer Jim Law ran a small slaughterhouse, killing not only his own pigs but those from other farmers near by, to supply more than forty butchers and restaurants in the area with pork of the highest quality.

As early as 1990, Mr Law had been told by MAFF officials that, with the new directive on the way, his slaughterhouse fell short of what would be required to achieve the 'EC export standard' necessary to stay in business after January 1993. Not, of course that Mr Law wished to export his meat anywhere except locally; nor were his premises in any way unhygienic. They were simply not constructed according to the 'standard' the Ministry required.

Mr Law's initial response was to seek planning permission to build an entirely new slaughterhouse, closer to his farm. But when local authority officials discovered that the road to the projected site passed a primary school and the children might have to see truck-loads of pigs being driven to their deaths, permission was refused. Left with no other option than to 'upgrade' his existing slaughterhouse, Mr Law took advice from the ministry and spent £200,000 on a complete refurbishment. Only then was he told that his licence would be refused simply because his abattoir was 'too small'.

At this point he asked for our assistance. Inspection of his immaculate premises confirmed that here was a perfect test case to demonstrate that the Ministry's policy was not motivated by a genuine concern for hygiene. An appeal was lodged against MAFF's refusal to grant a licence and the resulting case in the summer of 1995 was easily the longest ever heard by the three Ministry nominees on its supposedly independent meat tribunal.

Thanks to pressure brought to bear on ministers by our allies in both Houses of Parliament, it was agreed that MAFF officials directly responsible for Mr Law's case would be available for cross-examination. Over many days, in a Manchester hotel room in that stiflingly hot summer, I took the three officials, Messrs Hewson, Cartwright and Wild, all veterinary surgeons, in minute detail through their reasons why Mr Law should be driven out of business. What my interrogation demonstrated, in a way which even the officials eventually found hard to deny, was that, in wanting to refuse Mr Law his licence, they were not actually enforcing the provisions of the directive or the regulations. They were picking out points from the *vade mecum* to find arguments to justify a decision they had already taken.

What gave away the officials' game more than anything was their suggestion that, under their rules, Mr Law might be allowed to stay in business, but only on what was known as a 'low throughput licence'. But this would so reduce his output as to make it impossible for his business to survive. The licence was based on the number of 'livestock units' (LUs) which a slaughterhouse could kill. Originally Brussels had ruled that a 'low throughput' slaughterhouse could process only twenty 'LUs' a week. As three pigs counted as 'one livestock unit', this meant that Mr Law's could only slaughter sixty pigs a week, barely a tenth of what he needed.

After pressure from the Germans, however, Brussels had ruled that seven pigs counted as 'one LU', which would at least allow Mr Law to kill 140 pigs a week. But as MAFF officials knew, this still would not be enough to keep his business viable and to justify employing twelve men. Nevertheless, the officials were absolutely determined that Mr Law should not be given a full licence, entitling him to work the five days a week he wanted. In other words, they were prepared to admit that his premises were sufficiently hygienic for him to kill pigs for three days. He could even kill 140 pigs in one day if he wanted to, but if he killed 141 in a week, spread over five days, his abattoir suddenly became unhygienic.

Faced with this Alice in Wonderland reasoning, the tribunal conceded that the regulations appeared to be 'extremely complex', and that there were 'inexplicable divergences' between the regulations and the directive. It agreed there was no 'logical reason' why Mr Law should be allowed to kill pigs on three days but not on five. Most tellingly of all, the tribunal even conceded that if the case were being heard under British hygiene law, it would have been necessary for the officials to prove that Mr Law's meat posed a genuine risk to public health, and that they had made no such case. But under EC law, the chairman pointed out, this principle did not apply. All that mattered was whether the slaughterhouse complied with the letter of the law. And although the tribunal agreed that the officials had not been able to justify most of their case, it still concluded that, on three tiny technical points, Mr Law should be refused his licence. The face of the Ministry officials had been saved.

However, the case had aroused embarrassing public attention, and a few weeks later, after Mr Law had carried out minor works to deal with the three outstanding points, his licence was quietly granted. And the main point, over which the battle had been fought, had been conceded. The *vade mecum*, on which the officials had placed so much reliance, had been ruled an 'advisory' document by the tribunal. Its provisions were not legally enforceable.

Shortly afterwards, I visited a medium-sized slaughterhouse in the Midlands which was operating under the temporary licence. The owner, faced with a bill of £700,000 for upgrading his unit, had not yet started work. He held the premises on a short-term lease and the expense was not commercially viable. However, now that the role of the *vade mecum* had been clarified, it was possible to reappraise what was required by way of works. A new schedule was prepared, to which the MAFF inspector readily agreed. The total cost was less than £40,000.

The Most Hated Service

In the run-up to the Law tribunal, events had been proceeding apace in the industry as a whole. With the imposition, in 1992, of veterinary supervision, the meat inspection system had degenerated into chaos. Local authorities were having to employ private vets to provide coverage, sometimes having to hire them at whatever fees were quoted. Abattoirs in different areas were being confronted with a bewildering array of charges. Some were 'getting away' with as little as £22 per hour. Others were having to pay an extortionate £140 per hour, with additional hours tagged on for 'travelling time'.

Playing on the exasperation of the industry at the soaring and irregular veterinary fees, MAFF said that they would stabilise the fees and, overall, bring down the costs of meat inspection to the industry. Such a promise, however, would not be easy to achieve, if indeed it was at all possible. Any new service, in addition to paying its vets and inspectors, would have to fund a new bureaucracy, adding costs which the local authority service did not have to bear.

Nevertheless, the industry, represented by the major processors, with the full support of the NFU, bought the line and pitched in behind the ministry. In 1994 it was thus able to engineer a situation whereby, when the newly-appointed agriculture minister, Douglas Hogg, brought in industry representatives to canvas opinion about the new service, there was only one dissenting voice. That was the owner of a medium-sized abattoir near Bristol, Toby Baker, secretary of the Quality Meat and Livestock Alliance. Although he actually represented the majority of slaughterhouse owners, his voice was drowned in the chorus of 'ayes' from placemen supporting the idea.

Behind the scenes, however – as we later found out – the issue was being raised in Cabinet, where there was a spilt down the middle. John Redwood, then the Welsh Secretary, was firmly against the project, not least because officials had darkly implied that the EU was not in favour of local authority-based inspection and preferred a centralised system. But the apparent support of the industry undermined the opposition and what was to become the Meat Hygiene Service (MHS), was given grudging approval.

However, there was still one irritating little hurdle to surmount – Parliament. The House of Commons had to give approval to regulations bringing the MHS legally into being. There had been grave unease across all parties about the new service and such was the climate that – with the narrowing

Conservative majority – there was every expectation that the regulations could be voted down. Hopes were especially high when the Labour Party, headed by Tony Blair, his deputy John Prescott and the whole of the opposition agriculture team, tabled the 'prayer' which started off the parliamentary process of opposing the regulations.

When nearly a hundred MPs from all parties signed up, it was clear that the opposition was strong enough to force a debate, following which a vote on the floor of the House would probably have carried the day. But in a deft procedural move, agreed by junior agriculture minister Angela Browning, the government arranged for the debate to be held not on the floor of the House – where every MP would get a chance to vote – but in a House of Commons committee. There, the government could still muster an in-built majority.

When the debate was held, Labour MPs, led by Martyn Jones, supported by Eddie O'Hara, MP for Knowsley South, and Paul Tyler for the Liberal Democrats, plus others, argued cogently against the regulations. On the other side, Angela Browning made the case for the new legislation. None of the other Conservative MPs joined the debate. They sat and talked amongst themselves, laughed and joked, got up and wandered about. One had even laid his papers out beside him on the bench and was busily working on what appeared to be his constituency correspondence. When the opposition MPs had made their case, Browning gave a perfunctory response and a vote was called. To a man, the Conservative MPs came alive and, in swift succession, voted 'aye' – for the regulations. With their in-built majority, the deed was done.

There were about a dozen slaughtermen there to watch the travesty. For many, it was their first visit to the House of Commons and their first opportunity to see democracy in action. They had only one word for the proceedings – contemptible.

It thus came to pass that the Ministry finally launched its MHS in April 1995, setting up its head office in the regional headquarters in York. The task of inspecting meat businesses was taken from local authorities and placed in the hands of a thousand officials employed by the new agency, which would eventually be funded entirely from charges on the industry, amounting to over £50 million a year. True to its promise, how-

ever, the MHS – soon to acquire the sobriquet 'Most Hated
Service' – kept the costs down, at least to the large abattoir
owners. To do so, it consciously and deliberately broke EU law.
The way it did so was quite brazen. Clearly stated in Directive
91/497/EEC is a requirement that there should be a full-time
presence of an 'official veterinary surgeon' in each slaughterhouse. These officials have to be present from the moment
slaughter starts to the end of the work. Although the Ministry
had insisted that local authorities provide this 'hundred per cent
coverage', thereby upping their costs, almost immediately it had
been officially launched, the MHS came up with a new scheme
called the 'Hygiene Assessment System' (HAS). This was a
childish, checklist-based inspection system, on the basis of which
up to hundred points were awarded to slaughterhouses,
according to their supposed standard of hygiene. High-scoring
slaughterhouses were rewarded with reduced veterinary coverage, dropping down to as low as 25 per cent of slaughtering
time, saving owners substantial amounts of money.

Although this was in clear contravention of the directive, most
owners responded to the system with alacrity. By this means, the
MHS was able to keep its word, cutting back veterinary hours
and reducing the bills. By the time the EU Commission discovered the sleight of hand in 1996, and insisted that full coverage
be reinstated, the MHS was so well entrenched that it could
afford to comply. Only through strenuous lobbying by the meat
industry, with strong support from an alliance of country interests, was disaster averted. Government agreed to bear the extra
costs. Thus, as always, the British taxpayers ended up footing the
bill.

All the way along, therefore, the officials had the last laugh,
not least because key parts of their Hygiene Assessment System
were lifted straight out of our old friend, the *vade mecum*. The
Law tribunal notwithstanding, they had at last found a way of
enforcing their 'guidelines'.

Plus ça change ...

Before the final stage of this charade had been played out, there
had been a change of government. Although the new Prime
Minister and his deputy had placed their signatures at the head

of the 'prayer' against the regulations which brought the MHS into being, one of the first announcements by Dr Gavin Strang, the new agriculture minister – whose signature had appeared third on the list – was that the MHS would continue in operation. *Plus ça change* ...

14. The Global Power Broker

British agriculture, as part of the European Union bloc, has operated in a rigged market, protected from world competition by tariff barriers, quotas and a wall of rigorous 'harmonisation' standards. The combination of these measures has restricted the market access of third countries. Additionally, farmers have been able to benefit from a variety of measures which enable surpluses to be withdrawn from their domestic markets – thereby maintaining price stability. Not least of these measures is the export restitution system, which allows exporters to dump cut-price produce on the world market – thus undermining the vulnerable economies of Third World countries – and to claim back the difference between Community and world prices, by way of subsidy.

Of the various measures, tariff protection is now being dismantled and the restrictive quotas are being increased. World Trade Organisation (WTO) agreements currently limit the ability of the EU to maintain protective tariffs above the 3 per cent level, except where the Commission can prove that products are being 'dumped' on its member state markets.

Reduction of tariffs is seen by many free marketeers as an unalloyed good. Resort to protective tariffs has been regarded, historically, as one of the evils of the CAP and the EU in general, restricting free trade and creating artificial markets which allow less efficient producers to compete with specialists who can produce commodities much cheaper. Not least of the effects of tariffs is that domestic consumers have had to pay – at times – considerably more for their food than is paid on the world market, an aspect which is blamed for the overall excessive costs of certain commodities. Also, the erection of barriers denies Third World countries access to lucrative EU markets, thus limiting their economic development.

Nevertheless, reduction of tariffs has had a singular effect on wheat- and barley-growing in the UK, which, combined with the collapse of world cereal prices, has seriously affected arable farmers. After a period of comfortably high prices, these crops are now scarcely profitable.

Few would shed any tears for the 'barley barons'. Their 'prairie farming' practices – driven in part by the subsidies – are often held up as the classic example of how the CAP has gone wrong. However, like so many things, tariffs are neither wholly good nor wholly bad. While they may restrict global trade volumes, the effect on domestic producers may be to maintain farming practices which are strictly uneconomic on a global basis but which are environmentally advantageous and/or economically vital to the communities which rely on them.

Taking a neutral view, the farming industry can live with tariffs, and it can live without them. Whatever situation prevails, the industry can adjust, varying cropping patterns and farm structures to suit. But what farmers need, like any other business, is an element of stability and predictability. Whatever the regime, they need to know that the trading environment will be stable long enough to allow planning and reasonable forecasting. Investment decisions made must be allowed to come to fruition and returns on capital must be realistic.

Herein lies another of the terminal factors which have driven British agriculture on its way to becoming a corpse. This issue is essentially one of politics, where farming, which is difficult enough in the prevailing economic and policy environment, has become a pawn in a much larger, global political game, the toy of a global power broker. The game is played to an agenda pursued without any concern for the fate of any one industry, in which agriculture is an unwilling victim of the pursuit of grander objectives.

The sugar industry

A case in point is the British sugar industry. Here is a classic example of global politics reaching out to threaten the very existence of a thriving agricultural sector, all in the name of the global political aspirations of the EU.

In the broader context, it has to be said that growing sugar beet in the UK makes little sense. Beet is a relatively inefficient converter of energy into sugar and the crop, by global standards, is expensive to produce. Sugar cane, grown in tropical climes, is a much more efficient crop and delivers a product of much value to less developed countries in areas where alternatives would be less profitable. On this basis, that there is a sugar beet industry in the UK at all is an artefact of a protectionist regime. It makes the industry a wholly artificial creation, reliant on governmental support for its very existence.

Nevertheless, this artificial industry has grown and prospered, to the extent that, currently, it is almost the only farming sector that has remained profitable. In the UK it employs 23,000 people and pays £300 million a year to 8,500 farmers. The crop is processed by a monopoly enterprise, British Sugar, currently in nine plants spread across the country. It is grown on such a scale that it accounts for three-fifths of the 2.4 million tonnes of sugar Britain consumes each year.

Within its artificial framework, therefore, sugar beet growing makes a great deal of sense. Not only is it profitable but it is also particularly useful as a 'break crop', allowing cereal farmers to rest and revitalise their land without overuse of chemicals.

And, despite the continued and justified criticism of the Common Agricultural Policy, the sugar regime is perhaps the one example of the policy working, more or less successfully – at least from a strictly domestic perspective. After initial problems, the supply of white sugar within the internal market has been relatively well matched to demand and, owing to the self-funding arrangements which have been developed for export refunds, the burden on the EU budget has been minimal. The regime has ensured a stable income for sugar beet producers in a highly volatile world market. Sugar production in the EU has thus remained a major industry, accounting for some 23 million tonnes in the year 2000. About 14 million tonnes were consumed within the Community, 6 million were exported and 3 million were stored (for which aid was paid). Imports were approximately 1.8 million tonnes.

What makes the system work is tight control over production, backed by a regime that covers prices, quotas, and trade with third countries. There is also an intervention scheme – although this has not been used since 1986. Prices paid to farmers by sugar manufacturers are proposed by the Commission and fixed annually by the Council. Although they have been frozen since 1984/5, profitability has been maintained by dramatic increases in productivity. Compared with thirty years ago, only one-tenth of the labour is required to harvest the crop.

As to the quota system, there are two types of quota, fixed for each country and establishment. There is the 'A' quota which covers domestic production, and the 'B' quota which covers the export of excess sugar, for which export refunds are payable. Growers are also allowed to produce in excess of the A and B quotas, the so-called 'C sugar', which has to be exported without refund. Imports from third countries are heavily restricted, although, under a protocol to the Lomé Convention between the EU and ACP countries (former European colonies in Africa, the Caribbean and the Pacific), the EU pays above world prices to import 1.3 million tonnes of raw sugar annually from seventeen ACP countries, most of which (about 1 million tonnes) is refined by the UK.

EU exporters are paid refunds for sugar produced within the quota. These make up the difference between the Community and the world market price, which is currently quite large. This scheme is financed from a levy on the sugar industry.

Despite its success – from an agricultural policy perspective – the regime has also come under criticism. A lack of competition in the industry and its concentration have been attributed to EU intervention. The cost of sugar to the consumer is higher than if world prices were paid, and Third World producers are undermined by the export of surpluses. Food manufacturers, in particular, have complained about the higher costs of sugar, the Cadbury-Schweppes Group attributing extra annual costs of £7 million to the regime.

Nevertheless, the regime was neither included in the Agenda 2000 CAP reforms nor in the EU's year 2000 review of agricultural spending. Instead, the Commission reinforced the status quo,[1] concluding that it should continue until 2003 with only minor modifications (although attempts were made later to introduce further changes, which were rejected by the Council). Thus, in the short term, no major reforms were anticipated and the sugar industry settled down with the expectation of a period of stability. The minor modifications were formally announced in early October 2000, amounting to a 1 per cent overall cut in the A and B sugar quotas and a cessation of storage aid.

Enter Pascal Lamy

Although the management of the EU sugar regime was (and is) vested jointly in the Commission (under DG Agriculture) and the Agriculture Council, world sugar production had also been a key issue in the ongoing WTO negotiations, handled on behalf of the EU by Trade Commissioner Pascal Lamy.

Here, Lamy had his own agenda. He was the 'front man', having to fend off increasingly hostile attacks from world trading partners, irritated at the EU's continued dumping of surpluses on the world market. The major sticking point was agriculture. The United States wanted the EU to slash agricultural tariffs and eliminate export subsidies, and there were also long-running disputes over bananas and genetically modified foods.

In addition, Lamy – a Frenchman – had to deal with the indefensible action by France of favouring banana growers from its own former colonies, an action which had provoked the United States into invoking the WTO dispute procedure and imposing punitive trade sanctions against the EU as a whole.

Another potentially critical issue was the EU seeking to exclude, for health reasons, American beef from its markets, on the grounds that growth hormones were used. However, the WTO had not accepted the scientific evidence offered by the EU to justify the trade ban. Since the restrictions had been initially adopted under intense public pressure, European politicians were presented with considerable problems, especially when a WTO expert panel ruled that the embargo on trade was 'arbitrary'. Not without some justification, US producers suspected that the EU ban was more to do with protecting its own industry than it was about public sentiment.

Their suspicions were reinforced by reports of widespread illegal use of hormones in the EU and complaints that enforcement was erratic and ineffective. When Belgium had sought to clamp down on illegal hormone use, one of its officials, a vet, had been murdered and another had had his car torched. Inspectors subsequently had to make farm visits with police escorts. Furthermore, in late 1996, the US Grand Jury heard evidence of a massive smuggling racket into the US, supplying illegal growth hormones and other drugs to the US cattle trade. Named as a supplier was a Dutchman, Gerard Hoggendyke, for whom a request for extradition was lodged with the Dutch authorities. As a result, the US was applying considerable pressure on the EU to remove its ban, demanding either trading concessions or compensation for its losses – some $200 million per year.[2]

Lamy, therefore, needed a 'grand gesture' which would help dampen the chorus of disapproval of EU trade policies and divert attention from the growing number of trade disputes. Part of his strategy was to come up with a deal for Less Developed Countries (LDCs) which included amongst their number the world's poorest countries and many of those which had been heavily damaged by the continued dumping of EU agricultural surpluses. Almost grudgingly, the European Union Commission had already proposed a partial liberalisation of trade in the run-up to the WTO ministerial meeting in Seattle during November 1999 but the plans lacked conviction and were dismissed by activists. Stunned by the adverse comment, and seriously rattled by the street riots, which had dominated the media coverage of Seattle, Lamy had no option but to pull something out of the hat. And sugar was to be 'it'.

'Everything but Arms'

Even before the formal announcement of the revised sugar regime had been made by DG Agriculture, Lamy made his move. On 20 September 2000, he announced that the Commission had adopted 'a groundbreaking plan' to provide full access for the LDCs to the EU's markets. This was to be known as the 'Everything but Arms' scheme. It went far beyond all previous Community commitments, allowing duty- and quota-free access to the EU markets for 919 separate categories of products from forty-eight LDC countries. This amounted to 'essentially all' products from all LDCs, excluding only those relating to the arms trade. Crucially, because these LDCs were agricultural exporters, they were going to be allowed to sell sugar to the EU, possibly satisfying up to 40 per cent of the Union's demand.

The scheme, coming completely out of the blue, had a potentially devastating effect on Community sugar producers. Perhaps because it was due to be phased in over seven years, however, it was not immediately noticed by the farming community. But as news spread, the implications began to sink in. The

National Farmers Union estimated that the immediate effect would be between 2 and 5 million extra tonnes of sugar coming onto the market. And this was reckoned to be just the start of the problem: only eight of the forty-eight LDC countries actually produced sugar for export, but many of the others had the potential rapidly to expand their sugar industries. The worst-case scenario was that the EU could be importing an extra 5 million tonnes, with a 40 per cent quota cut being forced on domestic growers.

This additional production was forecast to be far more damaging to Britain than elsewhere, and the ruin of her sugar beet industry was predicted. As a taste of things to come, British Sugar immediately announced plans to close three of its plants, in Ipswich, Kidderminster and Lincolnshire, each of which, it claimed, 'plays a major role in the prosperity of the area'. Between them they provided up to 850 jobs, an income of nearly £70 million to 1,850 local farmers, and paid £1 million in business rates.

In the leading farming periodical, *Farmers Weekly*, on 19 January 2001, Marie Skinner, an arable farmer and beet grower, penned a highly critical piece about the Lamy initiative. A known, self-professed Europhile, she wrote, 'I believe in Europe,' but then added a broadside worthy of any Eurosceptic. '... its credibility fails when it indulges in such blatant, anti-democratic processes'. 'It is crazy' she proclaimed, that 'non-elected officials can destroy large chunks of the UK industry.' As a Euro-enthusiast, 'even I find it difficult to remain enthusiastic when my livelihood is put at risk by the actions of an un-elected technocrat'.

There it was. A support system which had sustained a whole industry was to be ditched for the sake of political advantage in a global arena. British growers felt particularly aggrieved. The UK sugar industry produced about 2.4 million metric tons of finished product annually, of which 1.4 million originated from sugar beet, the remaining million tonnes being refined from imported raw sugar derived from sugar cane. Thus, nearly half of the British market was already accessible to LDCs, with the UK-grown sugar satisfying only 55 per cent of its domestic market. Its 'A' quota was 1.04 million metric tons, compared with France's 2.53 million serving a smaller domestic market. British farmers felt that they were already 'doing their bit' for the impoverished Third World.

Worse still, it was by no means certain that any EU-wide quota cut would be imposed uniformly, and there were fears that the British industry could suffer disproportionately. In any event, with only nine factories processing sugar beet in Great Britain, it was certain that cuts could not be uniform throughout the island. Factories require minimum levels of throughput to be profitable, and the expectation was that their owner, British Sugar, would close down some factories and concentrate production in the remainder. This would make beet-growing uneconomic in large areas of the country, owing to increased transport costs.

Nor were other farmers immune from the effects of this devastating policy shift. Former beet growers would have to change to traditional arable crops and, with a larger acreage thus devoted to cereals, the subsidy 'pot' of area aid paid to such growers would be spread more thinly. All farmers would attract lower incomes for their arable enterprises.

British farmers, however, were not on their own. ACP countries, with their preferential access, were also opposed to the plan. So were other EU farmers, including the Italians, the third-largest producers after France and Germany. 'We are totally opposed to the plan and we think it is very dangerous,' said Carlo Biasco, President of the Italian Sugar Beet Association.[3] The plan would create artificial trade currents and sugar shortages in developing countries that sought to maximise the EU concession by exporting output needed at home.

Under sustained pressure from virtually all EU producing countries, on 17 January 2001 Lamy announced approval for what he claimed to be a 'fine tuning' of the EBA package.[4] It was a partial, but not complete climb-down. Sugar was not to be withdrawn from the initiative but the time-scale was put back to 2006-8, with LDC access to the EU market becoming completely free by 2008. The sugar industries had not been saved. Growers had merely been given more time to plan for their own demise. And it was only days later that British Sugar announced the closure of the three sugar beet processing factories.

For producers, EU-wide, Lamy had created a new period of uncertainty. Investment decisions had to be made, equipment had to be bought and plans had to be formulated but, for many farmers – and their suppliers – their horizons were to end abruptly in 2006 when the tariffs were to be reduced and the quotas changed. By then, with more advanced notice, some of the LDCs were expected to have geared up production, so it was feared that the immediate effects would be more severe than they would have been had the scheme been introduced earlier.

To add insult to injury, removing protection from the sugar sector was being presented as a beneficent EU indulging in trade liberalisation. Although it was a measure ostensibly aimed at helping poorer countries, its net effect would actually be to benefit a limited number of already powerful sugar traders, with very limited trickle-down to Third World producers. There would be some limited effect in bringing down consumer prices, but the small price reductions afforded would have minimal influence on finished product prices and would scarcely be noticed by shoppers, if at all by the time retailers had absorbed the differences.

But the effect on the arable sector would be devastating. For sure, many farmers had benefited from the protective measures in place, but it is not as if they had had a choice. Those who wished to grow sugar beet had to belong to the system. If they then complied with the rules of the system – which indeed they did – they were entitled to an element of stability and predictability. And while there may have been valid arguments for reform – or even elimination – of the sugar regime, any changes introduced should have allowed farmers, their customers and suppliers to have adjusted in good time.

Clearly, that was not the case with the original Lamy plan and, even though its implementation was delayed, in the nature of EU politics there were still no guarantees that the scheme would ever be implemented in its proposed form. Farmers – and all those dependent on their crops – had been faced with a period of avoidable instability and uncertainty. But those farmers had been given an important lesson – in the crucible of EU politics, their sector of the industry was expendable.

Bananas

The 'banana war' which had so preoccupied Pascal Lamy had been running for over eight years before the 'Everything but Arms' initiative was announced. The 'war' had predated the WTO agreement, when in 1994 the United States had complained to the disputes panel of the General Agreement on Tariffs and Trade

(GATT), which had ruled that the 'banana protocol' – part of the Lomé Convention between the EU and ACP countries – was 'inconsistent' with free-trade rules. In fact, EU member states were permitting exports of bananas from various small countries around the Caribbean, including the former British colonies of Dominica, St Lucia and Jamaica, at preferential rates.

Central to the dispute was the powerful American businessman Karl Lindner, who owned the world's largest banana firm, Chiquita. Although Chiquita already had 45 per cent of the European market for its so-called 'dollar bananas', mainly produced on large plantations in central America, what aggrieved Mr Lindner was that the EU allowed the Caribbean farmers 8 per cent of its market on preferential terms. But for these islands, the trade was vital to their survival. They depended on bananas not only for up to half their exports but also for the boats which provide the only way of shipping other goods to and from the outside world.

By contributing $5.5 million to the campaign funds of both President Clinton's Democrat Party and the Republicans, however, Mr Lindner had persuaded the US government to bring pressure on the EU to drop its preferential arrangements. This pressure brought the matter to the WTO disputes panel, which ruled the preferential arrangement illegal. This entitled the US government to impose prohibitive 100 per cent duties on $520 million-worth of EU-produced goods. These ranged from 'Pecorino cheese, from sheep's milk, in original loaves, not suitable for grating', through 'lithographs on paper or paperboard, not over 0.51 mm in thickness', to 'articles of a kind normally carried in the pocket or handbag, with outer surfaces of reinforced or laminated plastics'.

Some of the companies making the affected goods were British. One of them was Beamglow Ltd, which produced top-quality cartons for firms like Calvin Klein, Revlon, L'Oreal and Harrods. In April 1999 it had proudly installed a new £2.5 million printing machine more advanced than any in the world. Developed over three years with a Japanese manufacturer, Komori, this ingenious device would have put Beamglow ahead of all its competitors, not least in expanding sales in the USA, where it had just opened a New York office. Prospects for the firm, which, with its hundred staff and £7 million a year turnover, was the largest employer in the small Cambridgeshire town of St Ives, had never been brighter. A month later, the company became one of hundreds of small firms hit by the 'banana war'. Business ground to a halt and the plans for US expansion had to be abandoned.

For their directors, this was the start of a nightmare. They appealed to the British trade minister Richard Caborn, and were told the matter was in the hands of Brussels and Pascal Lamy. When they visited M. Lamy, he told them they should appeal to their own government, expressing the hope that their pressure would in turn move the UK to assist in resolving the dispute. It was clear that the affected companies were being used as pawns in the grand game.

Thus, because of its membership of the EU, the UK had been caught up in a trade dispute not of its own making, which it had no power to resolve. As a result, entirely innocent British companies suffered considerable economic damage. Although, this time, no agricultural enterprises were affected, the fact that the UK can become an unwilling party to such disputes demonstrates how much control this country has lost over its own trade policy. And, if it does not have full control, it is not in a position to protect its own industries, as indeed was shown by the Beamglow and sugar industry examples.

The 'Common Commercial Policy'

This absurdity stems from Article 133 of the Treaty of the European Union, part of the agreement on a 'Common Commercial Policy', in which the UK and other member states agreed to hand over power to the European Union to conclude international agreements on their behalf. The policy was based on

> ... uniform principles, particularly in regard to changes in tariff rates, the conclusion of tariff and trade agreements, the achievement of uniformity in measures of liberalisation, export policy and measures to protect trade such as those to be taken in the event of dumping or subsidies.

Power was given to the Commission to conduct negotiations leading to 'agreements with one or more States or international organisations', subject to authorisation from the Council, acting through a qualified majority vote. In effect, if enough member states so decide, they can overrule British national interests and agree unfavourable international trading agreements in our name, to which we are bound. That is the situation with the World Trade Organisation, where British interests are represented by a Frenchman nominally speaking for a fractious, divided trading bloc but actually working to his own agenda. The results are only too apparent.

15. Red Herrings That Don't Fly

So far, the list of those responsible for the damage to British agriculture is terrifyingly long. Not since Julius Caesar has it seemed that so many assassins have lined up to deliver their blows. Other possibilities are the 'greedy farmers' who are willing to despoil the countryside in pursuit of that quantity which brings the sneer of disdain to the lips of many a commentator – 'profit'. Farmers, it is held, in chasing filthy lucre, have contributed to the demise of their own industry.

In the same vein, supermarkets have come under frequent attack, evidence of that peculiar love-hate relationship we have with a phenomenon which has brought us cheap shopping, customer service *par excellence*, vastly improved food safety, and a massive improvement in the variety and choice of food available. But have they, as is commonly assumed, also contributed to the demise of agriculture? Certainly, it is well known that supermarkets drive down prices and take a disproportionate share of the final retail price of agricultural produce, but do they, in conjunction with intensive farming, qualify as assassins?

In exploring the possibility that both intensive farming and supermarkets are causal factors in agriculture's demise, an uncanny interrelationship between the two issues begins to emerge. From this exploration comes clear evidence that these two favoured culprits are, to an extent, red herrings.

The role of intensive farming

In evaluating the role of farmers as a putative cause of their own demise, it is important to appreciate how seductive and pervasive is the charge levied at farmers, that their progression towards more and more intensification has been, in effect, a form of suicide. The charge allows for an element of demonisation and, by positioning farmers as authors of their own misfortunes, clears the way for instant moralising and draconian solutions. It also legitimises the torrent of regulation which has been foisted on agriculture, while exonerating other, potentially more guilty culprits.

Quite how prevalent the charge has become can be seen from media output at the height of the foot and mouth epidemic. For instance, the headline of an editorial feature on foot and mouth disease in a tabloid newspaper proclaimed: 'Why have we killed them all?'[1] but, despite the headline's theme – questioning the all-embracing slaughter policy – author Michael Hanlon used the opportunity to attack intensive farming. He wrote:

> Modern farming encourages the spread of diseases by forcing farmers to pare costs to the bone and intensify production, meaning animals live in cramped conditions and feed on the cheapest foodstuffs. This is to beat off fierce competition from abroad. We will have to accept our meat is too cheap and pay more for the Sunday roast.

Similar sentiments were being expressed throughout Europe, the debate enlivened by the appointment of Renata Künast in Germany. She was demanding a complete reorganisation of food production geared towards organic production systems. Even in Norway these sentiments were being echoed, with a spokesman for the 'No to EU' campaign remarking, 'These food scandals must lead to politicians realising that BSE is a consequence of heavily industrialised food production ...'.[2]

What is so disturbing about the tenor of these outpourings is not so much the tired airing of prejudices which have been seen time and time again, but the economic illiteracy and the way the agenda fails to move forward. The articles written in 2001 were much the same as those penned in 1989, in the wake of the salmonella-in-eggs scare. Then, the *Daily Telegraph* published a piece by Geoffrey Cannon (Guild of Food Writers), under the title 'Paying the price for cheap food', with the sub-heading, 'The public's demand for inexpensive, mass-produced food has led to the current health scare ...'.[3] His view was that: 'The truth is that the severe outbreak of salmonella poisoning we are currently suffering is caused by our demand for cheap eggs. If we want cheap eggs, we will get mass production, by methods which will heighten the risk of disease; if we want safe eggs, we must be prepared to pay more ....'

In August 1997, the animal welfare charity Compassion in World Farming (CIWF) gained considerable headlines after issuing a report on 'factory farming', claiming that humans were being 'slowly poisoned by the animals we eat'. The culprit was, of course, 'unsafe intensive farming methods'.

But this report was nothing more than a recycling of sentiments expressed in 1996 – during the height of the BSE crisis, which were exactly the same as the denouncements in 1990 when the first major BSE 'scare' erupted, most of which had been aired previously in 1988/9 at the height of the salmonella-in-eggs scare.

Thus, when Hanlon declared that 'it is time to look to both modern science and old fashioned farming ways, if we want to have confidence in our food again', he had nothing new to add. Neither he nor his many predecessors were being constructive or helpful. Few commentators have even attempted to explore, much less understand, the economic stresses that force farmers into the positions which they so deplore.

The 'greedy farmer' myth

A classic example of the ignorance of those who criticise farmers is the myth of the 'greedy farmer' who turned cows – the 'gentle herbivores' – into carnivores by feeding them with 'cheap' meat and bonemeal (MBM), claimed to be the cause of BSE. What has never been properly explained is the reason why MBM was used. At issue is the natural – and generally laudable – business imperative to improve productivity. In the dairy sector – which was one of the biggest users of MBM – this translated into producing more milk per cow, which in turn required modifications to the feeding regime.

The immediate improvements, however, came not from the feed used but from continued and progressive genetic developments arising from selected breeding. This led to cows being bred with what was known as increased 'genetic potential' – the potential to produce more milk. The results were startling. Postwar, the typical annual yield of an individual cow was in the region of 1,000 gallons but, by the mid-eighties, cows were able to produce in the order of 2,700 gallons a year.

The technical problem for farmers was that cows' 'genetic potential' had increased to such an extent that it exceeded their ability to eat enough grass to realise their capabilities. Even if cows were fed grass all day long, they could not absorb enough nutrition to keep pace with their ability to produce milk. Therefore, to provide the nutrition the cows needed, it became necessary to feed them supplementary or 'concentrated' rations.

As to the 'herbivore' status of the cow, while it is true to say that cows, naturally, eat grass (although a cow will readily eat the placenta of its newly delivered offspring and close observation of feeding cows will reveal the occasional bovine relishing a tasty worm), the end product which they actually consume is protein. What happens in the rumen is that the grass mulch forms a nutrient broth for vast numbers of proteinaceous bacteria. It is those bacteria, not the grass, which are absorbed into the lower gut to provide the cow's sustenance. In other words, the herbivore, with its complex multiple stomachs, converts grass into bacteria which, being composed mainly of protein, then provide essentially the same diet obtained by carnivores by more direct means.

Thus, when it became necessary to increase the nutrition levels of cows to enable them to reach their genetic potential, there was every logic in bypassing the protein manufacturing plant in the cows' own digestive system and feeding 'pre-manufactured' proteins direct, proteins which they were well capable of absorbing. That logic was endorsed by government scientists, agricultural advisers and economists, lecturers, teachers and a whole raft of experts. No one demurred from the prevailing wisdom. Farmers did not invent the idea. They did as they were advised. And to have done otherwise would have been like buying Ferrari sports cars and running them on two-star petrol.

As to the source of the additional protein, this was available in the form of either fishmeal, vegetable protein derived from soya, or meat and bonemeal. Of the former, fishmeal was of limited use because of the taint it imparted to the milk. Processed soya was of similarly limited value: not only is it expensive, it lacks some of the essential amino acids the cows need, as well as calcium and phosphates. Furthermore, its bulk limits the amount which can be fed and the high oestrogen levels inherent in the processed product affect fertility. Meat and bonemeal – with a small proportion of fishmeal – became the ideal solution, with the added advantage that it converted otherwise valueless slaughterhouse waste into a valuable by-product, cross-subsidising the meat industry.

The point at issue is that meat and bonemeal was *not* a cheap option. When wheat – the main component of good quality supplementary feed – was £80 a ton, meat and bonemeal was £180. In fact, meat and bonemeal was the most expensive ingredient in the feed. With premium 'high genetic potential' cows costing £1,800 or more, however – and dairy farmers having to invest in two hundred or more of these animals – it would have been commercial suicide not to spend more on expensive feed to exploit the potential of these animals. The driving force was not greed but the simple economics of production geared to the marketplace.

Battery hens

A dynamic very similar to that applying to milk production also drives intensive egg production. Over many centuries, laying hens have been improved through selective breeding to produce an incredible number of eggs. Derived from tropical jungle fowl, which would perhaps lay six eggs in a season, by the time they are sixty-seven weeks old modern hybrids have laid over 280 eggs – just short of one a day for their brief laying careers. Clearly, without dramatically increasing the nutritional value of the feed, such performance could not be achieved. For laying hens too, MBM was used.

However, in the litany of denigration and condemnation, intensive egg producers are subject to even greater vitriol than their dairy counterparts for their practice of keeping hens in cages. But, as always, the myths do not reflect the reality. What most people are unaware of is that the practice of caging birds stems from pre-war times and entirely predates the intensification of the poultry industry, which occurred in the 1950s and '60s. The primary reason for caging, which was often done on a very small scale – no more than twenty to thirty birds – was simply to protect them from disease and from the depredations of foxes, which can execute horrendous slaughter on unprotected flocks.

It is nevertheless the case that most farmers would prefer not to keep intensively housed birds, although – on a relatively modest scale, say of five thousand birds to a house – so-called 'battery' units are by no means as offensive as animal rights campaigners would have us believe. Indeed, hens are afforded space no more than the size of an A4 piece of paper but, with four to a cage, they seem to manage, spending most of their time with their necks through the bars, 'talking' to their neighbours. We humans may see the bars but the hens – not known for their massive cerebral power – tend to be more concerned with their feed and water. Walking into a house, one can tell immediately whether the hens are contented. I know one farmer who, when the pressures get to him, retreats to one of his hen-houses and talks to his birds. Their soothing clucks and crooning have a singularly calming effect. On the other hand, enter a house populated by fractious birds and the squawks of alarm and outrage reach such a crescendo that remaining in the house is not an option for the intruding human.

I, personally, am less in favour of the massive industrial units where up to six million birds may be kept on one site, with giant, factory-style sheds housing 300,000 birds or more, their feed, environmental conditions and egg collection all managed by a computer, with little human supervision. This is all too impersonal, the hens just units in a profit-and-loss account. But it is this sort of unit which has survived and prospered as a result of regulatory pressure on the industry. Small-scale farming is simply no longer capable of keeping up with the costs of conforming with ever-changing welfare, hygiene and labour regulations.

In the current demonology the caging of birds is closely associated with widespread disease. Producers, of whatever size, are often accused of keeping their stock healthy only by resorting to massive use of antibiotics. Nothing could be farther from the truth. A measure of the fiction is that, in respect of salmonella infection in laying flocks, free-range birds are ten times more likely to be infected than their caged counterparts. The logic of this is indisputable. Salmonella bacteria are ubiquitous in the natural environment, finding hosts in a wide range of fauna, from foxes and sheep to rats and mice. They also infect all manner of birds, whether seagulls, carrion crows, magpies or starlings. In the free-range environment, hens cannot be segregated from these natural sources and readily succumb to infection.

Much is made, however, of the experience of Sweden, which has managed to eliminate salmonella infection from its industry – or so it claims. If Sweden can do it, so it is held, what is to stop the UK industry doing likewise? The inference is, of course, that 'greedy farmers' would prefer to poison their customers rather than spend the extra on ensuring that they produce disease-free birds. Once again, however, the reality is different. Sweden has a land area three and a half times that of the UK, with a population not much larger than Greater London and a poultry industry to match. Compared with, say, areas of East Anglia and Essex, where poultry units are 'wall-to-wall', Swedes are able to disperse their units widely, enabling them to limit infection spread. Arctic winters suppress wild animal and bird movements, giving long breaks in infection.

When a unit does go down, they demolish the buildings and take away the topsoil before rebuilding. Try that in the UK and – as experience has shown – within weeks the new units would be reinfected. Surrounded by infected fauna, with windborne organisms drifting in, the units have very little chance of totally excluding infection. Significantly, producers have also been reporting record levels of rat infestations, arising from the privatisation of the water industry, whereby the new water companies have been unable to agree fees for local authority sewer-baiting programmes. As a result, farmers have suffered massive incursions from – guess what – *urban* rats, bringing their infection into the countryside. And from where do the gulls, which are now seen deep inland, get their salmonella infections? Look at any domestic refuse tip or sewage works serving the urban populations, and you will see that it is white with feeding gulls. When they then visit farmland, they bring with them the infection, acquired in the first instance from man, the biggest natural reservoir of salmonellas of them all.

As regards dampening down ravening infection with antibiotics, any student of the economics of poultry husbandry will readily confirm that the price of such medication puts it out of the reach of egg producers. They would cease to be profitable if they relied on prophylaxis – in any event, there is 'zero tolerance' of antibiotic residues in eggs for human consumption, which rules out the use of most commercially available antibiotics and all the cheap products. It is the case, however, that young birds are often dosed with drugs known as coccidiostats, to prevent infection by a particularly damaging form of parasite, and these drugs have some antibiotic characteristics, but they are applied to meat birds only. Residues in eggs produced by commercial laying hens rule out their use in egg production.

The role of the supermarkets

Looking at the other popular scapegoat, the supermarkets, it is very much the case that the British have a somewhat schizoid love-hate relationship with these institutions. The 'hate' side was articulated by no less than Prime Minister Tony Blair, addressing a meeting of selected farmers at Hartpury Agricultural College on 1 March 2001. There, he criticised supermarkets for putting pressure on them. 'We all want cheaper food in our shops,' he said, 'but, on the other hand, the supermarkets have pretty much got an arm-lock on you people at the moment.' Later, on 4 March, the *Observer* reported that a 'crackdown' was to be announced on the way Britain's supermarkets used their power to manipulate the food industry.

According to the newspaper, a 'legally enforceable code' was to be drawn up which would require the large chains to have a 'fairer relationship' with farmers, who had complained about being bullied into providing food at very cheap prices. Supermarkets would face heavy fines if they failed to stick to the new rules. Agriculture minister Nick Brown – echoing the sentiments being expressed in acres of newsprint – said that it was time for a more fundamental look at the food industry. As well as the new code for supermarkets, the government said it would review 'just-in-time' supply chains which involve the high-speed movement of vast quantities of food around the country.

Blair and Brown were, of course, missing the point completely – perhaps deliberately so in order to divert blame from the main cause of the farmers' problems. And that cause was simply the distorted market created by the disparity in EU subsidies and other national support afforded to our trading 'partners'. The government itself, in robbing agriculture of its subsidies, is more to blame. How ironic – and even cynical – that the government should seek to use supermarkets as the alibi for its own disastrous actions.

In a nutshell, supermarkets operate in a competitive, price-sensitive market, driven by consumers who are mainly concerned with price, of whom few base purchasing decisions on quality, source or other attributes. This has been well demonstrated by consumer buying patterns for eggs. Despite saturation publicity on the evils of battery eggs and the relative merits of free-range eggs, the British public has been stubbornly resistant to accepting the higher premium attached to the free-range variety. More than a decade after the salmonella-in-eggs scare engendered by Edwina Currie, when free-range eggs were (wrongly) lauded as being a safer product, the market share of 'intensive' eggs remains at around 90 per cent.

Faced with the commercial realities, chain stores have no option but to offer food at competitive prices. If that food is available from foreign suppliers at significantly lower prices than can be delivered by domestic producers, the simple fact of life is that the supermarkets will source from those suppliers – especially for manufactured or processed foods, where the origin of the raw ingredients is less evident. However, inevitably, the situation is a little more complex. There is certainly a marketing advantage in maintaining a public relations profile that conveys support for British farming. Thus, most supermarkets are keen to buy a proportion of their stocks from domestic suppliers. But not at any price. To square the commercial circle, they exploit their buying power to drive down prices to market levels. And that market is international.

For many years I worked with the egg industry and I have been aware of the plight of egg producers confronted with the plainly unrealistic demands of supermarket buyers, calling for supplies at lower than the cost of production. Even when there has been rare unity amongst the producers, making a stand on a minimum price, the façade has crumbled when buyers have simply pointed out that alternative supplies are readily available at considerably lower prices from other EU suppliers. In the face of what some might consider to be a none too subtle form of 'blackmail', British producers have had to match prices or go out of business. But supermarkets do not set the prices. These are set by international competition. As regards eggs (to say nothing of beef), prices could be even lower if the United States had free access to our markets – producers could easily undercut the cheapest European prices by as much as 6p a dozen (in a market where a 0.5p price advantage can secure a contract). It is only EU quotas and tariffs which keep prices as high as they are, albeit not high enough for UK producers.

In view of the level of competition prevailing, there is no point in blaming the supermarkets for their behaviour, any more than there is any sense in blaming birds for flying – that is what they do. Nor, indeed, are the multiples always as black as they are painted. Days after Blair's 'sporadic outburst', Mr Richard Dain, a farmer-grower for over fifty years, wrote defending them.[4] After being squeezed out of the fruit market by cheap imports, he had planted cobnuts, working closely with Sainsbury supermarkets, who assisted him with advice on hygiene standards, farming practice, machinery and marketing. 'That advice was considered, balanced, informed and given with my best interests and those of my customers in mind,' he wrote.

Equally, there are horror stories. One lettuce grower, for instance, found several thousand pounds deducted from his payments for 'substandard' produce. He found he had fallen victim to an elaborate scam in which his supermarket client had offered a £5 voucher for any product returned by its customers. Unprincipled buyers found they could buy one lettuce and then, a week later, buy another, each wrapped in a loose polythene sleeve bearing a 'best before' code. They would then transfer the newer sleeve to the older product – by then long past its best – and return it to the supermarket for a 'no questions asked' replacement and the £5 voucher. But the sums paid out were deducted from the supplier's account, without him even having been told of the arrangement or being permitted to examine the 'defective' goods.

No doubt the supermarkets do unfairly exploit their positions, but they could not afford to mess around with suppliers who could give them highly competitive prices. British producers cannot. And the root cause of that is the unlevel playing field. It is the availability of cheaper, alternative sources of supply which gives supermarkets their power and the opportunity to exploit their domestic suppliers. On a truly level playing field, our farmers could compete with any in Europe. But so viciously has that field been tilted by the subsidy disparities that British farmers are caught in a classic squeeze. In order to stay in business, they have only two options – increase productivity or reduce incomes.

In fact, British farmers have been remarkably successful in improving productivity, but there has been a price. British farms are, on average, three times larger than their continental counterparts. They employ less labour, use more machinery and apply more fertiliser and pesticides. But this intensification is not the cause of the problem. It is a symptom. Farmers are not responsible for the demise of their own industry. Depending on the perspective, they are either victims or sensible businessmen reacting to market forces over which they have no control. It cannot be emphasised enough that the most powerful driver of the higher level of intensification experienced in the British countryside – compared with continental farms – is not supermarket pressure. The primary causes are subsidy and other financial disparities. And once productivity gains have been absorbed – as indeed they have been – the only give in the system is farmers' incomes, which have dropped with such disastrous effects. Those 'greedy farmers' have been paying out of their own pockets to keep their businesses afloat.

16. Quo Vadis?

The objective of the investigation in the first part of this book was to identify those factors and groups which have been responsible for bringing British agriculture to the point of death. Some have indeed been identified, but there may be even more. And, despite my defence of them, there are those who will continue to maintain that many farmers are the authors of their own misfortunes. A few indeed are. In any and every industry there are the very good, the good and the rotten apples. Farming is no different. But there are enough critics, with plenty of opportunities to vent their spleens; I am not inclined to add to their venom, not least because I believe that farmers, on balance, are more sinned against than sinning.

The same might actually be said of their representatives, particularly those of the NFU, known to its many critics as No F***ing Use. Too often, the union seems to be more interested in representing government's views to its members – which include less than 40 per cent of working farmers – than standing up for its members against government. The problem, however, is more complex and subtle than just inadequate representation.

It is a common and sinister development in modern governance that successive governments select and then favour particular trade groups – preferably one per industry or sector – granting them privileged access, flattering their representatives and routing favours and concessions through them. They then 'freeze out' rival groups – hence the experience of David Handley, chairman of Farmers for Action, recounted in the Prologue – ignoring their representations and snubbing their members. By this means governments 'capture', contain or neutralise possible dissidents. The approved trade groups thus end up acting as what Stalin described as 'useful fools'. The tragedy is that many farmers fail to realise how easily they are being manipulated and end up paying their subscriptions to finance their own subjugation.

However, while it would be possible to explore in more detail this and other contributors to agriculture's demise, the list is long enough to be going on with. More delving would confront the law of diminishing returns. The question now is where do we go from here?

We are faced with an unusual situation in that, having established that agriculture is dying, we want to bring it back from the brink and then protect it from the attentions of assassins who, as yet, have not been brought to book. They are still out there, unchecked, ready to negate any attempt at resuscitation. Thus, any plan for a 'new' or revived agriculture must address two central issues: how to neutralise the factors which caused its demise in the first place, and how to create conditions which will enable it to expand and prosper.

The central problem here is that success on either or both of these fronts demands commitment not only to deal with agriculture but with the broader political issue of our membership of the European Union. Demonstrably, to address agricultural problems we must remove those factors which have destroyed farming and then start with a 'clean sheet' in order to build anew. But inasmuch as many of the destructive systems identified in preceding chapters are an integral part of the EU – and we cannot opt for an *à la carte* menu – any attempt at 'clean sheet' engineering is doomed from the very start without either the ability to mould the EU's agendas to our needs or the political will to leave the EU altogether.

Some, including Conservative Party strategists, would have it that a halfway house could suffice; that we could live with the broader objectives of agricultural policy being set by the EU and settle for repatriation of the CAP, leaving Britain to manage its domestic affairs within a framework set by the EU. This dangerously seductive option is bolstered by the claim that politics is 'the art of the possible', the argument being that repatriation is attainable, albeit in the long term. The only trouble is that it will not even begin to solve the manifest problems of agriculture.

Most of the adverse influences on agriculture attributable to the EU come not from the CAP but from other sources. The single market, the integrationalist ambitions of the EU, the protectionist ethos which we saw in response to BSE and again to foot and mouth, the damaging effects of harmonisation, and the EU's global ambitions – all have far more influence on the health and prosperity of British agriculture than the CAP, to say nothing of the burden of red tape and regulation emanating from Brussels. Thus, even if the impossible happened and CAP reforms were negotiated entirely to the satisfaction of the British government, we would be no farther forward in revitalising British agriculture.

Therein lies the ultimate and possibly insoluble dilemma. We cannot develop a sustainable policy within the framework of the EU. Nor is there any realistic prospect of member states suddenly deciding to run their affairs in accordance with the wishes and desires of British farmers – notwithstanding Blair's 'positive engagement' in Europe. Also, there is no mainstream political enthusiasm for our withdrawal. Not least, the farming community itself is far from convinced that we would be better off out. Many remain enthusiastic about our continued membership.

This enthusiasm stems from our earliest negotiations for entry into the then Common Market, when most farmers favoured British membership. The fear at the time was that UK governments – and in particular Labour governments – would be unlikely to provide continued financial support for farming, or would drastically curtail such support. Membership, it was felt, would lock British agriculture into a support system dominated by the French, who would not only be more inclined to back their farmers but would prevent successive British governments from cutting subsidies. For the agricultural community, therefore, membership of the Common Market was a means of protecting British agriculture from British politicians.

In the early years of our membership, there can be no dispute that some farmers prospered greatly. Nevertheless, it is a moot point as to whether they were the beneficiaries of the massive increase in productivity in agriculture that coincided with our entry, or whether their prosperity was solely a result of the subsidy system. Either way, in the early years there was very little vocal complaint about the system, and it was only after the MacSharry reforms of 1992 – which switched from direct production support to a compensation-based system – that a surge of red tape brought about real complaints. The protectionist attitude of the EU to BSE also provoked considerable complaint and, from there, farmers have seen an explosive growth of bureaucracy combined with – latterly – a drastic fall in incomes.

That notwithstanding, it is probably true to say that, despite the acknowledged and manifest faults of the CAP and other crushing problems, farmers look at the current Labour government – which is perceived as profoundly 'anti-countryside' – and surmise (probably correctly) that, under British control, the situation could be much, much worse. When agricultural votes account for less than 1 per cent of those cast, they reason that they would have little chance against populist politicians. Few of these would think twice about arguing for spending the bulk of the £3 billion or so paid in subsidies on improved healthcare or some other populist causes. More hospitals or 'feather-bedded farmers'? No contest!

There is also, currently, another factor – either the 'strong' pound or, depending on your perspective, the 'weak' euro. Either way, since its launch in 1999, the euro has undergone a 28 per cent devaluation against the pound, giving continental exporters a massive competitive boost, enabling them to undercut still further the prices of UK producers in their own markets. This has given a stronger impetus for further integration, with the NFU firmly behind the campaign to abolish the pound, in order to remove the competitive disadvantage. It says something for the dire, myopic view of the NFU that it fails to recognise that early entry would be on the basis of the current exchange rate, locking in for all time the competitive disadvantage. And while farmers have been systematically cheated of their 'agrimoney' compensation – which was supposed to compensate in part for the drop in value of the euro – the NFU has been less voluble on this issue than it has been in support of abolishing the pound.

So tortuous and contentious is the EU issue that we have almost reached a stage where it has become a taboo subject. Many commentators simply ignore it altogether, for all the world behaving as if they were attending a surreal cocktail party where an elephant dominates the centre of the room, crapping on the carpet. They all act as if it were not there and step over the steaming piles without comment. But the elephant cannot be ignored. Even on a national scale, many of the problems that could be addressed have an EU dimension. There is, for instance, the shortfall in financial support, relative to other member states, which has put British agriculture at such a competitive disadvantage. Then there is the lack of national support schemes, which are so common in other countries. This is a problem that exists only because we are locked into the single market and obliged to give open access to the produce of our 'partners', who benefit from more generous EU and national support.

Even in the vexed problem of red tape and over-zealous officials, which so afflicts the industry, there is a strong EU element. And then there is also the pressing need to curtail the malevolent role of scientists, and to insulate the industry from the fall-out from turf-wars between different government departments. But both of these issues have an increasing EU element, especially when – as we saw from the Belgian dioxin crisis – events across the Channel can have a serious impact on British farmers.

However, where there are issues that lie wholly or mainly in the domain of the UK government – which do not therefore depend on EU approval for their remedies – it would be reasonable to expect action. But even without the dead hand of the EU, one still cannot be at all sanguine that any lasting action will be forthcoming. The signs are not good when the Labour government tells us it will expand the Rural Development Programme when it is only paying some £230 million a year, contrasted with Eire's £500 million, Germany's £1 billion and France's £1.2 billion. Furthermore, since the programme is fixed until the year 2006, there is no prospect of the UK increasing the funding in the short term. All that can be realistically expected is more of the same, a cruel, never-ending game of musical chairs where small amounts of money are continually moved around for purely political advantage.

Given that the whole reason for the parsimony is to protect the EU rebate and therefore minimise calls on the Exchequer, neither is it likely that the government will look kindly at national support schemes – common in other member states – which would aid farming and rural communities without offending EU rules.

There can, therefore, be no realistic expectation that government will give serious money to agriculture. Even though, at the time of writing, the UK was still in the grip of foot and mouth disease, with the whole of agriculture effectively closed down, the only aid on offer – apart from the statutory compensation for slaughtered animals – was £152 million 'agrimoney' compensation for the year 2000, leaving £1.2 billion still unpaid. Additionally, promises had been made that money would be 'pulled down' from the rural development fund. However, pig producers, who had taken the brunt of earlier losses, did not qualify for 'agrimoney' compensation. Therefore, according to Agriculture Minister Nick Brown, speaking to the National Pig Association on 28 February 2001, 'the Government was very limited in the help it could give'. He added, 'What I am trying to do is find some other means that would be legal – that would conform to the state aid rules – and be of practical assistance to pig farmers.'

All he could suggest was that '... money that would have been spent in two years time helping pig farmers to leave the industry under a restructuring scheme would be spent now on aiding those who felt they had had enough'. To do this, though, he would have to reallocate some of the cash from the paltry £230 million annual rural development fund. Lamely, he concluded, 'This is the best I can do in short order to try and find something that will help pig farmers ....'

But what appears to be a UK issue is not as simple as it looks. Once again the dead hand of the EU lurks behind the scenes. The clue that explains Brown's inertia was his reference to 'state aid'. Anything by way of compensation, other than to farmers who have had animals slaughtered under the control programme, is illegal unless cleared with the EU Commission. However, it was not only Britain's farming industry which had the begging-bowl out. On mainland Europe, in the winter of 2000-1, the BSE crisis ravaged the beef industry, precipitating a Europe-wide 27 per cent decline in consumption. In France and Germany, the extent of the crisis was equal to that level experienced during the height of the British crisis in 1996-7. So serious was it that, at an EU agriculture ministers' council on 26 February, France made it clear that in the absence of EU subsidies it would use its own money to bail out 40,000 struggling cattle farmers. However, any such resort to national funds would also be illegal, as were attempts to compensate Dutch and German farmers in the wake of a massive swine fever epidemic three years ago.

If the Commission is holding the line on swine fever and BSE, there is no way it can permit support for British farmers. As has been the case so many times, Nick Brown's hands, those of his fellow ministers and their civil servants, to say nothing of his successor, Mrs Beckett, are tied. The only meaningful activity being practised in Whitehall is 'group bondage'. Farmers cannot be compensated because the Commission will not allow it. Thus, after being systematically short-changed on subsidies for so many years, British producers are now having to compete with an EU awash with cut-price meat – not least surplus beef which continental consumers have been unwilling to buy.

With the unwanted surplus being dumped on British markets at prices that our own farmers cannot match, they can no longer compete in their own domestic markets. Had subsidies and other support measures been more generous in previous years – matching those of our competitors – and had the current administration committed to a higher level of rural development funding, the industry would have been better placed to withstand the FMD shock. There would have been more money in the agricultural economy. But after the years of neglect and indifference, agriculture is on its uppers, and ministers cannot help – even if they wanted to.

How typical, therefore, for want of any constructive activity, that the government should devote its time to rearranging the deckchairs on the deck of the Titanic – changing MAFF into the Department of Environment, Food and Rural Affairs. But this was far from curtailing the activities of this odious ministry. As Charles Clover of the *Daily Telegraph* argued on 12 June 2001, a reverse take-over had been completed. 'Environment' had not taken over 'Agriculture' – MAFF had taken over 'Environment'. Or, as an anonymous senior MAFF official put it, 'We had hoped we would get a steak out of the new reforms, but we ended up getting the whole cow.' And he was not talking about Mrs Beckett. To all intents and purposes, MAFF lives on, with Beckett 'in charge of efforts to revive farming and reform of EU agricultural policies'.

If this is one of the first outcomes of New Labour's second term in office, there can be little optimism that the new government will even attempt to lighten the burden of 'red tape' and regulation on agriculture. But then, not least because much of the burden emanates from the EU, there is minimal scope for action. Nor indeed did the earlier Labour administration show any inclination to reduce that part of the burden which lay within its control. Since 1997, the year of the first Labour victory, to the declaration of the 2001 election, over 15,000 new regulations have passed into law. The year 1999 was vintage, with the record for any single year being broken by a comfortable margin, a grand total of 3,501 regulations being passed. That compares with 2,336 in 1986, 2,667 in 1990 and 3,359 in 1992, when the number rose above 3,000 for the first time. For a government committed to 'better regulation', 'better' equals 'more'.

That leaves us with the vexed subject of 'scares', which have caused so much damage and destruction to farming. The key to dealing with these is to understand that they are not natural but engineered phenomena, created by groups pushing their own agendas. Whether, however, understanding will be matched by action remains to be seen, especially as there is a strong whiff of political incompetence in their handling. In any event, governments as much as other agencies benefit considerably from the scare dynamic, exploiting the 'beneficial crisis' aspect for political gain. And, as we have seen, the Belgian dioxin scare casts a long shadow. In this context also, the phenomenon has taken on a sinister international dimension, whereby UK agriculture suffers the fall-out not only from its own domestic alarms but also from scares on the continent, in which is has no direct involvement. However, there is one comfort we can draw from the dioxin crisis. No matter how bad the handling of our own scares, it does not even begin to compare with the disastrously inept conduct of the Belgian authorities.

This apart, the picture so far painted is uncompromisingly negative. The view has been advanced that there is little prospect of securing changes to EU systems, which dominate agriculture in a bewildering variety of ways. Neither is there any realistic prospect of immediate withdrawal from the EU, allowing the UK to formulate its own policies and run its own affairs. Nor is there any confidence that, if the UK were to run its own affairs, the result would necessarily be better – and there is a distinct possibility that the situation could get considerably worse. As to 'micro-policy', i.e. those few areas of policy which the EU in its munificence still allows us to operate, it is highly unlikely that New Labour in its second term, or any successive government, will acquire the wit or political will to make a difference.

Given this prospect of unremitting gloom, one has to pose the question as to whether there is any salvation for British agriculture. An honest response must confront the reality. The answer is no. And to admit that, paradoxically, is to pave the way for a future. The central problem afflicting agriculture is self-delusion, on the part of governments, of politicians, of the media, the people and farmers themselves.

The only way things are going to happen is when people decide they are going to happen. When enough of us decide we are no longer going to take the diet of gobbledy-gook dished out by politicians, there will be change. And, in the final analysis, there *will* be change – there has to be. There are more of us than there are of them.

Change, however, must be driven by vision. The curse of the current situation is that, bogged down as we are in the minutiae of current affairs, and in denial over the pervasive influence of the EU, there is little in the way of a coherent message reaching those who yearn for a better world. In my experience, these people have very simple demands. Whether they live in the country, the towns and cities or the suburbs, by and large they all want one thing, the same thing – the freedom to get on with their lives with minimum interference from the state, or anyone else. That is my vision.

Needless to say, in the real world, no freedom can be absolute. And, like their counterparts in the towns and suburbs, rural communities and farmers lay claim to large amounts of public money (though less in total, perhaps, than inner-city welfare claimants draw down). No case can be made for the wholesale disbursement of funds without accountability and some defined return, necessitating some curtailment of freedom. As long as public money is involved, there must be some state interference, however benign. But it can be benign.

This, perhaps, prejudges the issue in that some would advance the thesis that agriculture – and even the rural economy – can do without subsidies, that it can survive without public finance. Thus, the case for continued financial support is explored. But support can come in many different forms, so options are considered by which the state could support agriculture and the rural economy without becoming so intrusive and domineering that it changes, or even destroys, the very nature of the things it is trying to preserve. Any such systems have to lie within the realm of that Holy Grail of good administration, 'joined-up government', working to realistic, imaginative and sensible policies.

17. Joined-up Government

Inasmuch as the Common Agricultural Policy is in part responsible for the demise of British agriculture – even if, as the preceding chapters demonstrate, that part is relatively minor – its central flaw is the mistaken belief that there can be a *common* policy for the whole of the European Union. It is impossible to have a single policy which can successfully be applied to the arctic tracts of northern Sweden and Finland, while dealing at the same time with the Irish dairy regime, the wine producers of Languedoc and the olive cultivators of Italy – to say nothing of the goat breeders of Greece and the Spanish vegetable growers.

But whether the CAP is the main problem or not, the very concept of pursuing a *common* policy provides an object lesson. On the same basis, it cannot be acceptable that there should be a single regime covering the widely disparate farming styles and economic circumstances in the UK. In their own ways, the needs of the dairy farmers of Cornwall, the beet growers of Suffolk and the hill farmers of Cumbria, Wales and Scotland are as different as those of the farmers of the different countries of the EU. Accordingly, even on a national basis, it is unwise to embrace – except within only a very broad policy framework – a common agricultural policy for the whole of the UK.

A second – and fatal – limitation of the CAP is that it is an *agricultural* policy. Agriculture supports – and is supported by – a large and diverse rural economy, as has been highlighted by the foot and mouth epidemic. In fact, agriculture constitutes only 6 per cent of the British rural economy. Thus agriculture should be seen as an integral part of that wider economy, and be treated as part of it. A separate policy for agriculture divorces farming from its hinterland, from its economic and social infrastructure, treating it as a separate entity, which it is not.

Furthermore, farming enterprises traditionally have rarely been solely reliant on income from agricultural produce. Many enterprises are kept afloat by what is known as 'off-farm' income (which has been the saviour of Dutch agriculture). At one level, farmers, their wives and children may have jobs in the community, the income from which often helps support the farm. A whole range of other enterprises may be carried out, from bed-and-breakfasting to light engineering. As we saw during the fuel crisis, many farmers also run haulage enterprises. In other words, many farms themselves are mixed economies. To deal with only one aspect of the income stream seems perverse.

Taking the macro and micro situations together, therefore, it is both logical and essential to address rural affairs in a holistic way, with the focus on the whole rural economy rather than on agriculture, *per se*. In other words, in order to facilitate the survival and prosperity of agriculture, we need that much-vaunted but elusive animal – 'joined-up government' – to formulate a sound and effective rural policy.

The objectives of a rural policy

If it is accepted that effective strategic management of agriculture requires the formulation of a rural policy, it follows that the objectives of such a policy should be framed more broadly than those which deal with agriculture alone. If that fact is self-evident, it still needs stating because the basic premise is that agriculture should be treated as an integral part of the rural economy. Therefore, a sensible rural policy is not a farming policy with the rural 'bit' bolted on. The whole must be treated as a single, seam-free entity, each part being interdependent and, therefore, inseparable.

During the course of the year 2000, I and a group of colleagues held several meetings in a room in the London office of the European Parliament and, starting with a blank sheet of paper, constructed what we thought a rural policy should include. This is what we came up with.

It should:

1. encourage a healthy, prosperous and sustainable rural economy, which meets the needs and aspirations of rural inhabitants and their dependants, and of those who visit it and who otherwise contribute to and benefit from it;
2. promote and assist in the development and maintenance of

economic diversity and variety, while fostering traditional values and cultures;

3. encourage improvements in the quality of the countryside and its flora and fauna; to ensure equitable levels of access and to conserve our archaeological heritage;

4. facilitate the production of a wide variety of high quality, healthy foodstuffs and other agricultural products, in a manner compatible with the need to maintain good environmental conditions, animal welfare and the long-term fertility of our soil;

5. maintain a strategic capability of largely feeding ourselves.

It is instructive to compare the differences between the first objective and the common agricultural policy set out in Article 33 (formerly Article 39) of the Treaty of the European Union. The latter reads:

> ... to increase agricultural productivity by promoting technical progress and by ensuring the rational development of agricultural production and the optimal utilisation of the factors of production, in particular labour.

It continues:

> Thus to ensure a fair standard of living for the agricultural community, in particular by increasing the individual earnings of persons engaged in agriculture.

It is worth noting, in passing, that continuing emphasis on production, against static demand, eventually means oversupply which, with price-inelastic commodities, inevitably results in a collapse in prices and thus reduced margins. Almost Soviet in concept, the promotion of production without reference to demand was always going to be a recipe for disaster. Then to link increased productivity with a 'fair standard of living' was absurd. The inevitable collapse in prices could only lead to reduced incomes.

It is for that reason we decided on the need to 'encourage a healthy, prosperous and sustainable rural economy', making prosperity the key objective, without stating the particular means by which that should be achieved. With flexibility being the watchword in agriculture – and the economy in general – this offers scope to respond to changing circumstances with different strategies, without having to change the fundamental policy objective.

Crucially, however, we added the second objective, to 'promote and assist in the development and maintenance of economic diversity', an objective which is completely absent from the CAP objectives. In fact, economic diversity is the key to sustainability. The drive for productivity promotes specialism, monoculture and eventual decline. Furthermore, the 'economic diversity' objective encompasses not just agriculture but the whole of the rural economy.

The remaining objectives are fairly self-explanatory, each leaving the means open as to how they can be achieved, with the possible exception of the last – 'maintaining the strategic capability of ... feeding ourselves'. This, at first sight, would appear to equate with the CAP objective of assuring 'the availability of supplies', but there is no direct parallel. The objective of the CAP was rooted in postwar political reality, reflecting the near-starvation resulting from the U-boat blockade of the North Atlantic and the dangerous shortage of food on mainland Europe after the cessation of hostilities.

While our objective might also seem a throwback, we were not actually seeking to anticipate a similar problem, but simply felt it wise to adopt precautions to deal with the possibility of interruption of food supplies. We have no means of predicting what might cause such an interruption but, in this uncertain world, it is best to be prepared. There is, for instance, what some believe to be a worrying trend towards redirecting primary agricultural production eastwards, to former Soviet satellites such as Poland. While this may, in the short term, afford the UK a source of cheap food, it also exposes us to potential dangers. From being supplied largely by sea routes – particularly from former colonies such as Australia and New Zealand – the UK would, for perhaps the first time in its history, be more reliant on land routes for its food supplies. Traffic would pass through Germany, the Low Countries and possibly France before crossing the Channel. Crucially, we are without the means to protect these routes, and would entirely depend on other nations to do the job for us.

A long memory is not necessary to recall the sudden and devastating effects of the Channel blockades in the autumn of 2000, when a combination of fishermen, truck drivers and farmers brought Channel traffic to a standstill. Nor is it easy to forget that the French police stood by, unable or unwilling to act. One can remember also, in Germany, the extraordinary scenes when protesters sought to prevent the movement of one consignment of nuclear waste to a reprocessing plant, and the massive police effort that was required to ensure its safe passage. Given the real possibility of civil unrest being directed against commercial traffic, for whatever reason, the 'land bridge' with what could become our primary food suppliers begins to look alarmingly fragile.

Nevertheless, we were not advocating a policy of 'Fortress Britain' whereby this country should seek to maximise its output and minimise its reliance on imported foods. What we were actually focusing on was *capability*. We felt, simply, that an infrastructure and organisation should be maintained which could enable the very rapid expansion of indigenous food production, should the need arise. This would entail maintaining the knowledge base which would allow increased numbers of people to work on the land, together with the training structures which would be needed to make this happen. There should also be provision for enlarging farms, to maximise output – with sufficient reserve stocks of seed and machinery to enable large increases of staple crops to be grown at very short notice.

The national rural and countryside policy

In addition to examining the CAP objectives, it is also worthwhile looking at the Rural White Paper, published in the autumn of 2000, in which was set out, for the first time, the government's statement of its overall aim and its objectives for rural and countryside policy. The overall aim was 'to sustain and enhance the distinctive environment, economy and social fabric of the English countryside for the benefit of all'.

The government offered five national objectives:

1. to facilitate the development of dynamic, competitive and sustainable economies in the countryside, tackling poverty in rural areas;

2. to maintain and stimulate communities, and secure access to services which is equitable in all the circumstances, for those who live or work in the countryside;
3. to conserve and enhance rural landscapes and the diversity and abundance of wildlife (including the habitats on which it depends);
4. to increase opportunities for people to enjoy the countryside;
5. to promote government responsiveness to rural communities through better working together between central departments, local government, and government agencies and better co-operation with non-government bodies.

It is instructive to note from this that the (Labour) government could not bring itself to use the word 'prosperity'. Yet economies are about money, and dynamism depends entirely on maintaining a level of prosperity which can support the activities in an area. And although the government's policy also offers competitiveness as an objective, it does not indicate whether this attribute relates to the local or global stage. Exploring the detail offers no clues. All that is on offer is an economy which is 'competitive, diverse and flexible' and 'better able to respond to changing market opportunities', whatever they might be.

However, the central defect of this policy is so stunningly glaring that one wonders how it can even qualify for the title 'rural and countryside'. On offer are 'aspirations' that the countryside should be 'responsive to consumer wishes, for example concerning the welfare of animals, and the quality, source and value of produce'. It should be 'environmentally responsible' and should also be 'managed as an integral part of the rural economy'. But nowhere is there any mention of producing food or other agricultural produce. It is almost as if the government believes that milk comes from a carton on a supermarket shelf.

Thus, completely lacking is the understanding that the countryside is a by-product of the primary activities of agriculture, the production of food and non-food produce, like timber, wool and flax. The objectives of 'conserving and enhancing rural landscapes and the diversity and abundance of wildlife' and increasing 'opportunities for people to enjoy the countryside' depend entirely on the style, nature and profitability of the agricultural economy, the methods of farming employed and the structure of the industry.

Decentralisation

Since the entry of the UK into the (then) Common Market, and through the transition to the European Union, MAFF has been responsible for implementing and administering agricultural policy. As policy has been increasingly dictated by the EU, we have seen the Ministry become more and more integrated into the EU system, to the extent that it has become little more than a branch office of Brussels, implementing policy rather than creating it.

At the same time, the Ministry has become both increasingly centralised and 'anti-farmer', unresponsive to the needs of the farming community, and at the same time failing to represent its needs to ministers and to Brussels. The internal culture of the Ministry has now developed to such an extent that the farming community can have no confidence that it can effectively represent and foster the interests of agriculture, much less the rural community as a whole. Even without the foot and mouth débâcle, therefore, there are sound reasons for the abolition of MAFF.

To implement rural rather than agricultural policy, it makes sense in any event to have a ministry which is charged with administering rural affairs as a whole. To that effect, there is a strong case to be made for a new department of state. Such a possibility has been given currency in the form of the Department of Environment, Food and Rural Affairs.

However, simply amending the nameplates on the doors of offices in Whitehall and spending a small fortune on a new logo will not change anything. From a local perspective, a central government department is still central government, whether it is MAFF or the Department of Environment, Food and Rural Affairs. And if it is logical that – in the same manner that the EU's Common Agricultural Policy cannot succeed because it encompasses so many disparate systems – a common UK policy cannot succeed (nor even can separate English, Scottish and Welsh policies), it makes absolute sense to have local flexibility and a strong element of local autonomy. Accordingly, while there is an important role for central government in setting the overall framework, there is also a very strong case for devolving as much of rural policy as is possible and practicable to lower tiers of government, either county or unitary councils.

The broader policy infrastructure

However policy is administered, there is a danger in focusing on rural and countryside issues in isolation. No policy of any nature exists in a vacuum, unaffected by the main policies of state. This applies with some force to rural policy. Furthermore, the interplay between different facets of other policies can have as dramatic an effect on rural prosperity and wellbeing as can those which are ostensibly directed at the specific sectors.

To take a case in point, a magnificent and imaginative rural policy could be devised which, on its own, could have the potential dramatically to improve prosperity. But if the funding and resources this policy made available were subsequently clawed back in discriminatory taxes, the original policy would be to little avail. This is, in fact, very much what is happening. When the cost of diesel on the Continent was 45/46p per litre, the pump price in the UK was, on average, 67/68p. This differential, which continues to this day, imposes an extra cost on the transport of finished goods. A similar differential in petrol prices – and the paucity of reliable or frequent public transport – similarly imposes an unacceptable burden on rural inhabitants. Higher road fund taxes on commercial vehicles, some £4,000-£5,000 per lorry, also impose a massive burden. The complex income tax and benefits system discourages the employment of labour, especially in small enterprises; the rigorous control of casual workers prevents flexible use of the labour force; and a complex and inflexible VAT system for non-food products discourages diversification. The structure of Uniform Business Rate (UBR) penalises small businesses and damages low-margin enterprises like slaughterhouses and vegetable processing plants.

This effect is at its most pronounced in the rural public house, hotel and restaurant. The combination of UBR and VAT at 17.5 per cent on restaurant sales (without which few rural pubs would survive) means that they become milch-cows for the Revenue, which extracts taxes from businesses irrespective of their ability to pay. They are thus driven into the ground by taxation levels, which they cannot afford, not having the ability of their urban cousins to increase margins. Unsurprisingly, four rural public houses are closing every working day – twenty a week – leaving villages without a focal point or amenity for passing tourists.

Clearly, if rural policy is to be effective, other policies must not work against it. On the contrary, all the policies must work in harmony. Rural needs, therefore, require recognition in the broader policy infrastructure which only 'joined-up government' can supply. In a book of this nature, however, it would not be possible or desirable to explore all of these matters. But it is worth discussing, by way of illustration, two completely different aspects of rural need, thus demonstrating the complex interrelationship between broader policies and rural affairs: rural policing and public transport.

Rural policing

After the incident in which Tony Martin, an East Anglian farmer, shot and killed a juvenile burglar, there has been much debate as to whether the so-called 'explosion of crime' in rural areas is real or perceived. Either way, crime is a matter of great concern to rural communities, as indeed it is elsewhere. At the heart of the problem, perceived or otherwise, seems to be the increased detachment of police forces from their core duties – fighting crime – and their increased bureaucracy, which keeps constables off the beat.

Specific to the countryside is the added perception that the police have given up on crime and have retreated to their urban 'bunkers'. They are seen only when they venture out in their expensive patrol cars and 'rapid response units' to deal (tardily) with reported crime or, more commonly, when they are persecuting motorists and terrorising farmers when they fail to acquiesce to the demands of MAFF killing squads. Many will take some convincing that the police are short of resources to tackle crime when they can afford to dispatch fifty officers to assist in the slaughter of fourteen goats and three sheep at the Mossburn animal sanctuary, or when they announce their latest 'blitz' to entrap another million motorists on the nation's motorway system – or, for that matter, when they ostentatiously park their cars outside the village pub, intimidating customers, while crimes elsewhere go unattended.

Additionally, it is a matter of amazement that police forces make such limited and ineffective use of modern technology, in particular by failing to exploit fully computer-based intelligence which can assist in identifying crime patterns. Even now, there is no integrated national database for recording police intelligence and where, as is more likely than not, rural communities are affected by the activities of criminals who operate across police force borders, there seems no effective co-operation, or even communication, between forces.

Notwithstanding technical improvements and broader policy issues, however, there can be no doubt that, of all the facets of policing, the one thing rural communities would like to see is the reintroduction of rural police stations, with police houses attached, bringing the police back into the communities they serve. There have also been suggestions that there should be an extension of the Special Constable scheme, bringing in part-time, paid constables who are given a higher level of training than is afforded to normal 'specials', sufficient to equip them to patrol without being accompanied by full-time constables. Such a scheme would have the merit of providing useful income to some country dwellers.

Another important issue is the systematic and progressive disarming of the countryside. Rules relating to shotguns and other firearms are becoming more and more draconian and, while crimes involving the use of firearms are at record levels – with increasingly armed police seeming ever more willing to shoot unarmed citizens, with no comeback – sporting and farming usage of firearms is being criminalised. The Tony Martin affair raised deep unease as to the relationship between the police and country people, and the broad feeling is that where, as is manifestly the case, the police are failing to provide adequate protection for rural communities, not only should shotgun ownership be encouraged but their use in defence of life or property should not be regarded as an offence.

Public transport

In the days before I had acquired enough money to be able to afford a car, while working in the London Borough of Croydon, I was courting my wife-to-be, who at the time lived in a remote village called Skelton-on-Ure, in North Yorkshire, midway between Ripon and Boroughbridge. Getting from London to York by train was no great hardship but, no matter which train I caught, it just missed the Ripon bus at the other end. An hour's wait, plus a dreary hour crawling through every village and hamlet on the way to Skelton, turned what is an easy twenty-minute drive into a dismal marathon.

Such an experience is by no means untypical and it is therefore no surprise that, if they can afford it, every country-dweller acquires a motor vehicle and avoids public transport like the plague. The result is a downward spiral. Transport provision becomes less used so services become progressively more uneconomic until they are withdrawn. Those who, for whatever reason, are obliged to rely on public transport are more and more isolated, spending more for increasingly unreliable, expensive and inconvenient services.

Given the obvious utility and convenience of the private car, however, there can be no reasonable expectation that people will be persuaded to abandon this form of transport and voluntarily patronise public transport, thereby improving the lot of those who are without personal mobility. Nor is it possible to expend unlimited amounts of public money to subsidise rural transport. Nevertheless, without better provision rural dwellers are at a serious disadvantage compared with their urban counterparts, some of whom are well-served by reliable and easily accessible public transport.[1]

One scheme that has been suggested to encourage the use of public transport is a substantial increase in road tax, perhaps as much as £1,000 for luxury cars, the difference between the normal and luxury rates being handed back to the car-owner in the form of vouchers, redeemable only on local public transport services. With a 'pot of money' available in each locality, private operators would then be incentivised to run services to mop up the available cash. Another option is the 'Cherut' taxi in Israel, and its counterparts in other countries. Essentially, these are mini-buses, running continually on fixed routes but to no set timetable, which can be hailed like a taxi anywhere on their routes, with set-down at any convenient location.

In Strasbourg, where public transport benefits from heavy

public investment, one particularly attractive feature is the 'electronic bus stop' which displays accurate information as to the position of buses on the route and continually updated information on the arrival time of the next bus. There have also been schemes which make this information available on the Internet so that potential bus users can check the time of arrival of their transport at their local stop, thus eliminating unnecessary waiting time.

One thing that is clear, however, is that there are no 'quick fixes' and no universal solutions to the transport problem. What is needed is imagination, flexibility – and local money under local control.

The role of local authorities

To an extent, many of the answers to rural problems lie with local authorities. Provision is already made by central government in respect of local authority funding to give special attention to areas of social deprivation, managed through the charge fund settlement – whereby central government tops up local authority finances. However, there are considerable disparities in the per capita funding made available. Shire counties – with considerable social need – often fare less well than certain urban areas. Any 'joined-up' policy should rectify this imbalance.

Another major problem is that, since local government reorganisation in 1974 when rural and urban district councils were merged to form the district councils we know today, many rural communities have lost their voice in local government. Their interests and needs were drowned out by the clamour of the more populous urban communities, with disproportionate amounts of local spending going to urban centres.

Classic of this dynamic is the long-running saga of Harrogate District Council, which now runs the administration of the formerly independent City of Ripon and all the villages in between, with which it has absolutely no affinity. Despite their own needs, the charge-payers of these habitations are saddled with a massive debt to bail out the Harrogate International Conference Centre, the result of over-ambitious attempts by local (urban) politicians to put Harrogate 'on the map'. Delightful though the building may be, hard-pressed rural residents are somewhat jaundiced at the prospect of having to part with their own cash to fund this extravagance. Their resentment is especially piquant when it is realised that the 'investment' brings them no economic benefit and some of them are so isolated that they have no bus connection with Harrogate and could not visit the centre even if they wanted to.

To provide some form of redress, it is arguable that each local authority with any sizeable rural community should be required to draw up specific plans for supporting their rural economies, identifying specific needs and measures which will improve conditions. Funds made available through the charge fund settlement from central government might then be 'ring-fenced' and kept available for keeping the shops, mobile shops and sub-post offices trading, the buses running, and local schools open. Part of this settlement might also fund a significant reduction in the uniform business rate levied on rural shops, pubs and other rural enterprises.

A more desirable option might be to reverse the 1974 reorganisation – which has never worked – and restore to local communities their own local governments, splitting urban and rural administration and allowing local people to run their own affairs within their own budgets.

18. Subsidise or Die

Within the broad framework of rural policy, there is the narrower but still vital question of financial support for agriculture. Opinions vary widely as to whether public support should continue and, amongst those who agree that it should, there is an equally wide range of opinions as to how monies should be disbursed. A very few would prefer maintenance of the status quo, but most accept that much of the funding has to be refocused on environmental rather than production support.

Those who would dispense with subsidies altogether often cite in their own support a unique experiment in which, more than a decade ago, New Zealand phased out agricultural support. Despite predictions of mass bankruptcies, farmers deserting the land in their droves and the collapse of the system, this country's agriculture is now thriving, demonstrating that there is life after subsidies. As a result, the New Zealand experience is often heralded as applicable to the UK, with subsidies being completely abandoned, creating a truly free market in agricultural produce.

One writer who is clearly in favour of this option is Graham Harvey, former scriptwriter and agricultural editor for *The Archers*, BBC Radio's somewhat tarnished 'soap' about far-from-everyday country folk. In his book, *The Killing of the Countryside*,[1] he tackled the 'landowning lobbyists' who 'have long argued that a free market would ruin agriculture'. He argued:

> They raise the spectre of the depressed 1890s when railways and refrigerated transport brought cheap food flooding into Britain from New Zealand, Australia and the prairie lands of North America.

To counter this doomsday scenario, Harvey cited Christopher Haskins, chairman of Northern Foods – a company which is a major supplier of ready-meals to supermarkets, using him to argue that world commodity prices will remain buoyant and that the emerging nations of South-East Asia are likely to soak up any surpluses. In this fantasy world, Harvey postulated that organic farming is the way forward, in which context:

> ... UK farmers possess one priceless asset – a market of 55 million people within a few hours' driving time. For the overwhelming majority of British farmers long-term security will rest on their success in supplying the people of these islands with fresh, safe, nutritious food.

Given a 'free market and a taxation system that charged polluters [i.e. intensive farmers] the full cost of environmental damage', in Harvey's little world 'organic farming would thrive'. And clearly, if this solution could be applied, it would be highly popular with the taxpayer who would be relieved of a substantial financial commitment, liberating significant funds for other purposes.

Even with his eyes firmly on the 'emerging nations of South-East Asia', however, Harvey failed to see that, at the time he was writing, the 'tiger economies' were moving into recession and were in no position to soak up agricultural surpluses. Nor, evidently, was he aware of the massive agricultural restructuring going on in the region, to the extent that Thailand has become a major exporter of cheap, intensively reared poultry meat, adding to the stresses affecting world trade.

More importantly, he seems to have failed completely to see the colossus of the continental EU nations with their CAP subsidies and structural surpluses, who enjoy the same 'market of 55 million people', a mere tunnel or ferry crossing away, to which they have unrestricted access. The costs of transporting container-loads of produce over the Channel are little more than it costs to move produce off British farms to urban markets. Translated into costs per pound of apples or dozen eggs, the differences are infinitesimal.

Thus, while UK intensive farmers would be taxed into oblivion under the Harvey regime, leaving the handful of survivors to retreat into the bucolic ideal of organic farming, our competitors would flood our shops – and the Northern Foods of this world –

with cut-price goods. Our own farmers will have been priced out of business. Nor could they protect themselves from EU imports. The guardian of the single market, the European Commission, would soon intervene and UK Plc would be on its way to the European Court of Justice.

Nevertheless, there are other advocates of the free market scenario,[2] but these seem to rely on two premises: that the CAP has not worked and is unreformable (a point with which I have no disagreement); and that the subsidy-free option has worked in New Zealand.

The New Zealand experience

Before running away with enthusiasm for the New Zealand option, however, it must be recognised that the topography, climate and soil conditions are wholly different from those prevailing in the UK. Furthermore, New Zealand is an uncrowded island, largely rural, with an isolated landmass of over 100,000 square miles, housing a population of less than four million. That compares with the UK, which occupies 94,000 square miles with a population of sixty million, relying primarily on industry and services.

The uncrowded countryside of New Zealand and a more relaxed regulatory regime permit low-input, extensive livestock production – and milk and dairy production – at costs which make them highly competitive on the world market. And although Britain's entry into the (then) EEC deprived New Zealand of a lucrative – almost captive – market, as a major exporter of agricultural produce she found valuable alternative customers in Japan and other Far Eastern countries. With new relationships forged, she retained her position as a leading exporter of agricultural produce, but changed from a low-cost, high-volume base to a high-value, high-quality, speciality producer. In this, the industry has been assisted considerably by a currency devaluation of over 40 per cent in the period since subsidies were abandoned.

The UK, by contrast, is a major net importer of food with a strengthening currency compared with its major agricultural competitors. It is a large, attractive and liberal market for agricultural producers, especially for EU farmers, who are organised on a co-operative basis, maintaining their own centralised marketing schemes. The UK's supermarket system, with its central buying and central distribution, accounting for around 80 per cent of food sales, actually makes our market in some ways more accessible than the relatively decentralised systems in other member states.

Attractive as it may seem, therefore, there is no evidence that the subsidy-free experiment could be a success in the UK. It has only worked in New Zealand because of very special – if not unique – circumstances. Absence of support would leave British agriculture unable to compete with imported produce, in a highly vulnerable position. Even the *Economist* magazine,[3] no friend of subsidies, recognised that if a higher cost basis were adopted, Europe's farmers might be ' ... much more vulnerable to competition from elsewhere; imports from less regulated intensive farms in places like China and Brazil might soar'. Although couched in terms of 'Europe' and non-EU suppliers, the caveat applies equally to the UK in its relations with the EU.

If we even tried to compete, the effects would be unacceptable. Any industry which emerged from the wreckage of the current situation would have to be allowed unrestricted freedom to make as its absolute and sole objective the production of food – and other agricultural produce – at prices which were competitive on the world market. We would have to stand back and allow this 'new industry' the freedom to manage its affairs accordingly. We would expect these industrialists to rip out all the fences and hedges – far more than have already been destroyed – creating massive fields on massive farms, minimising labour and making best use of artificial fertilisers, herbicides, pesticides and machinery. We would have to tolerate minimal regulation, especially in the expensive animal welfare field, and expect massive, centralised production plants to add maximum value to farm produce, at minimum cost. In other words, we would have to allow industrial agriculture on a grand scale, irrespective of its impact on the environment and our way of life.

Thus, no good case has been made that British agriculture can survive and prosper in a completely free market against unrestricted global competition, allowing free reign to cheaper imports, without the countryside suffering even more environmental degradation than has already been experienced.

A North American view

A more sanguine review of modern agriculture comes from a commission with members appointed by the United States President and Congress. It has just concluded a major two-year study on the role of government in support of production agriculture,[4] in which it set out the reasons for continuing subsidies. Its authors wrote as follows:

Support for US agriculture has been sustained, in large part, because of the recognition that production agriculture is an inherently volatile industry. The source of this volatility is twofold. First, the demand for agricultural production is highly price inelastic. That is to say, when prices for agricultural commodities decline, the quantity of agricultural products purchased does not increase greatly. In addition, the supply of agricultural products is, at least in the short term, also highly price inelastic. As farm prices decline, producers, faced with relatively fixed land and machinery resources, may not be able to cut back on overall production in the short run. As a result, small changes in the demand for agricultural products and/or the supply of agricultural products lead to large swings in commodity prices and, hence, farm incomes. Producers, however, may change the crop mix and in the long run gradual adjustments in quantities supplied and demanded occur.

The forces leading to change in the demand for, and supply of, agricultural products are for the most part out of the control of individual producers. Agriculture is a biological production process requiring months from planting to harvest for crops and livestock to achieve marketable weights. Over this period, producers are subject to often variable weather patterns and outbreaks of disease that can affect their supply of products dramatically. In an increasingly global market, economic forces such as relative exchange rates can change dramatically between the time producers invest in the production of a commodity and when they bring it to market. In addition, farming and ranching are characterised by a large number of producers who can do little to influence market prices by reducing their own supplies.

The authors concluded:

> Given the importance of agriculture to the general economy,
> the inherent volatility of the sector, its reliance on markets
> that transcend national boundaries, and the inability of
> individual producers to have an impact on the overall forces
> of supply and demand, the federal government will likely
> remain involved in activities which directly affect the mar-
> ketplace for agricultural products and the economic
> well-being of producers.

The other side of the coin

Comparisons are frequently made between farming and other
industries such as coal mining, steel production and car manufacturing. Why, some say, should agriculture be subsidised when
other industries are left to go to the wall? To an extent, the question is valid, but any extrapolation is less so. Just because these
industries are not subsidised is no good argument that agriculture should also be deprived of support.

Crucially, the problems with the coal and steel industries have
arisen precisely because of the problems currently besetting
British agriculture – disparities in subsidies. It has long been
known – and accepted by the EU Commission – that German coal
is subsidised to the tune of £10 billion a year. If the far more efficient British industry was supported to the same extent, it could
afford to give away its coal and would still make more profit than
it does at present. Equally, while the British steel industry is
acknowledged to be the most efficient in the world, it has to compete against other industries, variously subsidised to the extent
that they are able to undercut the market. The answer to these
industries' plights, therefore, is not to visit the same grief on
agriculture, but to level the playing field in the affected sectors.

More particularly, the situations simply cannot be compared.
Beef farmers, for instance, will have invested a considerable
amount of money in land and infrastructure before they can
bring animals onto the land. The land is the 'factory', the equivalent, say, of a motor car factory or a steel plant. Between the
two, however, the level of investment per unit produced is far
greater for the farmer who can only produce – on an extensive

system – perhaps one animal per acre valued at – say – £500-£800 when it reaches marketable weight.

While the motor-car manufacturer may spend hundreds of millions on a plant, he will expect to churn out thousands of cars a year, each valued at £5,000 plus, or even more. He will buy components on fixed-price contracts, at knock-down volume discount rates, and offer his cars at a market price, each produced in a matter of hours after the components arrive at the plant. If his cars do not sell immediately, he can store them at very little cost without them deteriorating and, if there is a prolonged market downturn, he can lay workers off and shut his plant.

The farmer, on the other hand, has to wait nine months for his cows to produce their offspring. The costs of his 'inputs', such as labour, supplementary feed, veterinary services, fuel, equipment and all the other purchases which are involved in running a farm, will be determined by suppliers far larger than he, who can impose price rises at will – or, in the case of labour, wage rises, which are imposed by the Agricultural Wages Board. The calf will have to be nurtured for as many as thirty months to bring it to marketable weight and, if it does not die or get struck down by disease, the farmer will expect to sell it for a price which will reflect his outgoings and make him a profit.

Days before he is ready to sell, prices may drop to levels below that which are needed for the farmer to recover his costs. But he cannot store his beasts, in the hope that prices will recover. He cannot close the farm down and wait for a better time – the animals are still there. They have to be fed and cared for. If he slaughters them, he gets nothing. The farmer has to take the price offered and hope that his next batch of beasts fetches higher prices. If it does not, he must take the loss. Then, just when prices seem to recover, the country is hit by foot and mouth, or was it BSE? That is the reality of modern farming, the human face of what is described in the dry prose of the US Congress and Presidential Commission.

The subsidy chain

The unpredictability of agriculture was clearly to the forefront when in 1947 the Attlee government passed the Agriculture Act, which introduced a permanent subsidy system. By giving farmers price stability, the Labour government hoped that farmers would be encouraged to increase their production to feed a hungry nation. The scheme worked. Farmers delivered what was asked of them and, for a time, were rewarded for their labours.

But Harvey argues that the Atlee government learned precisely the wrong lessons from the wartime performance of British agriculture. Its quick response to sudden changes in the nation's food requirements, he writes,

> ... revealed an industry not in need of public support, but one which was adaptable and intrinsically healthy despite years of recession. The threat of German U-boats in the Channel [*sic*] produced a sharp increase in food prices. Farmers responded by ploughing up their grazing pastures and sowing their land to wheat, admittedly with some goading from the government. It was the classic response to a clear price signal: the 'cashing in' of twenty years' fertility built up under grass to achieve a rapid boost in output.

Even taking this account at face value – neglecting, for instance, the fact that, under emergency powers, farmers were told what to grow, labour was provided (by the girls of the Land Army) and prices and markets were rigorously controlled – farmers were operating in a rigged market, 'protected' from cheaper foreign produce by the U-boat blockade and benefiting from government price controls.

Harvey would have it that farmers, having profited from the wartime price boom, should have been 'allowed' to readjust to the less frenetic price regime of peacetime. In other words, farmers, having suffered a pre-war recession arising from a free market in agricultural produce in the middle of a world depression, and having recovered as a result of a protected market, were supposed then to prosper from the uncertainties of a return to free-market conditions, while investing heavily in increased production.

That they were rewarded with subsidies, Harvey maintains, was to lead to untold damage to the countryside and was to fail the very farmers they were designed to help. That the subsidy regime adopted then – and the different regime imposed by the (then) EEC – caused incalculable damage is beyond dispute. But a distinction must be drawn between the principle of state support for agriculture and the type of support offered. Harvey may have a case for arguing that the wrong regime was applied. He makes no convincing case against state support in general.

The case for state support

There is a simple and persuasive argument for state support, to which even free-marketeers such as Ruth Lea, Chief Executive of the Institute of Directors, subscribe. The case rests on the premise that, in addition to providing food and other produce, farmers manage the countryside, delivering as a by-product the environment that is so treasured by our own population and visitors. That public amenity, Lea writes,

> ... is, however, a 'public good' which is not 'paid for' by the 'consumer'. There is, therefore, 'market failure' in economists' parlance. 'Society' should, therefore, pay for the public good we all enjoy.[5]

There can be no dispute that a well-managed countryside is a real and tangible asset, accessible to the whole community – urban and rural. Its beauty – where this has survived – adds, to use an old-fashioned phrase, to the gaiety of life, providing a backdrop for recreation, sport and other country pursuits which are regarded as essential antidotes to the pressures of urban life. Furthermore, it sustains an important and growing recreation and tourism industry, attracting significant foreign and domestic earnings which, according to the English Tourist Council, amount to some £12 billion a year.[6]

Therefore, the countryside is not just a machine for producing food and other essentials. An industry currently worth £1.8 billion provides an essential backdrop for a much larger enterprise. Furthermore, in a strict sense, it is not even an industry, as it provides more than just work. For many of its participants, it is a way of life, a defining occupation that supplies income, housing, entertainment and food. For the nation as a whole, it forms part of our national heritage. Its character and use and management are of interest – and value – to everyone.

But despite the tangible and direct economic good accruing from the countryside, farmers rarely benefit directly from it – apart from marginal earnings from bed and breakfast operations and similar small-scale activities. Therein lies the case for providing continued financial assistance to the farming community.

It is generally accepted that the whole nation has an interest in the countryside and expects to have a say (through the medium of government, as well as more directly) in the use and management of farming land, to the extent that its intervention involves imposing restrictions on the economic freedom of farmers – the freedom to generate as much income from their investments as is lawfully allowed. Under these circumstances, it is entirely reasonable that the state should offer financial support (or payment) to compensate for revenues lost.

In a relatively undeveloped and underpopulated country like New Zealand, where the extensive style of livestock management has, in any event, limited impact on the environment, the restraints on farmers are minimal. But in our crowded island, where pressure on land is acute, things are altogether different. If we want small farms and diversity of production; if we want beautiful scenery and rural structures which can only arise from the style of farming we demand; if we want high and increasing standards of animal welfare; and if we accept that our labour force has rightful expectations of high living standards – or at least as high as its urban equivalents – then it is entirely justifiable to expect farmers to be paid for their work in providing the social structures and in maintaining the countryside in the condition we expect.

We can pay for it in subsidies, in higher food prices, or we can pay directly for services rendered. But pay we must. We cannot expect a free ride, on the back of increasingly impoverished and alienated farmers.

Crisis measures

Prime Minister Tony Blair, at the Hartpury Agricultural College meeting referred to earlier in this book, pledged a 'long term future for farming'. But a farmer in the audience warned that there would not be any farms left to support because of collapsing prices. Without very large injections of cash, there *is* a long-term future, but that future belongs to foreign farmers.

British farmers who are not on the dole or sweeping the streets under some 'New Deal' programme will be paid by the government to dress up in peasants' smocks and chew straw. They will stand at the picturesque gates of their 'theme parks', directing tourists in a heavily accented brogue to the carefully sanitised pens holding the last remaining examples of the animals which used to inhabit the countryside – like sheep and cows. The industrial units which produce what passes for food on the highly intensive 'agricultural holdings' will be owned and managed by multinational corporations.

The point is that, whatever the long-term aspirations for farming might be, they simply will not materialise, given the unprecedented crisis that has been made inestimably worse by the foot and mouth epidemic. Immediate aid is needed to stabilise the situation – an injection of large amounts of taxpayers' money. We are not talking about the pathetic £100 million pledged by vote-hungry Liberal Democrats in the run-up to the 2001 general election, but substantial sums, in the order of billions.

It has to be said here that a benefit of withdrawal from the EU would be that such largesse need not impose any additional burden on the taxpayer. In approximate terms, we contribute nearly £6 billion a year to Community funds, in order to receive back something less than £3 billion in agricultural support. This is paid in a devalued currency called the euro which, at the time of writing, was dropping in value faster than at any time in its troubled history. Therefore, even if only for a short period, we as a nation could afford to double the funding to agriculture alone, with no increase in taxation or curtailment of other government spending plans – provided we left the EU.

It is important, however, that any additional money should be properly targeted yet be distributed quickly, with the minimum of bureaucratic delay and obfuscation. The infrastructure for making payments to farmers is already in place and funds could be disbursed very quickly. With £3 billion available, a fixed sum of £10,000 could be sent to every one of the 300,000 registered holdings in a matter of weeks. Since this is something less than is paid (in cash and kind) to the average single mother on benefit, these individual sums would be a small price to pay for saving an industry which is the custodian of 85 per cent of our land area, which defines the character of the whole country, and which underpins rural tourism to the value of £12 billion and an 'added-value' food processing industry worth £60 billion annually.

19. Agricultural Support

The global case has already been made that continued payment of public money is needed to keep agriculture afloat. But long-term monies paid do not have to be in the form of subsidies – as such. The very term 'subsidy' applies to cash handed over to support uneconomic or otherwise uncompetitive industries which, without the injection of these additional funds, would not survive.

As an article of faith, British agriculture is neither uneconomic nor uncompetitive, as long as it is allowed to compete on the fabled 'level playing field'. Agriculture's problem is, on the basis of Ruth Lea's analysis, that it is not only producing tangible goods for which it is paid but also highly valuable 'intangibles' – the countryside and all it contains – for which it receives very little or no payment.

Many forms of 'environmental support' have been envisaged to address this problem but farmers, rightly, tend to display little enthusiasm for schemes which relegate them to the role of park-keepers. They have still less enthusiasm for governments which seem to regard the countryside as little more than one vast open-air theme park. The farming community considers that its primary task is to grow food and other produce, and is justifiably proud of its record in improving the range, quality and availability of its produce, and the productivity of its industry. Whatever its intrinsic value, farmers regard the 'countryside' as a by-product of farming. They are not wrong. Without farming, the countryside as we know it would not exist.

Differential payments

To 'level the playing field' against competitors who do not bear the overhead of maintaining the countryside to the same degree, and to give farmers a decent standard of living, it is a relatively simple matter for society – through the medium of government – to pay farmers for farming in such a way that the 'intangibles' are preserved or improved. On this basis, farmers would be paid for services rendered. They would not be (or be seen as) beneficiaries of unearned state handouts. Instead, they would remain farmers but, in addition, become valued contractors providing services which the taxpayers want and are prepared to pay for. In this way, support for agriculture could be politically sustainable.

The basis of such a scheme could be quite simple. Notionally, any farm is capable of yielding a certain income. Arguably, it could be managed solely on business lines with a view to maximising that income. This level of 'efficiency', however, could have significant adverse impact on the visual environment and on the survival of flora and fauna. To maintain or improve the environment and/or the amenity would demand less 'efficient' farming, and thus involve loss of income. Payment from public funds could, therefore, be arranged to make up the difference in income between farming practices devoted to maximising efficiency and those which are more environmentally and socially acceptable. In effect, such 'differential payments' would be made on the basis of a contract between society and individual farmers to manage the land, producing food and other produce, but in a way which met the expectations of society as a whole.

Political justification

In illustrating how differential payments could be justified politically to the weary taxpayers who have to provide the funds, it is instructive to focus not on farming, but on a completely different industry – say car production.

By any measure, a car factory is a blot on the landscape. No matter how carefully designed and landscaped, the end result is a big, squat, ugly building. It is surrounded by car parks, for its workers and for the finished cars it produces. It must have manoeuvring areas for trucks and transporters, delivery bays, security cabins and all the rest of the paraphernalia that goes with a modern factory. One can hardly imagine that there will be a thriving bed-and-breakfast trade alongside, dedicated to providing accommodation for people who come from miles around to admire the view and enjoy the tranquillity of the walks. Far less will people travel to the site for the recreational amenities it affords, and those who demanded right of way right down the middle of the production line would get short shrift from the security guards.

Now imagine that society required of factory owners that they should operate in a wholly 'environmentally friendly' and socially acceptable way. First to go would be the large factory buildings, to be replaced by a widely dispersed group of traditionally built structures, each constructed of local materials so that they blended in with the landscape. Gone too would be the robots – this is 'intensive' car-making. Instead, each car would be made from scratch by groups of workers, using traditional tools, mostly hand powered. At any time of day or night, work would have to be interrupted to allow wandering ramblers passage though the factories, and nothing dangerous could be left lying around in case they injured themselves.

Only the finest raw materials would be allowed, and government inspectors would have to be brought in to check their quality, as well as supervise the vehicle construction, for which they would have to be paid substantial hourly fees. All interior cladding would have to be made from food-grade material, just in case passengers happened to suck the dashboards or other parts on their way to their destinations. Paints, of course, would have to be 'organic' and water-based to avoid damage to the environment, and they would be brush-applied to minimise smell or fall-out from spray. Every single component would need to have a full record of its origin and history, available for inspection for seven years after each car had been finished, and the vehicle manual would have to include all these details.

Waste produced from each site would have to be stored in specially constructed buildings and only disposed of at certain times of the year. There would be a limit on how many cars could be produced each year from each building and, in the car parks, there would be minimum space for each finished vehicle, with special provisions for heating, lighting and supervision.

Of course, there is a public subsidy for each car produced – as indeed there already is for many of the automobiles produced in this country – and, with this support, these four-seat family saloons would sell for a mere snip at £14,000 each – but only because the factory owners would be ploughing their life savings into the business to keep it running, as well as working on the assembly line because they could not afford extra staff.

Naturally, imported cars would be on offer at £5,000-£6000 to the dealers and, quite unreasonably, they would expect these prices to be matched. When the public did not rush out to spend twice as much on the 'environmentally friendly' vehicles, they would be adorned with 'little red motor car' logos to denote their origin. Adverts would be created exhorting 'Buy British' to all those who would listen. The public would offer considerable sympathy – as they drove away from the showrooms in their foreign cars.

Parody this might be, but it reflects the reality of modern farming. Imagine Nissan, Rover, BMW or any other car manufacturer being asked to produce under this regime. How long would it be before they shut up shop and moved their factories elsewhere? And there is the difference. British farmers cannot move on. But their business does. If it is empty fields we want, all we have to do is maintain current agricultural policies. Alternatively, if we, as a society, want 'environmentally friendly' farming, then we as a society have to pay. The way to do it is to underwrite the difference between 'efficient' production and the type of farming we want, referred to here as 'differential payments'.

Implementation

In principle, this concept of 'differential payments' is not new. It is similar to environmental management schemes already in place in the UK, and not dissimilar to the Irish Rural Environment Maintenance Scheme (REMS). It embodies the best aspects of the Environmentally Sensitive Area Scheme and the countryside stewardship scheme, the latter having proved relatively popular with those farmers who have taken it up. However, widespread implementation is another matter. Many a scheme which is sound in theory founders on the difficulties of practical implementation.

A central feature of any viable differential payment scheme is that it would need to be voluntary. Arguably, other than in exceptional cases, such as sites of special scientific interest which are especially important to wildlife conservation, or areas of outstanding natural beauty, farmers should be able to choose whether they participate and be given the freedom to decide on the extent of their involvement. Then, the key to a successful scheme would be in the nature of any contract conditions applied, the precise mechanisms by which they were agreed, and with whom. And while some bureaucracy would be inevitable, any scheme that became too complex would be a non-starter.

Basic parameters could include the overall size of a farm, the size and possibly the shape of fields, the length and types of hedges or traditional walling, the proportion and type of woodland maintained, and the presence of other natural features such as ponds and lakes. Others could include types of crops grown, the crop mix, methods (and timing)[1] of cultivation, types of animal farmed, their stocking density and the types of husbandry. Pesticide, herbicide and artificial fertiliser usage could also be factored in.

There are, possibly, wider applications of a differential payment scheme. For instance, social factors could be included, such as employment levels, the supply of workers' housing, training opportunities and the provision of external education opportunities (such as entertaining organised school visits or granting research access). Public access, public amenity areas and specific wildlife conservation schemes could also be considered. Provision for renewable energy schemes, such as coppicing and the growth of crops for alcohol and other fuel sources, could also be accommodated. In order to maintain a strategic capability of largely feeding ourselves, maintenance of farms and their equipment, enabling them to be brought rapidly to a highly productive state, could also be a contract condition which would attract payment.

By graduating payments according to the degree to which the farming practice conformed with stated parameters, and the notional losses or expenses incurred, socially and environmentally desirable practices could be rewarded.

The 'one-stop shop'

Inevitably, to factor in all and every possible permutation would involve some complexity, especially in the initial stages when contracts had to be drawn up and agreed, *de novo*, but the great merit of a differential payments scheme would be the 'one-stop shop' aspect. All the other support schemes would go – IACS,

SAP, BSP, SCP, LFAS, ESAS and the rest of the alphabetical soup that characterises and dominates modern farming. And once agreed, any contract could be 'rolled over' year on year with amendments needed only to reflect changes in circumstances. In the longer term, bureaucracy could be minimal in relation to the expenditure involved.

Management of the scheme

In contrast to current agricultural schemes, which are administered centrally, the role of local administration would be crucial. Given a legislative framework, the overall shape of a scheme might be shaped by a strategic plan, prepared by central government – perhaps on a five-year rolling programme. The basis of this plan would be to address, amongst other things, the perennial problem of matching supply with demand. Having regard to consumption patterns, production capabilities, world prices, stocks and predicted imports, the government could set guidance on overall production targets. These would then be translated by local authorities into their own 'local plans' which would designate general production targets for their areas, having regard to the types of farming local authorities wished to be undertaken.

The development and implementation of these plans would borrow from town and country planning mechanisms already in place, with draft plans open to local consultation which would then be approved by central government, or rejected if they did not conform with the guidelines set by Parliament.

This exercise could thus set local and regional quotas, which would be enforced by withholding financial support in relation to specific products where a surplus was anticipated. For example, in the notoriously cyclical pigmeat sector, expansion or new entrants into a buoyant market – attracted by higher prices – often create overproduction which then results in a catastrophic fall in prices. Additional capacity would not be afforded any financial support (or would even be penalised), thus discouraging excess production. On the other hand, where commodity shortages were anticipated (which could not readily be made up from imports), special premiums could be arranged to provide incentives to farmers to increase or switch production.

Lands tribunals

In any system, there have to be checks and balances. To that effect, a mechanism for resolving disputes about the implementation of strategic plans is essential. These could be handled by local lands tribunals, following the pattern of existing tribunals. The classic pattern is a panel chaired by an experienced lawyer with 'lay' assistants. In this context, working farmers and an independent land-use expert would be a useful mix.

Such tribunals would give farmers a low-cost means of appealing against the decisions of local authorities. They could also be the local arbiters of whether contract conditions had been observed, where disputes arose. And, of course, since tribunals would be acting in quasi-judicial roles, any of their decisions would be amenable to appeal, by way of judicial review. Thus, a full range of checks and balances would be available to farmers, to prevent – or remedy – abuse or maladministration.

The scheme in practice

In its fully developed form, a differential payment scheme would be initiated by a farmer wishing to participate. In the first instance, the approach would be made to the local authority, a representative of which would visit the farm. Larger authorities, with a large number of participating farms, might employ their own agricultural experts, who would advise on the options available.[2] Smaller authorities might contract the work out to local agricultural surveyors. How the scheme would work in detail would then depend on the nature of the farm and the intentions of the farmer, but the end results would be unique contracts, specific to each farm.

As an illustration of how this might work, an admirable example would be an intensively managed arable farm, with large fields, few hedges, copses or uncultivated areas, heavily reliant on artificial fertiliser, pesticides and herbicides. In this example, the farm buildings are of the modern industrial type, and heavy machinery is used for cultivation and harvesting. Few crop types are grown, the main cash crops being wheat, maize and oilseed rape, with a 'break crop' of sugar beet. This is the classic 'barley baron' type of farm – even if barley is not grown –

of the type demonised by urban commentators and vilified by politicians as typical of the 'feather-bedded' subsidy-rich style of farming.

For the farm thus described, no public money would be forthcoming. However, if the farmer agreed to reduce the size of his fields, increase the field margins, plant hedges and set aside land for copses or woodland, or even plant permanent water meadows, the costs of these changes would be readily calculable in terms of lost yields and increased cultivation/ harvesting costs. Annual payments could then be made to compensate for these losses. Similar payments could be made to compensate for reduced yields arising from minimising use of pesticide, herbicide and artificial fertiliser.

But there are other possibilities. If, for instance, a farmer in a particularly attractive area agreed to replace industrial buildings with more traditional structures – or maintain existing traditional structures – in keeping with the rural surrounds, this would attract payment equivalent to the extra costs incurred over the expected lives of the buildings. For instance, if a portal-frame, asbestos-sheet-clad barn was replaced with one or more buildings constructed from traditional materials, in keeping with the architectural character of the area, notional additional annual costs – incorporating purchase and upkeep – could be paid under the scheme.

Depending on the local authority's overall 'local plan', additional payments might then be made for other changes. For instance, farmers might be asked to change their crop mix, grow specific crops, or combinations, or otherwise adjust farming methods (such as changing from winter wheat to spring-sown wheat) in order to promote wildlife. They might be asked to introduce livestock on the farm, turning it into a mixed farm, or even provide or maintain designated footpaths. Each of these changes would have calculable financial implications and, in all cases, compensation could be paid for loss of income. To prevent over-generous 'compensation', payments might need to be aggregated with possible provision for a 'cap' – a form of modulation – on the total sum payable.

Another example might be an intensive livestock producer, with a large tract of arable land dedicated to feed-wheat production or grass for silage. Apart from any other qualifying payments, compensation would be offered if the farmer converted to a more extensive husbandry regime and/or reduced stocking density, and reverted to more natural feeding.

One feature absent from the scheme is a capital grant payment system. Should capital expenditure be required, this would best be underwritten by annual payments which take into account the cost of capital. Farmers could obtain loans from commercial sources, at commercial rates, and be freed from the bureaucratic controls and restrictions which inevitably accompany government grant schemes.

Self-help

An important psychological function of the scheme thus far described is the attempt to wean farmers off their 'welfare dependency' culture, whereby they turn to government for solutions to every problem, usually in the form of cash handouts. The problem is that the malaise runs deep. It is not only money which the government supplies, but a vast range of technical services. These include research, technical advice, data collection, statistical services, disease monitoring and, as we have – or have not – seen with foot and mouth, disease control.

In this latter context, there is, of course a necessary and valid role for government in maintaining a watching brief on diseases which have public health implications, but the control of foot and mouth is undertaken for economic reasons only, the slaughter being financed by government in order to protect the interests of meat and livestock exporters. One wonders quite how enthusiastic the NFU and its fellow travellers would have been about the continuation of the contiguous culls – instead of a vaccination policy – if they had had to pick up the bills themselves.

Arguably, a more prosperous and sustainable agriculture could and should pick up its own bills. It should finance its own research (relying on neither government nor pharmaceutical companies), collect its own statistics and provide all the other basic support that a modern industry requires, independent of the dead hand of government. The mechanism for achieving this is the compulsory levy, with the different sectors of agriculture providing for their own needs. At stake is control. He who pays the piper calls the tune. Government is paying for too many of the tunes, and they do not make for easy listening.

Global trading

A partner of production support is often some form of import restriction. The simple rationale for this is that, if this country is heavily subsiding specific commodities, it makes no sense to allow in cheaper produce which then undercuts domestic producers.

The great advantage of differential payments is that farmers receive an income stream wholly unrelated to their production scale or type. Production and support are decoupled, the ultimate objective of modern systems. But with an assured income, farmers can cover their overheads and deliver goods to the market more cheaply than they could otherwise. The system therefore increases the competitiveness of the domestic producer, without the need for specific import controls.

However, as a global trader, this country cannot implement a regime that unfairly restricts access to our markets and, as long as this country subscribes to the World Trade Organisation, it must abide by international agreements. Future rounds of WTO negotiations will focus heavily on removing trade barriers, in particular production subsidies, but there is growing acceptance of the need for national environmental support schemes, the so-called 'green box' subsidies. Senior officials in the United States also readily concede that protection of the amenity value of the countryside is a legitimate target for support, and there is no reason to think that, should it be raised, this issue would not be treated favourably.

In this context, a 'differential payment' scheme is most likely to be the type of support acceptable to the international community. For instance, the scheme could be used to encourage farmers to move from winter wheat to spring-sown wheat, leaving the stubble from previous crops over the winter to provide cover for ground-nesting birds. If this practice were adopted by all farmers, it is estimated that the national yield would drop by some 3 million tons. Apart from being a far more constructive measure than the unpopular 'set-aside' scheme – and reducing substantially fungicide usage – this would, in effect, increase world trade. Any deficit would have to be made up from imported grain.

But there is a fly in the ointment. WTO negotiations are handled on our behalf by that Frenchman, Pascal Lamy. And, as we have seen with the sugar and banana regimes, the EU Commission's agenda is not necessarily one that will suit UK producers.

20. Better Regulation

Whatever the 'high ground' of support schemes, and the broader utility of rural policies, the point has already been made that 'joined-up government' is an essential prerequisite for a prosperous rural economy. Different policies must intermesh so that they do not conflict with or negate each other. No more so than in the case of regulation, which has the potential completely to undermine the agriculture industry.

But it is a measure of the complexity of the subject that farmers' complaints about regulatory burdens included 'yellow lines' in town-centre streets. Equally objectionable are the bijou pedestrianisation schemes in town centres, beloved by planners, which rob towns of their commercial vitality. Hampered by restricted parking or vehicle access, shoppers are less inclined to patronise high-street shops and will instead drive to local supermarkets. Since it is the high-street shops which provide an outlet for many farmers, parking regulations have a direct effect on the prosperity of some sectors of agriculture.

For my own part, I would rely on a laissez-faire attitude to parking, prohibiting it only if it obstructs access to emergency vehicles. Alternatively, local authorities should ensure at least equal provision for parking close to high-street sites as they do for the supermarkets which compete for the same business.

But let us return to the more central issues of regulation. In Chapter 6 I introduced the concept of different regulatory models, the 'penalty' and the 'intervention' models in particular, the one punishing people for transgressing the rules and the other fabricating ever more complex regulations to prevent people from breaking the rules, transgression of which becomes an offence in its own right. In terms of simplifying the regulatory code, reversion to the 'penalty' system, away from 'intervention', would do much to make everyone's life easier and happier. At the heart of such a move is an essential liberalism, in that the boundaries of acceptable behaviour are set by society but it is left to individuals to determine how they keep within those boundaries.

This contrasts with the objectionable aspect of the 'intervention' model – its sheer negativity. More and more, the state is seen as intruding into the 'nooks and crannies' of everyday life, dictating what can and cannot be done. It also creates an unavoidable conflict between the business ethos and compliance. Business is about making money – that dirty word 'profit' – while compliance with regulations costs money. Inevitably, when a businessman is confronted with technical regulations that impose significant costs, he will compare the costs of compliance with the risk of detection and the penalties. If the chances of detection are slight, and/or the penalties are significantly less than the cost of compliance, many will take the cost-effective option and ignore the regulations.

Alternatively, the businessman will seek another approach, encapsulated in the difference between what is known in the environmental field as 'BATNIEC' and 'CATNIP'. The former is an acronym which relates to the technology required to minimise pollution, plant operators being required to adopt the Best Available Technology Not Involving Excessive Cost. But, in reality, operators go for CATNIP – Cheapest Available Technology Not Involving Prosecution. Compliance is driven by the search for the 'minimum fix', which is not necessarily the best way of dealing with actual problems. But there is another way.

What is needed is a completely different approach to regulation, one which addresses real problems sensibly, with systems so devised that, if requirements are met, businesses actually save money. Then, regulation is working *with* the business ethos, rather than against it.

The 'third' way

To illustrate how an alternative system of regulation could work, I have drawn on a particular case history. This concerns a series of incidents which affected large numbers of farmers, particularly sheep farmers, who had severe health problems after using sheep dips formulated with organophosphorus pesticides (OPs).

On the face of it, these incidents should not have happened.

OPs, in common with all other chemicals licensed (or 'authorised', in the legal jargon) for use as pesticides on the farm, are subject to what appears to be one of the most rigorous regulatory regimes imaginable. In the first instance, products must be thoroughly tested to demonstrate that they satisfy extensive safety criteria. Then, manufacturing is rigorously inspected. Quality and consistency are checked. Labelling and containers have to be approved and the use of the products is subject to reams of health and safety laws. In theory, nothing can go wrong. In practice, it does.

Controlling the whole safety system is a regulatory agency, which qualifies as a 'sefra'. It regulates pesticides and drugs used on animals, for which it is able to charge substantial licensing fees, the source of its income. This is the Veterinary Medicines Directorate (VMD).

Specific evaluations of safety are conducted by the Veterinary Products Committee (VPC), which draws it membership mainly from scientists, most of whom have direct or indirect pharmaceutical interests in the very companies submitting their products for approval. Interestingly, in 1992, eleven of the seventeen members had professional links with pharmaceutical companies that made OPs.

As regards safety testing, for obvious reasons pesticides cannot be tried out on human beings. Tests are carried out on animals using what is known technically as a 'predictive model'. Animals are used as 'models' to predict whether humans might be harmed. To that effect, licence applicants negotiate with the VMD a package of safety tests. These are then carried out by the applicants, or commercial laboratories on their behalf, and the results are submitted to the VMD – and thence to the VPC – for scrutiny. However, the regulators have no means of independently verifying the results submitted to them.

The primary test used is known as the LD_{50}, which is usually expressed in mg/kg body weight of the test animal. It represents the concentration of a chemical required to kill 50 per cent of a test population, applied either orally or dermally. To assess oral toxicity, the laboratory rat is often used. For dermal toxicity tests, rabbits are the animals of choice. Survivors are often kept, sometimes for several months, to assess whether there are any delayed toxic effects. Percutaneous LD_{50} tests are often required. These involve injecting pesticides in measured doses under the skins of test animals (again usually laboratory rats). Inhalation tests are carried out when volatile or dusty products are being produced.

During these tests, known as 'primary toxicity tests', there is a requirement that any mutagenicity indications are 'noted', but carcinogenicity is evaluated mainly through longer-term tests. These involve exposing rats or mice to daily doses of the test substances for the natural lifespan of the test animals – two years in the case of a rat and eighteen months for a mouse. Doses are based on the maximum daily intake levels set for man.

OPs, however, are neurotoxins – they affect the central nervous system. Therefore, they must also undergo tests for neurotoxicity. Hens are used, a group being exposed to an LD_{50} level of the pesticide under test. The survivors are observed for a period of twenty-one days after the initial effects have worn off. During this period, disabilities commensurate with neurological damage are noted. The birds are then killed and examined.

Despite the extensive nature of these tests, however, they are inherently flawed. They rely heavily on the powers of science to predict risk, but there can be no assurance that what is harmful to animals and birds is necessarily harmful to man, and vice versa. In other respects, the tests are fatally inadequate – literally so in some cases – in that they focus on acute toxicity (the immediate effects) and ignore the potential for longer-term (chronic) damage. They also ignore the 'cocktail effect' – the effects of products when mixed with other chemicals or when users are also exposed to other chemicals, albeit not necessarily at the same time.

In these flaws lie great dangers. People are persuaded that a benevolent government has subjected chemicals to rigorous testing and has ensured that all the necessary information has been made available. The regulatory system is trusted to have done everything possible to safeguard the public interest. Users, not unsurprisingly, believe they are being offered, if not a guarantee, certainly an assurance of safety.

Nothing can go wrong ...

In reality, the situation is exactly the opposite of what it purports to be. Far from actually assuring safety for the user, the regulatory system is actually giving the manufacturers of the products an indemnity – an assurance that if or when a product does go wrong and people are harmed, they cannot be sued for damages. The manufacturers, faced with law-suits, simply fall back on the licensing system, arguing that the product is safe because the 'government' has said so by virtue of having licensed it.

Victims of what are known as 'suspected adverse reactions', who without product licensing could have sued the manufacturers directly – as they did with thalidomide – now have to determine the relative liability of manufacturers and the government licensing agency. This adds difficulties to an already difficult process, and effectively prevents all but a very few damages cases succeeding in the courts. And it gets worse.

Post-licensing surveillance

As a means of ensuring the continuing 'safety' of licensed products, the VMD records – or is supposed to record – all cases of alleged harm caused by these products, a process known as 'post-licensing surveillance'. However, if this agency is too zealous in monitoring for problems, and picks up large numbers of 'suspected adverse reactions', it may be criticised for licensing as safe a product which is subsequently proved to be otherwise. If this happens too many times, or even if large numbers of people are affected by a single product, the public – and government ministers – might start questioning the usefulness of the system.

Here we bump into the phenomenon explored earlier: 'self-maintenance', the all-pervasive pressure on bureaucracies – and such is the VMD – to protect their own interests and ensure their self-perpetuation. For the VMD, it is against its own self-interest – its self-maintenance ethos – to find something wrong with products it has licensed. And to make sure it does find nothing seriously wrong, the agency has constructed an elaborate charade whereby it appears to look for problems but in fact ensures that nothing damaging (to it) gets through the system.

The way this works is to transfer to victims of a pesticide contact the responsibility of reporting their own conditions and of *proving* that they have been affected by the product in question. They even have to report their 'adverse reactions' on an official form, without which a complaint is not recognised. Then, according to the VMD:

All suspected adverse reaction (SAR) reports should be acknowledged within three working days and summaries of all SAR reports are presented quarterly to the VPC. The target is for all SAR reports to be presented within ninety days of receipt to the VPC and for serious SAR reports to be presented within thirty working days or the next VPC meeting. Whichever is sooner. Follow-up action is taken based on advice received from the VPC.

In other words, some office functionary looks at the forms and summarises the contents. At three-month intervals, a compilation of the summaries – but not the original complaints – is presented to a scientific committee, made up largely of scientists with links to the chemical companies which have produced the offending products. Most often, these dedicated men of science do precisely nothing. In the rare event that anything at all is done, the victims are approached and asked to supply more information and evidence to support their complaints. Right through the process, it is up to the victims to prove their case.

Compare and contrast this scheme with the system for investigating food poisoning arising from commercially produced food. In the first instance, suspected food poisoning is a notifiable disease. On receipt of reports, verbal or otherwise, upwards of six thousand environmental health officers are available to carry out field investigations and to collect samples. These officials are backed by a network of microbiological laboratories, medical consultants employed by the health authorities, and MAFF veterinary officials. A response time might be expected in hours rather than days, and information is shared nationally through a network of interconnected computers, backed by a comprehensive list of publications. These combined forces track the source of the infection, and if they find the persons responsible, they are often prosecuted, following which civil claims by the victims are relatively uncomplicated.

For the pesticide victims there is no such luxury. The problems are made even worse in the case of OPs as the symptoms of adverse events are often 'non-specific' – ranging from headaches and blurred vision to life-threatening depression, where suicide is not uncommonly attempted – and there is no definitive, officially recognised diagnostic test. For the many people who claim to have suffered from OP poisoning, the search for diagnosis has taken many years of frustrating referrals from one medical specialist to another. And, all the time, the VMD and its advisers in the VPC are judge and juries in their own cause. They decide whether to accept an 'adverse reaction'. They decide whether the evidence offered is acceptable. They decide what action to take.

Regulatory capture

Here we confront yet another of the phenomena discussed in an earlier chapter – 'regulatory capture'. The VMD relies for the bulk of its funding on the companies it regulates. Thus, there is no longer a 'pure' relationship, as there would be, say, between the police and a suspected burglar. In fact the relationship is more akin to that between a supplier and a customer. In this context, it is notable that most 'sefras' call their regulated industries 'customers', as indeed does the VMD.

Where such a cosy partnership exists, the agency has a vested interest in the survival of its fee-paying 'customers'. It will tend to avoid actions which might prejudice their profitability, for fear of damaging its own revenue base. When the agency is also required to be 'cost effective' – at least showing a break-even on its operational account – it may be more interested in promoting the interests of those 'customers' that make a positive contribution – i.e. those that pay more in fees than they cost to regulate.

Of course, the larger 'customers' offer a positive contribution and are more profitable for the regulator. Smaller operations, which cost more to police than they contribute, are therefore discriminated against. Then the larger 'customers', who are aware of their financial contributions to the regulator – on which it relies for its survival – start taking over. This is the final phase of 'regulatory capture'. They exercise influence and even control over the regulator, sometimes subtly and sometimes crudely – by threatening, for instance, to relocate to countries where the regulatory regime is more amenable, unless their conditions are met.

A primary concern of these 'customers' is invariably to increase their own market share. Advertising and marketing are expensive, and it is often more cost effective to lobby for regulation that has a disproportionate effect on smaller businesses.

This leaves the market open to a 'regulatory conspiracy', where regulation is actively solicited by an alliance of the regulatory agency and its larger 'customers'. This benefits the agency by increasing its fees and gives equal benefit to the 'customers' by increasing the cost of competing in the market. Small competitors are driven out and new entrants are excluded. Regulatory costs can, of course, be recovered from product users who are forced to buy from a state-enforced monopoly which can charge whatever it needs to pay its regulators.

This situation is by no means theoretical. In 1995 a pesticide manufacturer (Aquaspersions Limited) sent a letter to the chairman of the 1995 Agriculture Committee concerning its product 'Hugtite'. Part of this letter is reproduced below.

About eight years ago my company, along with Humber Growers Limited in Humberside, developed an environmentally friendly pesticide based on modified potato starch. The product has been successfully patented in the UK, Europe, America and Japan.

For the last five years Hugtite has been slowly moving through the approval process at PSD [Pesticide Safety Directorate] having obtained an experimental permit for its use on cucumbers and tomatoes in 1990. All the indications from PSD last year were that an approval was likely by the year-end, on which basis a product launch was planned for January ....

Regretfully, late in 1994 we were told that the product had to go through a European approval process which demanded a considerable amount of extra data to be generated .... The cost of providing this data – minimally a further £250,000 and the three years necessary to generate it has caused [our marketing company] to withdraw interest.

This is a nonsensical situation. Had the product been marketed as an ingredient for soups, gravies, stews and sauces, for which it was already used, no approvals would have been necessary. Had it been sold as a glaze for protecting the cut edges of cucumbers or as a leaf-shine product, none of the data required would have been needed. In preventing this product reaching the marketplace, the regulatory authorities forced potential customers to use the existing licensed products. These were more dangerous than 'Hugtite' and had to be obtained from established manufacturers. By imposing tight controls on safety, not only does the regulatory machine create a dangerous situation, it also serves its customers' interests by reinforcing their monopolies.

The Alternative Model

The alternative to the disaster which is the regulatory system for dangerous chemicals is to use the system applied to food. In this case – with some exceptions – there is no requirement to license a new product. Anyone can enter the market, without any reference to the authorities. However, there are numerous, wholly independent enforcement officers in the field checking on compliance with standards. If products fall short of standards set, then prosecutions are instigated and, if the facts are proven, penalties are imposed. By this means, the regulators act as advocates for the victims, not as potential defendants protecting themselves against damages claims, as would be the case if they had licensed the products.

Manufacturers, in this 'model', might be allowed free access to the market, but this would be backed up by a specific 'duty of care', a requirement not to cause harm – with compulsory insurance held to cover any potential damages claims, without evidence of which a product could not be released. This arrangement would need to be supported not by a licensing scheme but by registration. Producers would be required to lodge with the regulator details of their products, the testing undertaken and the results, and to update information as it became available. No further direct control, prior to release, would be exercised, but the regulator would monitor product usage for adverse effects, including investigating claims and carrying out detailed field studies, with additional scientific research where necessary.

Borrowing from the food poisoning investigation system, it would be necessary to have a cadre of skilled officials capable of investigating adverse reactions. Where they found evidence of failure to exercise the 'duty of care', prosecutions could be undertaken, and massive penalties imposed. Victims would almost certainly have access to established facts on which to base their claims for compensation, and would not have to mount their own cases unaided, as is the situation at the moment. As a result of this, most manufacturers might settle out of court, their risks being covered by mandatory insurance.

And despite the absence of statutory pre-release licensing, a form of pre-release certification would still be carried out. No commercial company could release a product until it had carried out necessary checks to ensure that, as far as practicable, the product was safe to use, because it would not get insurance. For some products, like 'Hugtite', the test regime might be less onerous than that currently imposed. For others, it would be more severe. Where imponderables existed, such as the propensity to cause chronic damage – which is very difficult to measure – certain products already in use might have difficulty in getting cover.

A side effect of this regime would also be, through increased competition, a reduction in the costs of veterinary drugs and better availability of some of the cheap remedies (many of which have a long history of safety) that have been withdrawn because they are too expensive to relicense.

The 'insurance' model

Therein lie the bones of an alternative regulatory system. All businesses have to have insurance but many policies are what are known as 'all risk'. Given a requirement for separate policies for specific risks – such as food poisoning, health and safety, and the others that might affect farming and allied enterprises – the financial risk is carried by the insurance company and compensation is available for anyone harmed.

But there is a twist. With many risks, the chances of causing harm are so slight that insurance premiums would be negligible. There is no incentive to prevent harm. And although within the legal system there is provision to prosecute those who cause harm, again the penalties are often insignificant. But this could be changed. Firstly, penalties could be linked to turnover, say a multiple of the annual figure, and then – something which is not allowed at the moment – businesses could be permitted to insure against penalties. The insurance companies would then be at serious financial risk and would impose conditions before they took on clients. But, more importantly, low-risk operations would pay lower premiums. At last, removing risk would be linked to profitability. By improving safety, the business would make more profit.

Genetically modified organisms

New products always bear an element of uncertainty, an implied risk which cannot be quantified easily. Into that category fall genetically modified organisms (GMOs), which have caused considerable public controversy, to say nothing of widespread opposition. Interestingly, lined up alongside the companies that are seeking to market these products are governments, quick with their reassurances that legislation is in place to protect the public.

It should perhaps occur to those who oppose GMOs and demand more regulation that the legislation is not intended to protect the public but to protect the marketing companies. If they surmount whatever hurdles the legislators erect, they have immunity from public action, having acquired a licence to operate. Effectively, by submitting to regulation, marketing organisations enlist the support of whole governments, which are then compromised by their assent to the process.

If marketing companies are confident about the safety of their products – and their limited impact on the environment – then they should have the courage of their convictions. Rather than hide behind the skirts of governments, relying on conformity with legislation to give them immunity, they should take the risk of being wrong. What price the insurance premium for genetically modified maize, should any company be willing to underwrite the risk?

Freedom for all

Of course, the insurance model described would only affect regulation based on 'intervention'. But that, in itself, would afford considerable relief for retail food shops, markets and small producers, who complain that hygiene laws are applied far more rigorously in the UK than elsewhere. Since risk would largely be born by insurance companies, this would also deal with complaints about the risk-adverse Department of Health, which – sometimes with tragic consequences – is ready to close down businesses on the slightest pretext. It is one thing for the Department to take on a sole trader; it is quite another for it to confront a major insurer with a purse deep enough to fund serious legal challenges.

Removal of interventionalist legislation would also be of great assistance to slaughterhouses. They would no longer have to be licensed but 'registered', as are most other food premises. If they produced unfit food they would be massively penalised, but there would be no state inspectors on the premises to prevent that from happening. If slaughterhouse owners need inspectors to ensure that their products are wholesome, they should employ their own. This would remove the complaint of excessive MHS inspection costs and their disproportionate effects on small abattoirs.

It would also prevent hundreds of useless and uselessly employed vets wasting their time in slaughterhouses, costing the meat industry a small fortune. They could be redeployed in the State Veterinary Service, where their presence would reverse the rundown of the service. There, they could be usefully employed, monitoring the health of farm animals. Then, perhaps next time there is an outbreak of foot and mouth disease, it will not take six months or more to discover it.

Planning and other problems

There is more to regulation than simply interventionalist legislation, and again the wide range of complaints about 'regulation' – itemised in Chapter 5 – underlines the difficulties in addressing complaints about over-regulation. One of these complaints is about the town and country planning system. Planning laws are applied over-rigorously to farms, limiting their ability to diversify. Yet the controls themselves are based on a false premise, that it is necessary and desirable to 'zone' land usage according to pre-defined categories. Thus, agricultural land should be used for farming, industrial areas for industry, and so on.

The problem is that farming does not fit into the tidy little categories that the planners so admire. Traditionally, 'agriculture' has always been a mixed economy, and a wide range of work is normally carried out on farms, from administration in offices to repairing and maintaining vehicles, tractors and farm equipment. Farms can become 'depots' for quite sizeable transport operations, home bases for agricultural contractors, and sites for animal slaughter and the further processing of a variety of agricultural products. Redundant hen-houses and pig units are very often suitable for conversion to offices, warehouses or for light industrial use. In the main, the environmental impact of these developments is minimal and, in some cases, beneficial. Which produces more pollution – an intensive hen-house or the same building converted into offices?

By and large, therefore, subject to overall restrictions on scale, farms should be totally exempted from planning restrictions, free to adapt, convert and build as necessary to maintain overall economic viability. Such exemptions might perhaps be conditional on the environmental impact of developments being limited, but the onus of proof should be on the planners, working to guidelines set by central government.

As to distortions produced by the planning system, which give preferential treatment to supermarkets and out-of-town developments, there have been, of late, some controls. But these have been more a case of shutting the gate after the horse has bolted. In many areas the damage has already been done. However, with the ability to be flexible, and an emphasis on quality and niche marketing, most farm enterprises and small shops can compete with supermarkets, given a 'level playing field'.

Another important, if localised, aggravation is urban encroachment. It is quite inequitable that residential or other developments can be permitted adjacent to existing farming enterprises and for new residents then to complain about the flies, noise, smells and so on, which were there long before they arrived. Developers can be wickedly cynical about this, building new homes next to 'nuisance' sites in the expectation that the law will subsequently shut them down. And the residents also benefit. Often they acquire their properties at a significant discount because of the presence of adjoining operations, and then enjoy increases in value when the 'nuisance' is removed.

The obvious remedy is to carry out a 'nuisance' survey prior to development and, if the operation is deemed to present a problem to the new site, to give the developer the opportunity of buying out the nuisance at market rates. That way, the farmer is treated fairly and the true development costs are born by the new occupants.

Welfare rules, for both pigs and poultry and, to an extent, other livestock, also present a significant burden, but there are few farmers who would argue against them. Their concern is, once again, the unlevel playing field, where they are required to compete with producers operating to lesser standards. Farmers must be protected from this, by import restrictions based on common welfare standards.

The cost and difficulties inherent in disposing of 'casualty' animals are also a welfare matter. Much of this problem arises from a few misplaced and quite unnecessary prosecutions of farmers – and even vets – for permitting the transport of injured animals to slaughterhouses. Clearer government guidelines would resolve the problem. However, in terms of the broader problem of disposal, costs have escalated largely as a result of the BSE controls on knackers. There is room here for a public subsidy, on the lines of that available in France.

The 'harmonisation' programme also needs to be revisited. Clearly, it should be up to any nation state to decide what standards they apply to their imports (subject to WTO and other agreements), but it is plainly nonsense blindly to apply export rules to domestic producers. Why should a small egg producer be forced to grade his eggs according to rigorous marketing rules, and be limited to selling only Grade A eggs to the local shop, just because a multimillion-pound operation in France or Holland wants to compete for the business?

The same applies to the Christmas turkey trade and complaints that restrictive hygiene measures prevent small-scale seasonal production. It is entirely safe for a farmer, a few weeks before Christmas, to cover an old door with new plastic sheeting, and set it up on straw bales in a barn to use as a worktop to produce a couple of hundred dry-plucked, uneviscerated turkeys for local customers.[1] The income used to be a useful bonus for many small farmers, and there is no reason whatsoever why they should be forced to apply international rules devised for large-scale exporting processors. Therein lies madness, the madness of a regulatory system which is doing more harm than good.

21. Dealing with Scares

As a motivating force for increased and highly damaging regulation, there seems to be no more effective a device than the scare, effectively defined as 'a disproportionate response to a threat'. While there may be every willingness on the part of governments to avoid being 'bounced' into panic legislation, the pressure induced by the scare dynamic is so powerful as to be almost irresistible, forcing a disproportionate legislative response. The way to defuse scares is to understand them, thereby enabling early action to be taken to prevent the situation getting out of hand. This must be an essential element of any structure that aims to protect agriculture, which has been too long at the receiving end of scare-induced regulation.

In this context, it should be appreciated that the 'scare' phenomenon, known better to sociologists as 'moral panic', is not new. Similar dynamics have been recorded as early as the 1600s. The classic scare scenario can, in fact, be recognised in the 1678 Popish plot. Here, the central figure was Titus Oates, a failed Jesuit priest who put about a series of lies to the effect that the Jesuits were planning to murder the king and invite foreign powers to recover England for the Pope and Catholicism. In the ensuing panic, thirty-five entirely innocent people were executed. It was not until 1684 that the frenzy completely subsided.

Interestingly, this scare, indistinguishable in principle from modern scares, existed even before daily newspapers – much less television and radio – had been invented. This suggests that the media are not primarily responsible for the scare phenomenon, as is supposed by many commentators. However, in that the Popish plot ran for about six years, the indications are that the media intensify the scale of scares, while perhaps shortening their duration.

For an explanation as to why people respond to the threats which lead up to a scare, and why it is so difficult to counter them, reference can be made to none other than Shakespeare, who wrote in *A Midsummer Night's Dream*:

> Or in the night, imagining some fear,
> How easy is a bush suppos'd a bear.

Imagine walking down a path in the twilight in an unfamiliar area and happening upon a half-formed shape in the distance. The imagination will turn what is in fact a bush into one's worst nightmare: a bear. This illustrates an inherent facet of the human psyche: fear of the unknown. This, in itself, is a survival strategy, and it is entirely natural that humans should be afraid. It is also entirely logical that the imagination should attempt to rationalise the unknown and turn it into a more familiar threat against which a response can be formulated.

Therefore, at the heart of the scare is human psychology. But in the Middle Ages people were mainly concerned with moral corruption. Religious scares, such as the 'witchcraft' scares and the Popish plot, focused on loss of the immortal soul. Today, in a society in which religion is less important, the focus has shifted to the body mortal. In contemporary scares, therefore, we see 'mortal fear' of eggs, of contaminated cheese and of BSE-infected cattle. These threats invoked fear of bodily corruption.

On that basis, it is evident that scares, as such, will never be entirely preventable. It is in the nature of people to respond to very mild fears. Christopher Booker defined the substance of this phenomenon with an invented word: the 'nyktomorph', a composite of the Greek *nykto* and *morph*, meaning night-shape. It defines the source of that vague insubstantial fear – the bush which turns into the bear. In many ways, the root of all food scares is a nyktomorph: the food-poisoning bacterium, the unfamiliar *Listeria monocytogenes* or the terrifying 'prion' in BSE.

Interestingly, however, despite its psychological provenance – or perhaps because of it – the scare has a definite structure and follows rigid rules. All full-blown scares have what I have come to call 'scare elements', of which four must always be present. These are:

Universality
Novelty

Plausibility

Uncertainty

There are also other elements, but the above are essential to the scare dynamic. They merit detailed examination.

Universality

Specialist foods or branded products are rarely involved in a full-blown scare. Products implicated in scares have included eggs (about 30 million eggs are sold per day), cheese and, to an extent, cook-chilled meals, in the context of the listeria scare. But the 'mother of all scares' was beef. Again this was a generic product eaten by all except the 5 per cent of the population who are vegetarians.

Novelty

The essence of the scare in terms of the media response is defined by the very element for which the media exists – news. And news has to be 'new': there must be some facet of the 'nyktomorph' about which nothing has been previously written in the popular media.

In the context of the salmonella-in-eggs scare, salmonella was not news. The number of cases had been rising in the UK ever since statistics had first been formally published in 1945. There was nothing new in an increase in aalmonella; there was nothing new about people dying from food poisoning. But the 1988 scare was presented in terms of a new 'killer bug' – *Salmonella enteritidis*.[1] The fact that it was 'getting inside the egg' was also an apparently new phenomenon.

The same dynamic can be seen very clearly with cheese. It had become infected with a 'new', almost unpronounceable bug, again branded as a killer, *Listeria monocytogenes*. The fact that the organism had been discovered in 1926 was irrelevant. It sounded terrible, it was killing babies and, as far as the media were concerned, it was brand new. And BSE was also presented as a brand-new cattle disease, with the potential to kill thousands or even millions of people. The 'prion' identified as the putative infective agent was the ideal 'nyktomorph' – invisible to the naked eye and virtually indestructible, causing an incurable disease.

Plausibility

A threat does not have to be real. What is important is perception. If it is perceived to be plausible, a scare will develop. The principal means by which plausibility emerges is though the threat being adopted by authoritative sponsors, such as a well-known academic, an important civil servant (as in the Chief Medical Officer) or a government minister.

If there is evidence of people dying or becoming seriously ill, apparently as a result of exposure to the threat, this strengthens its plausibility. It is strongly enhanced if there is evidence of children or babies dying. Government warnings, or new regulations introduced to deal with the problem, also drive the scare dynamic, reinforcing the plausibility of the threat.

Uncertainty

Flying in aeroplanes kills people. Heroin kills people. Some 3,500 people die on the roads each year; over 5,000 a year are killed in NHS hospitals as a result of infection. As many die from adverse reactions to prescribed drugs (licensed as 'safe' by government) and medical negligence. But these are familiar and known risks. They are discounted and accepted as part of the everyday hazards of life. There is no debate, no uncertainty and no scare.

In the early stages of the egg scare, however, there was a major debate about how many eggs were infected. Estimates varied from one in 10, to one in 5,000, to one in 500,000, to one in 10 million. There were also arguments about whether there had been 20 or 700 deaths. The uncertainty fuelled the debate, whereas, had there been agreement on the issues, the scare would have died very quickly. Thus uncertainty drives the issue forward and keeps it in the headlines.

Government denials can create uncertainty, especially when an official spokesman warns of the threat and then tries to talk down the scale, or when different spokesmen present different versions of the same event. Equally, during the progress of a scare, scientific disagreement can create uncertainty.

Scares as an artifact

Scares are not accidental or random phenomena. They are invariably manufactured, and behind their creation is what could be described as a major industry. Behind the 'industry' are key persons and groups, known as 'agenda pushers'.

These 'agenda pushers', or 'pushers' for short, are individuals, or organisations, who have 'agendas' which they wish to promote. By harnessing the scare elements, deliberately, intuitively or even accidentally, they are able to advance their agendas, bringing them into the political arena in a way that conventional lobbying cannot. In a way, scare creation is a form of institutionalised queue-jumping, whereby legislators are forced to intervene in issues which would not otherwise warrant political attention.

However, there are also other 'players' in this game. These are called the 'blockers', groups or individuals opposing the scare tendency. In normal circumstances, there is equilibrium between the 'pushers' and 'blockers', and there is no scare. When the pushers gain temporary dominance, arising either from the blockers switching sides or from their failure to neutralise the pushers, and all the scare elements are in place, the full-blown scare will develop.

Typical 'pushers' may be academics, sometimes motivated by nothing more than a need to seek higher profiles for their specialities in order to raise research funding. Others have more personal agendas, such as a revulsion for intensive food production, and use their status to further their interests. Other very important pushers are the regulatory agencies who 'talk up' threats to further their own sectional interests, a mechanism for obtaining an increased share of public funding, more staff and a higher public profile. Also, professional bodies, especially those representing regulatory agency staff, are often strong agenda pushers. The greater the threat, the more likely it is that their professional members benefit both financially and in terms of status and numbers.

Then there are a number of loose-knit groups who dislike intensive farming, or even the exploitation of animals. Members are ready to link their agendas to the scare dynamic to pursue their own objectives. Individuals in the media can also use their positions to advance their own, or corporate, agendas.

Perversely, certain sectors of the food industry may play an important role in promoting scares, not necessarily intentionally. For instance, the Food and Drink Federation, through the early part of 1988, ran a publicity campaign seeking to reverse public hostility to preservatives by highlighting the microbial threats. The strategy backfired but, for a while, the food industry was actually highlighting the same threat as other agenda pushers.

As to blocking scares, predictably affected trade sectors will perform that role. The media may also play the role of the 'blocker', diminishing the impact of scares by spreading information based on good science. By being dispassionate, and giving time to different commentators to explore the issues, they can remove uncertainty. Politicians may perform either role, depending on their political orientations.

Independent scientists may be major blockers. Although the elements of the UK egg scare were present in America and Holland, where most people watch BBC1, in neither of these countries was there a major scare. In the United States, there was an East/West Coast division within the scientific community. East Coast scientists were pushing the scare while West Coast scientists were dismissing it. The American Egg Association was able to exploit the division and prevent the scare taking off. However, once the scare dynamic is up and running, such divisions can exacerbate a scare. In Holland, however, the industry had its own university links and a strong corps of supportive scientists. It was able to call upon these scientists to put the issue in context.

In the UK, however, the egg industry had no scientific backing to call upon. On the day Currie made her announcement, and for months afterwards, there were no scientists anywhere in the country who were prepared to support the industry. All the scientists who were prepared to talk publicly were on the other side.

The structure of a scare

In any full-blown scare there is a clear structure. There are five distinct phases. The first is the 'public phase', when the media 'catch' the story and give it high-profile treatment. It is covered on the front pages of the newspapers, becomes the lead story on all channels and is featured in current affairs magazines. It is the main item on chat shows and discussion programmes. This is the classic 'nine-day wonder' phase.

If the scare elements are not complete, after the initial outcry the scare dissipates. But, if they are, phase two starts. This is the 'reaction phase', where consumers take note and avoid the profiled product – for example, there was a 90 per cent drop over a few days in the consumption of beef after the 1996 BSE announcement. If the scare continues, it enters phase three, the 'political phase'. Here, the politicians start taking a real and then dangerous interest. If their interest continues, the executive responds by framing legislation. This is phase four, the 'legislative phase'. Finally, in phase five, the legislation is enforced by a variety of officials – the 'enforcement phase'.

The 'public' phase

The 'public' phase is fuelled by uncertainty. Coverage in the media is amoral: the 'story' is treated on its news merit, the level of coverage dictated by 'peer' activity and the news values of the media organisation. Television and radio journalists read the previous day's papers. In newspaper offices there are televisions showing every channel and journalists watch their rivals' coverage.

The 'reaction' phase

Consumer reaction may be immediate, perhaps apparent within hours. Days later, there is often evidence of a sales decline. But consumers are not a homogeneous group. Different groups respond differently. Household buyers revert to earlier patterns fairly quickly but institutional buyers tend to behave differently. They make buying decisions but do not suffer the consequences of their decisions. The school meals buyers, for instance, who decide to ban beef, do not suffer the consequences of this decision because they do not eat school meals. They can afford the luxury of being risk adverse, whereas the average houseperson (if there is such a being) comes under pressure from the family to provide familiar and popular meals. Following the egg scare, household consumer sales recovered to 90 per cent of pre-scare levels within weeks of Currie's statement. The same happened with beef after the March 1996 crisis. The longer-term drop in sales was due to institutional buyers avoiding the product.

The 'political' phase

Political activity is often delayed, but when party politicians react they most often respond along partisan lines. The real danger, however, is the 'closed loop'. When the media run the story, the politicians, in their little bubbles, follow the media and believe they represent popular sentiment. They then start reacting, and the media report them as if they were representing the public interest. The two then fuel each other, with occasional input from external figures. The 'debate' becomes self-referential. Consumers are no longer involved. For them, the scare becomes a spectator sport.

The 'legislative' phase

The effect of the political interest is to prolong the scare and, more dangerously, to create pressure for a legislative response. Rarely, however, does proposed regulation address the real problems. More commonly, it is focused on restoring 'consumer confidence' but the actual effect is usually to confirm to the consumer that there was indeed a problem. The perception is that, if there had been no substance to the 'scare', legislation would be unnecessary. New controls cause consumer confidence to dip, and sales drop again.

The 'enforcement' phase

Legislators see their role as creating legislation. But once they have completed their tasks, they move on, by which time media coverage of the original scare has subsided. They then tend to be uninterested in what the enforcement officials do. The trouble is that it may take time for the legislation to bite, but its impact can last for years, long after the crisis which gave rise to it has been forgotten.

It is the combined effect of the 'legislative' and 'enforcement' phases which does the most damage in triggering a renewed decline in sales and engendering costs of compliance.

Furthermore, the damage is not always financial. As part of the response to the 1996 *E. coli* outbreak, the Meat Hygiene Service launched a 'clean animal campaign', requiring, among other things, farmers to clip the bellies of cattle to remove long, soiled hair. This had no relevance whatsoever to the outbreak, which involved cooked meat. But two hundred workers have been badly injured trying to obey the new rules.

Limiting the damage

With food scares, prevention is better than cure. From an industry perspective, this requires good 'intelligence', as there is often early warning of a problem. The fatal mistake made by the egg industry was that it did not realise early enough that its product was being targeted. In June 1998, months before the 'public' phase of the scare, it was obvious from the growing coverage in a wide range of media that the issue was building up. The industry could and should have known that problems were emerging and appropriate action could have been taken to defuse the scare. Not least, once the 'scare elements' were seen to be coming together, and the 'pushers' were recognised, it should have been possible to start taking defensive action.

The appliance of science

Dealing with 'pushers' is, or should be, primarily a responsibility of government, inasmuch as, in many cases, they are government scientists. Here, the original driving force is the 'self-maintenance' dynamic, where the individuals or their organisations are seeking to engender and then exploit public concern for their own ends. This problem is one of the government's own making in that, effectively, science has been progressively 'nationalised' under successive administrations. Even supposedly independent universities are unhealthily reliant on public funding (or grants from drug companies, which are effectively in the 'pocket' of the governmental scientific establishment), to the extent that they are all too often beholden to sponsoring ministries which hold the purse-strings.

Being totally reliant on public funds, which are often erratic and – at least, in the opinions of their recipients – insufficient, workers are often forced to exist hand to mouth. The obvious and time-honoured route to increased funding is 'shroud waving', creating a scare, the solution to which is more research and more funding. One is forcibly reminded of the wit of that ferociously controversial American journalist, H.L. Mencken, who observed:

> The whole aim of practical politics is to keep the populace alarmed – and hence clamorous to be led to safety – by menacing it with an endless series of hobgoblins, all of them imaginary.[2]

Clearly, too many scientists have learned the art of 'practical politics'. One counter is more predictable and equitable funding, with proper financing of key functions. Infectious disease surveillance services, for instance – whether of human or animal diseases (as well as zoonoses) – must be properly funded. Their tasks are to watch, wait and warn, enabling speedy responses to emerging problems, to stop them becoming major problems. All too often, the government acts like a miserly factory owner, paying off security guards – or reducing their pay – because no burglars have broken into the premises. Small wonder the scientists invent 'burglars' to keep themselves in funds.

But to avoid these people exploiting their monopoly of information, the industry must take on a much greater role in funding its own science. It cannot afford to rely on the 'free' science funded by the government. It cannot afford again to be in the position it was when the salmonella scare broke in the media. Then, the egg industry had no scientists to represent it and, faced with demands for a media presence, all it could offer was the president of the NFU and the chairman of the British Egg Industry Council. Against the Chief Medical Officer, MAFF spokesmen, Professor Lacey and other scientists, they were totally out of their depth and were 'creamed'. Earlier, during discussions with the Department of Health, before the scare had broken, the industry again lacked its own scientists to negotiate with government counterparts. Then,as later, industry representatives were totally out of their depth.

Here, the example of the Dutch could well be followed. In Holland each industry sector is represented by its *produktshap*, which raises a statutory levy from its members to fund research.

Scientific effort is superbly co-ordinated. Vets in the field have immediate access to industry-funded research institutes and, where these cannot handle the problem – or longer-term work is needed – they can refer to specialist university departments, also funded by the industry. The system is seamless. It can recognise and deal with problems early, before they reach a critical stage. Furthermore, should a serious problem emerge, beyond the immediate resources of the industry, the *produktshap* can apply, as of right, to the government for a new law which, if granted, releases funding for any measures introduced.

On the other hand, it will come as no surprise that, when it came to researching the meat inspection system, no funds were forthcoming in this country to demonstrate quite how useless it was. The research which demonstrated that inspectors were the most important source of avoidable contamination in the slaughterhouse was funded by the Dutch and Danish meat industries. There was no possibility that MAFF was going to fund work which would damage its own political ambitions.

The Dutch system gives its farmers another advantage. Their research institutes collect a great deal of data for the industry – such as on the incidence of animal diseases – a function carried out in this country by MAFF. Not only does this mean that the better information is collected, free of the whims and capabilities (and incompetence) of government agencies, but control is retained over its release. In the post-salmonella crisis, when I worked for the egg industry, we were often 'bounced' by the Ministry releasing figures which we only found out about by reading the newspapers. We in the industry were the last to know what was going on. This is not to imply that the Dutch industry does not publish its figures; it is obliged to do so. But it is able to have its response ready when the information goes to press and is not caught 'flat footed'.

Neutralising the scare elements

One of the easiest issues to address is novelty. Both government and industry can play a part by being wholly open about emerging problems. Almost counter-intuitively, the best strategy is to flood the media with press releases. Editors and journalist quickly get bored and treat the issue as routine, robbing the subject of its novelty value. This is something that has been learnt by the motor industry, which routinely publishes information on vehicle recalls. When a company initiates the action itself, this is taken as evidence of responsible management. If a recall is forced by adverse publicity, as happened with the A-series Mercedes when stability problems were highlighted in the media, this can be very damaging.

Nothing can be done about 'universality' – a product is either widely consumed or not, and any generic product will always be vulnerable to scares. But 'plausibility' can be addressed. The key, once again, is good, independent science. So much of the science driving the scares has been second rate; in the salmonella scare, some of it was distinctly fraudulent.

Given access to the same data as government and its payroll scientists, industry and independent scientists can at least review these data and provide an alternative to the 'spin' offered by self-interested advocates of a particular line. This, of course, depends on the information being made available. It is interesting to recall that, in the run-up to the salmonella scare, the PHLS was making data from its 'Communicable Disease Reports' freely available to selected journalists but, for people like myself, at the time an independent food safety consultant, the publication was 'confidential' and not available. When the PHLS was finally forced to circulate its publication more widely, it imposed a not insignificant charge and reduced the amount of information given. The report became useless as a source of information.

Similarly, food poisoning outbreak reports, which could provide valuable data for the food industry, enabling problems to be identified and solutions formulated, are often treated as the private property of their authors, to be used freely for their own purposes but withheld from other interested parties. Freedom of information for this type of data is essential.

Dealing with uncertainty also requires good science, but it also relies on advance intelligence and the ability to identify issues of potential concern. The antidote to uncertainty is information, but often this will not be available when new problems are emerging. Therefore, there must also be a highly responsive system which enables funding to be made available for research, without the delays that have been experienced in previous incidents. At the very least, this allows the development of timely and effective control measures and reduces the need to rely on knee-jerk or scattergun measures.

Scares in progress

Once a scare is 'up and running' it is very difficult to affect is course but, at the very least, the 'players' can avoid making the situation worse. Here, without infringing on what is sometimes whimsically called the 'freedom of the press', there is room for the media to play a more responsible and informative role. I recall in the early days of the salmonella scare the *Observer* lovingly detailing the experience of a man who had breakfasted on fried eggs and, two hours later, had fallen ill.[3] According to this newspaper, the man was another infected egg 'victim', except for one minor problem. The incubation period for salmonella food poisoning – the period between exposure to the infective agent and the onset of symptoms – is at least eight hours. No responsible newspaper – or other medium – should lend its name to such utter tosh.

But the main injunction must be directed at the legislators, ministers and civil servants. Difficult though it may be, they must learn restraint. The answer to the problems highlighted during scares is not necessarily new law. In any event, law made in haste is often bad law. There are other ways of solving problems, some of which were explored in the previous chapter.

Above all else, both the legislators and the media need to recover a sense of cynicism. Too may otherwise sensible MPs (if there are such things) and journalists seem to melt at the sound of scientists or law enforcement officials holding forth about the latest threat. But, just as all that glisters is not gold, not every scientist in a white coat who warns of impending, horrible deaths is necessarily telling the objective truth. Nor are they necessarily speaking for the good of humanity. Scientists, like all of us, have their own agendas. In their world, as in the 'jobsworth' mind of the enforcement official, scares are extremely good for business.

The Food Standards Agency

In this context, the continuing existence of the Food Standards Agency should be seriously questioned. Its very existence is a reward to those who have promoted previous scares. But what makes it very dangerous now is that, having taken over many of the duties and responsibilities of MAFF, it lives under the wing of the Department of Health – and the European Union Commission – and works to a mainly urban agenda, or, at least, espouses what might be called urban values. In working to that agenda, it effectively formalises the artificial and divisive distinction between the 'urban' consumer and the 'rural' producer.

Another disadvantage of maintaining the agency was neatly summed up by Stephen Dorrell in January 1997 at the prestigious Oxford Farming Conference. He told delegates that he was opposed 'to any proposal that executive responsibility should be shifted from ministers to some executive agency. Responsibility belongs to Parliament and the Government.' In effect, the Agency creates a screen between government and ordinary people, confusing the issues of responsibility.

In a dangerous way, it also unnecessarily politicises the science of food safety by controlling the flow of information. Therein also lies the danger of 'self-maintenance' in that, should the occasion arise when the Agency falls out of favour with the government and attempts are made to cut its funding, it may well react in much the same way that the PHLS did. It will use its privileged access to information to engineer another food safety crisis, thereby demonstrating its worth to society. In effect, as long as the Agency remains in place, there is a potential 'scare factory' waiting in the wings.

Essentially, there are two crucial areas of concern to a government in pursuit of high food safety standards: policy and enforcement – both relying on good scientific and, above all else, neutral information. For information provision to be neutral, it has to be well separated from the mechanics of government and be freely available to all comers. Governments should govern and information providers should do just that – provide information. The roles should not be confused. The role of government would be made a great deal easier if it had a constant source of good, up-to-date information, thus reducing the uncertainty which has dogged so much of the food safety debate.

Therefore, policy – and policy advice – should be returned to where it properly belongs, with the traditional instrument of government – the ministries. Research and information on risk and emerging food safety threats could be more properly provided by an entirely separate scientific institute, funded through different channels and keeping outside the policy and enforcement 'loop'. What would be ideal would be a 'national institute of food safety', accorded the status of a university with both research and teaching duties. Its task should be the promotion of good science and the provision of accurate information on food safety issues to all comers. We do not need professional spin-doctors using the spurious authority of a government agency to legitimise partisan interests.

That, of course, leads to another question, the proposed establishment of a European Food Authority, regarded as 'an essential pillar of food safety policy in Europe'. By any measure, this is a retrograde step, diminishing rather than improving food safety. Here, it is germane to note that, of the last four major food safety threats, three – *Salmonella enteritidis* in eggs, *Listeria monocytogenes* and *E. coli* O157 – first emerged in the United States and were evident elsewhere the world before affecting the UK. Therefore, control of potential food safety threats needs a wider perspective than 'little Europe'. For surveillance and risk assessment data, there is already the World Health Organisation, with a European outpost in Berlin. And for the WHO, 'Europe' is twenty-seven countries, including Russia and Israel. There is nothing the EU could offer which the broader perspective could not do better.

22. In Paradisum

The last movement of Fauré's *Requiem* is the hauntingly beautiful piece called 'In paradisum', a work which calls on the angels to lead us into paradise. That is the fitting end to many a fictional investigation when the hero – and the compulsory heroine – ride off into the sunset to live happily ever after. But this book is no work of fiction. Heroes and heroines there may be, those men and women who work the land and who, under incredible handicaps, denigration, abuse and plain slander, produce the bulk of our food. For them there is no happy ending – no waiting paradise.

That said, there are solutions which could turn farming back into a happy occupation – if not actually a paradise – and I have sketched out some options which could make the system work incomparably better. In so doing, despite having rounded on the advocates of 'fantasy agriculture', I have indulged my own fantasies, dignified by the more sober appellation of 'vision'. But fantasies they are because without the political will – of which there is no sign – there is not the slightest chance of any of my proposals being adopted.

But even if they are fantasies, they are at least constructive. Better that than the attitude of Christopher Haskins, the government's 'Red Tape Tsar', who in May 2001 confidently predicted that 'Europe' was on the brink of the most radical legislative reform since the birth of the EU as France, Germany and Britain came close to agreement on key changes to agricultural policy and farm subsidies.[1] It will be highly instructive, in the year 2006, to revisit his and all the other confident predictions on the reform of the CAP, when yet again the system groans, thrashes around and fails, once more, to deliver.

If there is to be any reform, the likelihood is that it will not favour British producers. To reduce the crippling burden of the CAP on the EU budget, Chancellor Schröder of Germany is in favour of more 'co-financing', in particular through the extension of rural development schemes. That would afford the British government the opportunity to pay even less to its farmers than it does already.

In terms of this and my other gloomy predictions, I have to say that I started writing this book determined to be strictly neutral on the role of the EU. I have no truck with that brand of Euroscepticism which sees all problems as emanating from 'Europe' and the solution to everything lying in that simple, seductive dictum 'better off out'. Nor do I have any truck with the 'World Order' conspiracy theorists, who hint darkly that the EU is part of a dastardly plot by the Bilderburgers, the hamburgers or even the 'Big Macs' to take over the world and destroy British agriculture. From what we have seen of the Ministry of Agriculture, it is quite capable of doing the job unaided and, by and large, is succeeding.

As for conspiracies in general, there have been endless rumours that the response to foot and mouth disease has been determined by the EU as a means of executing a plan to rid the UK of its livestock industry. Although the mass slaughter of stock has been highly fortuitous for the Community, saddled as it is with massive overproduction, I can nevertheless find no evidence that such a plan exists. However, our 'partners' must be rubbing their eyes in disbelief at their good fortune, that the UK should so obligingly reduce its farm animal population at no cost to Community funds.

Apart from the fact that MAFF – with the full assent of the NFU – sees small farmers as 'inefficient' and has always sought 'rationalisation' – i.e. their removal – nor do I see any evidence within the national frame that the ministry has deliberately set out to engineer the destruction of farming. Never, I have always counselled those who would claim otherwise, underestimate the incompetence of MAFF. More to the point, rather than some grand 'World Order' or even national conspiracy, with a 'Mr Big' sitting in a penthouse suite, somewhere in Brussels, New York, or wherever, stroking his cat while plotting the demise of civilisation as we know it, the essential problem is that no one is in charge.

I am reminded of an interview I had with Mr (now Lord) Freeman in 1996, when I sought to brief him as Chancellor of the Duchy of Lancaster – and nominally in charge of the Cabinet

Office – on the chaos overtaking the implementation of the 'over-thirty-month' cattle destruction scheme. Looking over Horse Guards from the window of his capacious office, from the very heart of Whitehall in which so much power supposedly resides, he likened his post as a senior Cabinet Minister with that of a sig-nalman in an old-fashioned signal box. He invited me to imagine the ranks of gleaming control levers, all lined up ready to respond to his actions – his 'levers of power'. But, he said, – not without a certain bitterness – 'I have all the levers, but they are not connected to anything.'

That lack of connection characterised the response to the foot and mouth disease. Where we needed a clear line and firm, enlightened leadership, authority was spread between numerous agencies in the British government, in Brussels and elsewhere, bogged down in that soggy grey mass that passes for modern gov-ernance. Effectively, with everyone dabbling – all with their own areas of power to play with, their own levers to pull with uncer-tain connections – no one was in overall charge. The diffusion of responsibility and the lack of clarity, more than anything, were responsible for the mess.

In this context, the European Union probably does its greatest damage just by existing. It dilutes and confuses lines of authority and responsibility. In so doing, it creates a vacuum of power, rather than surfeit, which is exploited by those lesser beings who have their own agendas, the Commission officials, the SVC mem-bers, Council representatives and the self-important, posturing phalanxes of MEPs, all of whom feel they have a right to meddle in our affairs.

But if there is an even more damning aspect to the EU, it is that it permits domestic civil servants to dispense with the tire-some apparatus of democracy. Should they be blocked in their designs by ministers, they can simply turn to their colleagues in 'Europe', who will obligingly prepare the necessary legislation which will allow them to circumvent their political instructions. Rather than 'Brussels' dominating our affairs, therefore, the true masters are our civil servants, who use the EU for their own purposes. The politicians are still allowed to posture and pontifi-cate, for all the world like puppets in a Punch and Judy show. They may squeak and squawk, but their power has been drained from them by the unseen puppet-masters, those smiling 'Sir

Humphreys' who have at last found a way of saying 'No, Minister'. Their catch-all phrase had become 'Brussels wouldn't allow it'.

Thus, try as I might, I cannot see any salvation for British agriculture within the framework of the European Union. The confusion of responsibility and the power given to civil servants apart, it is not just the CAP that is the problem. As I have so carefully argued, it is the single market, harmonisation, integration and regulatory agendas which are also so lethal. So damaging are these influences that the effects of the CAP almost pale into insignificance. Additionally, there is the greater problem – or 'opportunity', as some would put it – of globalisation. Here, membership of the EU puts not only our agriculture but also our relationships with other trading blocs and nations at risk.

Nothing has more aggrieved the international community than the damaging effect of the EU dumping its surpluses at knock-down prices on world markets while, at the same time, maintaining rigorous trade barriers to insulate its own producers from the effects of that dumping. While the United States is guilty of similar malpractice, there is a strong whiff of hypocrisy from the EU when it complains about the Americas, causing eternal friction in international fora. Britain, identified with the EU bloc, is increasingly being involved in trade wars not of its own making.

But in terms of the survival of our domestic industry, there seems to be no salvation in the warm embrace of our own government either. One tends to feel like Corporal Fraser in *Dad's Army*, rushing around declaring 'We're all doomed!' But we are not doomed, not if we still believe that what is left of the democratic process is capable of bringing change. I must believe in that process because the only alternative is to break out the Kalashnikovs and man the barricades. Thus, the fate of agriculture is intimately bound up with the fate of democracy itself. The CAP and all that goes with it exists only because we are members of a profoundly anti-democratic system. How else can one describe a system which perpetuates for decades a policy which is roundly condemned by friends and enemies alike, which causes massive damage and is so expensive? We have a system which not only does not respond to the popular will but is incapable of so doing.

The reform of our farming support system in a way that would meet with popular approval and satisfy the needs of our farmers and rural communities would be a major step towards restoring democracy – reinstating clear lines of authority and accountability. The one cannot be achieved without the other. On the other hand, if – as I fear – we continue to witness the steady decline of British farming, we will also be marking the destruction of our political systems and, even more importantly, the loss of our freedoms. To an extent, that is fitting. It is only the development of agriculture and the ability of the workers to produce more food than they consume which free people to undertake other activities, so creating the conditions for the emergence of an advanced society. By the decline of our agriculture, we will be able to measure our own. By our failures in this key industry shall we be judged – no civilisation has ever survived the loss of its agricultural base.

Notes

Prologue: Death and Destruction

1. S. Ransom, *Plague, Pestilence and the Pursuit of Power – the politics of global disease* (Credence Publications, Tonbridge, Kent, 2001).
2. *Guardian*, 9 May 2001.
3. Matthew Parris, *The Times*, 9 May 2001.
4. 13 May 2001.
5. Letters to the Editor, 12 May 2001.

1. Introduction

1. Personal communication.
2. BBC Radio 4, *PM* programme, 28 May 2001.

2. Danger – Maffia Killing Fields

1. In 1990, in order to challenge the validity of an Infected Place Notice, based on what we thought were 'false positive' tests, I committed a technical breach of the Animal Health Act in order to bring a test case to court (there being no appeal provisions). My defence was thrown out on the basis that the Infected Place Notice was 'proof unto itself' and I was convicted of a breach of the Act, acquiring a criminal record in the process.
2. House of Commons Committee on the Parliamentary Commission for Administration (1993), Third Report, 'Compensation to farmers for slaughtered poultry'.
3. Commission Decision 2001/145/EC.
4. Chapter 2.1.1.
5. One member of the SVC is Jim Scudamore, the British Chief Veterinary Officer. By an odd quirk of the EU system, therefore, Scudamore wears two hats. On the one hand, he is a British civil servant, and his role is to implement the policy determined by his minister. But, on the other hand, as a member of the SVC, he is partly responsible for telling his minister what to do. Depending on which hat he wears, therefore, Scudamore is either servant or master. He judges the adequacy of British action, formulates policy and then goes home to implement it.
6. N. Dixon, *On the Psychology of Military Incompetence* (Jonathan Cape, 1976).

3. Enter the Reformers

1. Reported in the *Daily Telegraph*, 7 March 2001: 'Blair denounces outdated CAP as bad for everyone'.
2. *The Sacred Cow* (Grafton Books, 1987).
3. G. Harvey, *The Killing of The Countryside* (Jonathan Cape, 1997).
4. Rider Books, 1991.
5. 7 May 2001.
6. *Daily Telegraph*, 27 September 1997.
7. 9 January 1998.
8. 23 March 1998.
9. Ambrose Evans-Pritchard, *Daily Telegraph*, 26 May 2001.
10. *Financial Times*, 16 May 2001.
11. Memorandum on the Reform of Agriculture in the European Economic Community. Supplement to Bulletin No. 1-69.
12. 2001 election manifesto.

4. Murder on the Fontainebleau Express

1. Directorate General for Research, European Parliament Working Paper: 'The Future of Young Farmers in the European Union', Agri 134 EN, 2000.
2. European Commission, 'Financing the European Union'. Commission report on the operation of the own resources system, 1998.
3. H. Young, *This Blessed Plot – Britain and Europe from Churchill to Blair* (Macmillan, 1998).
4. European Commission, op. cit. in n. 2.
5. European Commission, op. cit. in n. 2.

5. Red Tape and the Mad Officials

1. J.A.S. Watson & J.A. More, *Agriculture*: *the Science and Practice of British Farming*, 10th ed. (Oliver & Boyd, 1956).

6. The Deregulators

1. P. Selznich, *TVA and the Grass Roots* (Harper Torchbooks, 1966).
2. 'Improving Management in Government: The Next Steps', a report to the Prime Minister (Ibbs Report) (HMSO, 1988).
3. J.D. Rimington, 'Coping with technological risk: a 21st century problem', Engineers and Society – the CSE lecture (Royal Academy of Engineering, 1993).
4. C.M. Blight & S. Scanlan, 'Regulating cakes and ale: agricultural intervention and health', in Digby Anderson (ed.), *A Diet of Reason* (Social Affairs Unit, London, 1986).

5. An incident led to murder in New York State when a customer shot a burger-bar cashier for serving pickles with a burger despite having been specifically asked for it to be pickle-free (*Sunday Times*, 17 September 1995).

6. Lord Robens, 'Safety and Health at Work. Report of the Committee 1970-72' (Cmnd 5034) (HMSO, 1972).

7. 6 November 1995.

7. Mad Scientists and 'Killer' Eggs

1. 18 November 1987.

2. M.E. St Louis, D.L. Morse, M.E. Potter, T.M. De Melfi, J.J. Guzewich, R.V. Tauxe & P.A. Blake, 'The emergence of Grade A eggs as a major source of *Salmonella enteritidis* infections', *Journal of the American Medical Association* 259: 14 (1988), 2103-7.

3. R.A.E. North, J. P. Duguid & M.A. Sheard, 'The quality of food-poisoning surveillance in England & Wales, with specific reference to salmonella food-poisoning', *British Food Journal* 98 (1996) 2/3.

8. Hysteria Rampant

1. 12 October 1988. Editorial.

9. The Politics of Incompetence

1. Unless otherwise indicated, the source material for this and the subsequent chapter was drawn from the BSE Inquiry Report and/or the transcripts of proceedings.

2. M. Thatcher, *The Downing Street Years* (Harper Collins, 1993).

3. Cited in the *Financial Times*, 18 May 1991.

4. The speed of light.

5. J.P. Duguid, B.P. Marmion & R.H.A. Swain, *Medical Microbiology*, 13th ed., vol. 1: *Microbial Infections* (Churchill Livingstone, 1978).

10. The Department of Stealth

1. The Spongiform Encephalopathy Advisory Committee, successor to the Tyrrell Committee, set up on 3 April 1989, with Tyrrell at its head.

12. The Integrationalists

1. Doc. 50 0018/007 3 March 2000 Chambre des Représentants de Belgique, 'Rapport fait au nom de la Commission d'Enquête par MM.

Peter Vanhoutte et Luc Paque. Enquête Parlementaire sur l'organisation de la production de viande, de produits laitiers et d'oeufs en
Belgique et sur les responsabilités politiques dans le cadre de la crise de
la dioxine' (unless otherwise indicated, material is drawn from this
source).

2. The Rijks Kwaliteit Instituut voor Land en Tuinbouwproducten
was the reference laboratory in the Netherlands charged with quality
control of agricultural and horticultural produce and associated raw
materials. Working for the Ministry for Agriculture, it had for ten years
been researching the problem of dioxins in milk originating from the
environment surrounding an incinerator in Rotterdam. RIKILT had
gradually developed specific expertise in dioxin analysis, being able to
detect dioxin concentrations in milk samples as well as in samples of
feedstuffs and animal fats. It was one of the rare European laboratories
able to carry out such analyses. Thus, the Dutch laboratory was the
obvious choice. No laboratory in Belgium could test for dioxin in under
three months.

3. Only later did officials find a number of 'administrative irregularities' which, on 12 April, were reported to the Belgian public prosecutor.
He allocated 60 gendarmes to the case and, in June, Lucien and Jan
Verkest, and two managers from Fogra, were charged with fraudulent
merchandising.

4. The Health Ministry's general food inspection service (IGDA) was
not informed until 28 May. The omission arose through the assistant
director of the IEV, who also acted as general adviser and liaison officer
to the IGDA. He was actually informed on 30 April but was convinced
that the problem related only to the IEV. He did not, therefore, trouble
to inform the IGDA operational service.

5. The IGDA also received the 'Note Destickere'. It was faxed by the
minister's office and also sent by courier to an IGDA health inspector,
marked 'urgent'. However, the inspector was on detachment at the time.
When he returned, he was told by an IGDA director that it was 'IEV
business' and put it on one side, despite it being marked 'urgent'. He
received no instructions thereafter, neither from the minister's office
nor from his director, and did not, therefore, see any reason to follow it
up. As a result, the IGDA's operations unit only learned of the crisis on
27 May through the media. The department did not go into action until
after the crisis had broken in the press on 28 May 1999.

6. It also partly explains the severe response of the EU to Belgium.
Belgium was being 'reproached' for the lateness of its notification. The
attitude of the Commission was also influenced by the failure of the
Belgian authorities to advise the retail trade to withdraw products, and
their failure to impose any prohibitions. However, while the parliamentary inquiry conceded that the attitude of the European officials
reflected concern for preserving public health, it observed that '... economic and industrial interests also played a part in the decisions at the

European level'. Furthermore, the inquiry noted plaintively, 'As the Commission was located in Brussels, it could follow the Belgian press far more meticulously than it could have in other Member States'.

7. Verbatim record of proceedings.

8. European Commission, 'A Strategy for a New Europe', COM (2000) 154.

14. The Global Power Broker

1. COM (2000) 604 final, 'Proposal for a Council Regulation on the common organisation of the markets in the sugar sector', Commission of the European Communities.

2. Ironically the UK government had raised no objections to the use of growth hormones, although farmers were against their use, fearing a backlash from consumers sensitised by BSE. The UK, therefore, was in the interesting position of being exposed to possible US sanctions because of the EU stance, while its own producers were complaining that the illegal use of hormones in the EU was putting them at a trading disadvantage. Cattle fed with growth hormones showed extra weight gains of between 5 and 20 per cent, with feed efficiency increased by 5 to 12 per cent.

3. 23 January 2001.

4. Press briefing: Fine-tuning for 'Everything but Arms' package to speed approval, European Commission.

15. Red Herrings That Don't Fly

1. *Daily Mail*, 5 March 2001

2. EU Observer (website), 6 March 2001.

3. 11 February 1989.

4. Letters to the Editor, *The Times*, 8 March 2001.

17. Joined-up Government

1. Although Londoners may complain about the inadequacies of the tube system, country visitors are amazed at the speed, convenience and frequency of the service, such delays as are experienced being as nothing compared, in some rural districts, to a three-day wait for the only bus to the nearest market town.

18. Subsidise or Die

1. Op. cit. in ch. 3 n. 3.

2. In particular, R.W.M. Johnson with a commentary by Richard

Howarth, *Reforming EU Farm Policy: Lessons from New Zealand* (Institute of Economic Affairs, 2000).

3. 'From bad to worse, down on the farm', 3-9 March 2001, p. 44.

4. Commission on 21st Century Production Agriculture, 'Directions for Future Farm Policy: The Role of Government in Support of Production Agriculture' (January 2001).

5. 'CAP: a catalogue of failure. The need for radical reform', IoD Research Paper.

6. Cited in the *Observer*, 11 March 2001.

19. Agricultural Support

1. Such as an agreement to avoid winter wheat and a commitment to leaving winter stubble, with spring ploughing and sowing.

2. A side-effect of the scheme is that it would provide useful local employment for agricultural college graduates, who would form the nucleus of any 'agricultural department' in the local authorities administering land management contracts. We would expect a natural exchange of personnel between farm and authority, building bridges between the two, and increasing the level of expertise in both.

20. Better Regulation

1. 'Food safety' officials think otherwise. Industrial scale processing, however, involves 'wet plucking', with the use of a machine comprising rapidly rotating rubber 'fingers' which strip carcases of their feathers. These machines become highly contaminated in use, imparting high levels of bacteria on carcases. 'Hot' evisceration, by machine, causes a proportion of the birds' intestines to be torn, liberally spreading contaminated gut contents over the machine and subsequent birds processed. By contrast, in the traditional process, the bird is left to cool and evisceration takes place days later. By then, the mesenteric fat has hardened and the gut forms a smooth 'bolus'. It slides out easily, intact, with very little chance of tearing and, therefore, minimal chance of contamination by gut contents. Bacteriologically, the traditional bird is far superior. The problem is that the officials confuse visual appearance of the processing environment – cleanliness, finishes, etc. – with the 'hygiene' of the finished produce, believing that there is a correlation between the two, and opt for a high standard of the former, heedless of the quality (and safety) of the finished article.

21. Dealing with the Scares

1. Although it was presented as a virulent killer bug, a study carried out by Manchester Medical Teaching Hospital discovered that in terms of sequelae, i.e. full-blown septicaemia from which death often arises, *S. enteritidis* was low on the scale, relative to other species. The more familiar *S. typhimurium* was at the top. When it is remembered that *S. enteritidis* replaced *S. typhimurium*, the missing fact of the 1988 scare was that a more benign salmonella had replaced one that was actually more potent. In fact, pro rata, the death rate dropped.

2. 11 December 1988.

3. Cited in S. Ransom, op. cit. in Prologue n. 1.

22. In Paradisum

1. *The Times*, 31 May 2001.

Index